Third Edition

PROJECT PLANNING, SCHEDULING, AND CONTROL

A Hands-On Guide to Bringing Projects in On Time and On Budget

JAMES P. LEWIS

McGraw-Hill

New York San Francisco Washington, D.C. Auckland Bogotá
Caracas Lisbon London Madrid Mexico City Milan
Montreal New Delhi San Juan Singapore
Sydney Tokyo Toronto

Library of Congress Cataloging-in-Publication Data

Lewis, James P.
    Project planning, scheduling, and control / by James P. Lewis. — 3rd ed.
      p. cm.
    ISBN 0-07-136050-6
    1. Industrial project management.   2. Scheduling.   I. Title.

  HD69.P75 L493 2000
  658.4'04—dc21   00-058433
                                                                      CIP

McGraw-Hill

*A Division of The **McGraw·Hill** Companies*

4 5 6 7 8 9 0 DOC/DOC 0 9 8 7 6 5 4 3 2

ISBN 0-07-136050-6

The sponsoring editor for this book was Catherine Schwent, the editing supervisor was Paul R. Sobel, and the production supervisor was Modestine Cameron. It was set in Palatino by Judy Brown.

Printed and bound by R. R. Donnelley & Sons Company.

McGraw-Hill books are available at special quantity discounts to use as premiums and sales promotions, or for use in corporate training programs. For more information, please write to the Director of Special Sales, McGraw-Hill, Professional Publishing, 2 Penn Plaza, New York, NY 10121-2298. Or contact your local bookstore.

This publication is designed to provide accurate and authoritative information in regard to the subject matter covered. It is sold with the understanding that neither the author nor the publisher is engaged in rendering legal, accounting, or other professional service. If legal advice or other expert assistance is required, the services of a competent professional should be sought.
—From a Declaration of Principles jointly adopted by a Committee of the American Bar Association and a Committee of Publishers.

This book is printed on recycled, acid-free paper containing a minimum of 50% recycled de-inked fiber.

This book is dedicated

to

Alan Mulally
and the team that designed and built
The Boeing 777 aircraft.

Working together, they demonstrated what
teamwork and good project management can accomplish.

CONTENTS

SECTION THREE

PROJECT PLANNING

Chapter 6

Project Strategy: You Can't Develop a Good Implementation Plan Unless You First Have a Proper Game Plan

Chapter 16

Managing Meetings   443

PART SEVEN

MANAGING YOURSELF

Chapter 17

Managing Your Time   459

Chapter 18

Building Personal Effectiveness   477

Appendix

SCHEDULE COMPUTATIONS   490

PREFACE

By the time this book goes to market, it will be nearly 10 years since I wrote the first edition. It seems like yesterday that a fellow in one of my seminars suggested it. I will be forever grateful to him, because writing that book was one of the best things I ever did. *Project Planning, Scheduling, and Control* has become a very popular book, and I have been very pleased with the e-mails, faxes, letters, and reviews that I have received from readers telling me how much they like the book. Most of all, their main comment is that it is down-to-earth, readable, and understandable.

That was my objective. I absolutely hate reading books that are hard to understand. So my purpose in life has been to translate topics that may be a bit difficult into understandable, bite-sized pieces that people can digest. This has become my trademark, or brand—the thing that differentiates me from many other writers and instructors, and I hope it will remain so.

When it came time to revise the book this time, I could have simply tweaked it a little, but, instead, I decided to rewrite it more or less completely. You will find some material carried over from previous editions, but most of it has been written from scratch, and I haven't even consulted previous editions to see what I said then. I hope that will make the book useful even to people who have previous editions of it.

I have also tried to do something new with this book. In the nearly 20 years that I have been teaching seminars, I have always tried to present principles that people can use to guide them in solving problems. However, I have found that some individuals don't want to learn principles. They want me to tell them how to deal with a specific problem. They think that if they could just solve that one problem, they would have gotten their money's worth from the program, and perhaps

> The cause of all human evils is
> not being able to apply general
> principles to special cases.
> — Epictetus, c. 60–120

that is true. The thing is that, as soon as they encounter another problem, what worked to solve the first one won't necessarily solve the next one, and they are left wondering what to do.

People would also like to turn project management into a fill-in-the-blank process. "Just give me some forms to fill out that will walk me through the entire planning, scheduling, and controlling thing," they say. Unfortunately, it just won't work. It's like the belief that scheduling software will make you an instant project manager. It won't. Unless you understand the principles behind the scheduling activity, the software will only help you document your failures with great precision. The software is a tool. Giving me a saw won't make me a carpenter.

If you learn a *principle*, however, you can apply it to solve all problems of a certain kind. It is like the saying that if you teach someone to farm, you won't have to keep feeding him in the future. So if you know how to add and subtract, you can use those principles to balance your checkbook, do cost accounting for your company, or make change in a supermarket.

No doubt you have heard the story about the truck that gets stuck when trying to go under an underpass. The truck is bigger than the opening. To get the truck out, one of two things must happen, you must make the opening larger or the truck smaller.

Everyone is pondering the problem and neither course of action seems possible. You can't raise the bridge. And you can't shrink the truck.

A small boy ponders the situation for awhile, and then suggests, "Why don't you let some air out of the truck tires?"

Of course! That will work. You can't make the truck smaller in and of itself, but you can make it occupy less vertical space by lowering it! In doing so, you have applied a principle.

Another one. Once you know that using a lever allows you to lift a very heavy load with very little force, you can use that principle in a lot of different situations.

So here's the deal. I have tried to present the principle that applies to every step in managing a project so that, if you grasp the principle, you can apply it to your own unique situation, your own unique project, and it will work! I promise. It may not work the first time, but if you think about it, there may be many different ways to actually implement a principle, so if you try several different approaches, you will eventually find one that works.

Throughout the book, then, you will see principles in sidebars. You can do a quick read of the sidebars and get the real "meat" of the book from them. (Of course, the supporting text should enhance your understanding of the principle.)

It is my hope that you will find this the most practical, down-to-earth project management book you have ever read. Let me know. Visit my website, www.lewisinstitute.com or send me an e-mail. Or you can use snail mail or the phone to contact me (see the end of this Preface).

Finally, I have dedicated this book to Alan Mulally, who is now president of the Commercial Airplane division of Boeing, and who was the project manager for the model 777, an airplane considered by the experts to be one of the most technologically sophisticated ever built. Because of his superb management of the project, Alan was named Engineer of the Year by *Design News* magazine in 1996.

I am often asked if I know any organizations that really practice good project management, and I can say, without hesitation, that the 777 project represents project management at its best. Alan emphasized what I consider to be the key ingredients of good project management–attention to tools, systems, and people. No one by itself is enough, you have to attend to all three.

You can see some of this in how he ran program meetings. As the author of the Design News article about Mulally explained:

> At the weekly program meetings that chartered the progress of the 777, Alan would insist that his staff observe a set of 'principles and practices,' which managers have now carried over to other projects. Among these ideas:
>
> - Use facts and figures, "because the data will set you free."
> - You can't manage a secret. Get problems out in the open.
> - Whining is okay—occasionally—but be ready to propose a plan.
> - Listen to each other. No side conversations are permitted when someone is speaking.
> - Enjoy each other—and the journey. (Maloney, 1996)

If you want to learn more about the 777 project, I suggest you read Sabbagh's *Twenty-first Century Jet* (Sabbagh, 1996), Dimancescu's *The Seamless Enterprise* (Dimancescu, 1992), and watch the PBS video entitled *21st Century Jet*. It is a great case study for all of us to learn from.

Good luck with your projects.

Jim Lewis
302 Chestnut Mountain Drive
Vinton, VA 24179
Tel. 540-345-7850
e-mail: jlewis@lewisinstitute.com

ABBREVIATIONS USED IN THIS BOOK

ACWP	actual cost of work performed
AOA	activity-on-arrow
AON	activity-on-node
BAC	Budget At Completion
BCWP	budgeted cost of work performed
BCWS	budgeted cost of work scheduled
CEO	Chief Executive Officer
COPQ	cost of poor quality
CPI	cost performance index
CPM	Critical Path Method
CR	critical ratio
CSSR	Cost-Schedule Status Report
C/SCSC	Cost/Schedule Control Systems Criteria
DaBS	days before software
DIF	data interchange format
DU	duration
EAC	estimate at completion (see also $EAC)
EEO	equal employment opportunity
EF	early finish
ES	early start
FF	finish-to-finish
FMEA	Failure Mode Effects Analysis
GM	General Motors
HBDI	Herrmann Brain Dominance Instrument

IF	intermediate frequency
ISO	International Standards Organization
ITT	International Telephone and Telegraph
JIT	just in time
KISS	keep it simple stupid
LF	late finish
LRC	linear responsibility chart
LS	late start
MIS	Management Information System
NTSB	National Transportation Safety Board
PAF	prevention, appraisal, failure
PC	personal computer
PERT	Performance (or Project) Evaluation and Review Technique
PCTS	performance, cost, time, and scope
PMI	Project Management Institute
QFD	quality function deployment
ROI	return on investment
RPN	risk priority number
SPC	statistical process control
SPI	schedule performance index
SS	Start-to-Start
SWOT	strengths, weaknesses, opportunities, threats
VIP	Vision-involvement-persistence
WBS	work breakdown structure
WIIFM	What's in it for me
$EAC	monetary estimate at completion

LIST OF FIGURES

LIST OF TABLES

ACKNOWLEDGMENTS

As is true for any book of this type, there are countless people who have contributed to it. Since the first edition of this book was released, I have taught another few thousand individuals, and much of the new content comes from questions that they have asked or suggestions they have made. To all of those nameless individuals I want to say "thank you."

There are some individuals that I do want to thank personally. They include my newly married acquisitions editor, Catherine Dassopoulos, with whom I have worked for several years. She has always enthusiastically supported my projects. In addition, Paul Sobel, the production editor, has overseen production of the book, in a cheerful, professional manner, and made the job fun for me and everyone else. To these and all of the McGraw-Hill people that I may not know personally, thank you for a job well done.

Judy Brown has now typeset three of my books, and she did such a nice job on the previous two that I asked that she do this book. Her work is highly professional, and we now have three books that have similar styles, thanks to her hard work.

To Bill Adams, of Adams Graphics, I want to say "thanks" for translating my wife's ideas into finished computer artwork that has a very clean, professional look. He put in a lot of hours on this book, and made it look really nice.

As usual, my wife, Lea Ann, has spent more hours than she can count reading the text and developing illustrations that we hope will make the end result a better product for you, the reader. She has a knack for capturing a point with art so that it jumps off the page at you, and my books have benefitted greatly from her talent.

These are the people who have made the book the quality product that it is. Any shortcomings are, of course, my own.

INTRODUCTION TO
PROJECT MANAGEMENT

CHAPTER

An Introduction to Project Management

The news traveled from the palace to the valley of the kings with incredible speed—Nefertari, beloved wife of Ramses the Great, nineteenth dynasty pharaoh of Upper and Lower Egypt, had just borne him another son. The messenger was out of breath as he entered the murky darkness of the burial chamber and greeted Ashahebsed, builder of the tombs for the family of the great king.

"The new child has just arrived," he announced breathlessly, "a son." He need not tell Ashahebsed who he meant by "new child." Ashahebsed was well aware. The pregnancy of Nefertari, one of two *royal* wives of Ramses was well known throughout the kingdom.

Ashahebsed shook his head. Another tomb would have to be added. How many was this now? At last count, the king had sired 30 sons and as many daughters. With two royal wives, two Hittite princesses acquired through diplomatic marriage, and four of his own daughters whom he had married, following Egyptian tradition, Ramses was more than prolific. He was already 60 years old and still fathering children at an alarming rate.

The news traveled at incredible speed that the child had arrived.

"By the great god Amun," Ashahebsed exclaimed, "at this rate, I'll never finish this project!"

"You're right," said the messenger. "I have been instructed to inform you that Isetnofret is pregnant again."

"The second royal wife of Ramses," thought Ashahebsed. "And so are the two Hittite princesses," he groaned.

"Don't forget Bant-Anat," the messenger offered.

Isetnofret's child, one of the four daughters the pharaoh had married.

"It is clear that I will be on this project until pharaoh dies," said Ashahebsed.

"It looks that way," agreed the messenger, as he turned to go out into the blinding Egyptian sun.

Ashahebsed may not have managed a project with the grandeur of the great pyramid, but he may very well have suffered the greatest number of scope changes, over the most extended period, of any project manager in history. Ramses the Great had more than 100 sons and daughters spread over a 90-year life. He was pharaoh for nearly 65 years, and no doubt the building of tombs for his progeny extended over much of that time. The best that can be said is that Ashahebsed had job security. The worst is that the project just kept on going and going and going. . . .

WHAT IS A PROJECT?

The textbook definition of a project is that it is a one-time job that has a definite starting point, definite ending point, clearly defined scope of work, a budget, and is multitask in nature. Unfortunately, textbook definitions often don't agree with the real world.

> A project is a one-time, multitask job with a definite starting point, definite ending point, a clearly defined scope of work, a budget, and usually a temporary team.

Ashahebsed's project might have had a definite starting point, but the scope kept changing, making the ultimate completion date slide out further and further until it disappeared over the horizon. And of course the budget had to change accordingly.

This was certainly no textbook project. In fact, if any of you ever find a project that conforms to the textbook definition, please send me an e-mail about it, so I can write a case study.

About the only part of the definition that fits all projects is that they are one-time jobs that are multitask in nature. A repetitive job is not a project. Neither is performing a single task over and over. Nevertheless, that leaves a huge number of jobs that qualify as projects. And it means that a large number of people are managing projects (or trying to at least).

Tom Peters (1992) argued that much of the work done in organizations can be thought of as projects. This means that, even though everyone is not called a project manager, the people managing projects are de facto project managers anyway. And, although they may not need the formality of critical path schedules and earned value analysis, they do need some skills in project planning and control.

Joseph M. Juran said that a project is a problem scheduled for solution. I like this definition because it makes us realize that a project is conducted to solve a problem for the organization. However, the word problem almost always conveys something negative. When someone says, "We have a problem," that is usually bad news. But developing a new product or software program is a problem—a positive problem. So the word problem is being used

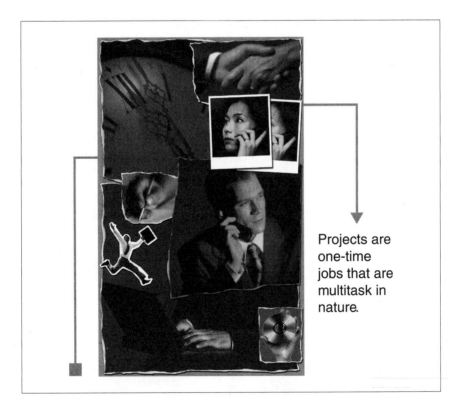

Projects are one-time jobs that are multitask in nature.

here in a very broad sense. Environmental cleanup projects might be thought of as solving the "bad" kind of problem: thus projects deal with both kinds of problems—positive and negative ones.

> A project is a problem scheduled for solution.
>
> — J. M. Juran

WHAT IS PROJECT MANAGEMENT?

This is a book on project management.

You knew that.

But what do you think it is about? That is the real question.

For that matter, what do you think management is?

Instant Pudding Project Management

In December 1999 I had a meeting in Germany with the parent company of a client that I have back home. I wanted to compare notes with one of the managers there to determine if project management in Germany was the same as in the United States.

I showed him my model of project management, which I call the Lewis Method™ and compared it to his process. To our delight, they were nearly identical.

"I have been trying to explain project management to senior management here," he said, "but I'm afraid with very little success." His face was sad.

"In one meeting, one of our vice presidents got very frustrated and said, 'I don't understand why we don't just buy Microsoft Project™ and do it!'" He added, "meaning, of course, why don't we do project management."

I almost laughed. "It's the same in the U.S.," I assured him. "Senior managers there also assume that project management is just scheduling, and that if they buy the tool for everyone, they will have instant project managers." He looked a bit more relieved.

"I think we should put the scheduling software in a box and rename it *Instant Project Manager*," I said. "On the side of the box, the instructions would say, just add water, stir, shake, bake, and you will have instant project managers—sort of an *instant pudding* approach to project management."

He thought for a moment. "That's actually what we are doing now, isn't it? Practicing instant pudding project management!"

"Yes," I agreed. "And I can tell you that it is an approach followed throughout much of the world."

Tools, People, and Systems

Project management is not just scheduling.

It is not just tools.

It is not a job position or job title.

It is not even the sum total of all of these. But my experience shows that not many people understand this. They believe project management is scheduling, and that if a person can do some technical job (using the word technical in a very broad sense), then that individual can manage.

This is a pervasive problem. We forget that there are two aspects to all work, including projects—the *what* and the *how*. The *what* is called the "task" to be performed. *How* it is to be performed is called "process." But process also applies to how the team functions in total—how they communicate, interact, solve problems, deal with conflict, make decisions, make work assignments, run meetings, and every other aspect of team performance. The tools they use—such as scheduling software, computers, project notebooks, and daily planners—help with both the what and the how. But the tools do not make an instant project manager of a person who has not been trained in the *how*. See Figure 1.1.

Notice also that organizations and project teams are *people*. I think we forget this. An organization has capital equipment, buildings, inventory, and other paraphernalia for the sole purpose of enabling human beings to do work that will result in desired organizational outcomes.

Project Management Is Tools, People, and Systems

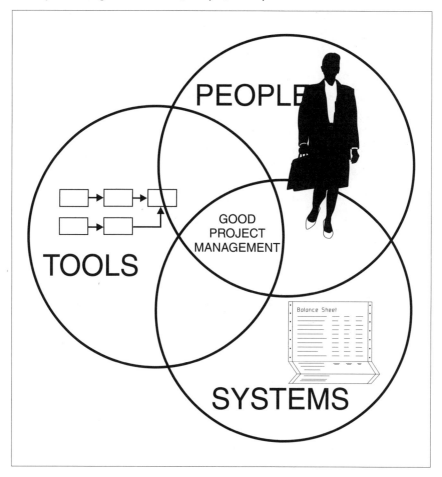

Yet managers often focus on everything but people. I am in England writing this section, and I was talking with someone yesterday who said he knew a manager who was brilliant with computers, but absolutely horrible at dealing with people. The manager in question was rude, condescending, and dictatorial. He was also passive in response to situations that he should be han-

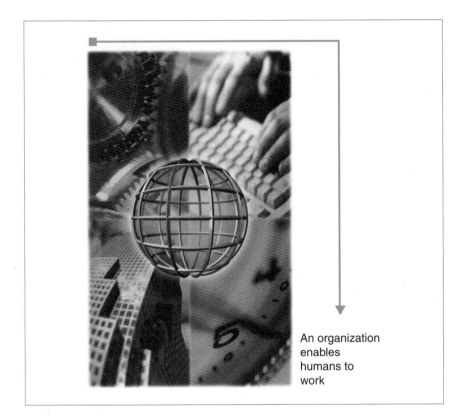

An organization
enables
humans to
work

dling. I have heard such stories both at home and abroad and I
sometimes wonder how organizations survive.

In any case, the message should be understood—organizations are people, and people engage in processes to get results. If the people do not function well, neither will the processes, and if the processes don't work, task outcomes will suffer.

This is another lesson that many managers have not learned—*process will always affect task performance!* We have understood this in manufacturing for many years. We have applied statistical process control (SPC) to manufacturing to detect process problems. We have worked to improve processes, to eliminate non-value-added steps, to reduce scrap and rework, and we have even begun to recognize that non-manufacturing processes should be improved. This realization may have been championed by Hammer and Champy, in their book *Reengineering the Corporation* (Hammer and Champy, 1993).

Project management deals with *tools, people,* and *systems.* The tools are work breakdown structures, PERT scheduling, earned value analysis, risk analysis, and scheduling software (to name a few). And tools are the primary focus of most organizations that want to implement project management.

However, the tools are a necessary but not sufficient condition for success in managing projects. The processes or techniques are far more important, because without employing the correct processes for managing, the tools will only help you document your failures with great precision.

A simple example is that you give a person an automobile so that he or she can get around. However, you give him no training in how to drive the car. He must learn by trial and error. By the time he has become competent in driving (if he ever does), he has battered up the car pretty badly, and in the process done quite a bit of damage to others. This is what happens when you give people scheduling software with no training in how to use it properly.

> Project management is facilitation of the planning, scheduling, and controlling of all activities that must be done to meet project objectives.

On the other hand, giving someone training in how to drive when she has no car is a waste. The training is irrelevant, absent the car that she needs to execute the training.

So what is project management? I define it as facilitation of the planning, scheduling, and controlling of all activities that must be done to meet project objectives.

The Four Project Constraints

Ever since I got involved in project management, it has been common to talk about the triple constraints in project management—performance, time, and cost. Colloquially, they are often referred to as good, fast, and cheap, and the saying most commonly used is, "Good, fast, or cheap—pick two." The message is that you could dictate only two of them, and the third will have to vary.

When I wrote my first edition of this book, I realized that there was a fourth constraint—scope. The magnitude or size of the job is also related to the other three, and I started pointing out that you could assign values to any three of them, but the fourth must be allowed to vary. In fact, it is scope changes that probably cause more missed project deadlines and cost overruns than anything else—except defining project requirements correctly to begin with.

> **Scope:** the magnitude or size of the project.

I have learned during the past couple of years that a lot of people are confused by the term *performance,* so I want to clarify it here. A project is intended to produce a result of some kind. Construction projects produce buildings for people to occupy or roads for them to travel on or dams that provide water to communities. Product development projects provide products for people to use. Software projects do the same.

There are two kinds of performance requirements, which are collectively called specifications. One is functional requirements. These tell what the thing being delivered is supposed to do. The other kind of requirement is technical requirements, which describe the features of the deliverable. They may specify dimensions, weight, color, speed, horsepower, thrust, or any of a million other specifications that can apply to a deliverable. As a former engineer, we used to ask if a change would affect the form, fit, or function of a product. You can see how this relates to what has just been said.

Defining requirements in a project is a major part of project definition, and doing so incorrectly or inadequately is—I believe—the single most common cause of project failures. I was once told a story by a fellow that illustrates this beautifully. He had a friend over at his house one day and they were doing some yard work. He said to his friend, "You see this small tree in front of my house? How about trimming the limbs off this tree to a height about like this" (which he indicated by holding his hand a certain distance above the ground).

He then left his friend to trim the tree and went to the back of the house to do some work. When he returned to the front of the house, his friend had just finished the job. It was nicely done, except for one significant detail. His friend had cut all of the limbs off the top of the tree, down to the proper height, when what the fellow wanted was to have the limbs trimmed off the trunk of the tree from the *ground up* to the height he had indicated!

Now what happened here is all too common. *Trim the tree* meant something different to each of them. We say this is a communication problem, and it is. And because it happens so frequently, it says we had better take care to achieve a *shared understanding* of what is supposed to be done in the project. We will talk about how this is done in Chapter 5.

Elsewhere I have said that project management is facilitation of the planning, scheduling, and controlling of all activities that must be done to meet project objectives. These variables are the constraints on every project, no matter how large or small, and because you can never escape them, you need to understand how they interact.

P = performance requirements: technical and functional

C = labor cost to do the job. (Note that capital equipment and material costs are accounted for separately from labor.)

T = time required for the project

S = scope or magnitude of the work

The relationship between them is given by the following expression:

$$C = f(P, T, S)$$

In words, this expression reads, "Cost is a function of performance, time, and scope." Ideally this could be written as an exact mathematical expression. For example:

$$C = 2P + 3T + 4S$$

However, we are always estimating the values of these variables, so the exact relationship is never known.

The Eternal Triangle (Not the Love Triangle)

One way to think of the relationship that exists between the PCTS constraints is to consider a triangle, as shown in Figure 1.2. P, C, and T are the lengths of the sides, while S is the area. If I know the lengths of the sides, I can compute the area. Or, if I know the area and two sides, I can compute the length of the third side.

What is important about this illustration is that I cannot arbitrarily assign values to all three sides and the area. If three are specified, the fourth can be determined, but if you try to assign values to all four, they will only "fit" by accident.

In projects, however, it is common that the project sponsor or some other manager wants to dictate values for all four. This is, in

F I G U R E 1.2

Triangles Showing PCTS Relationship

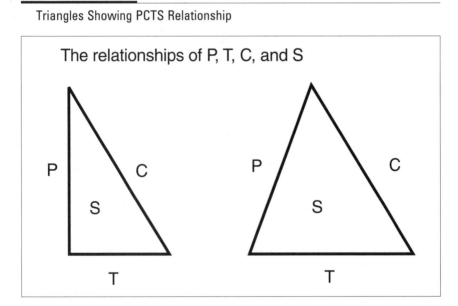

fact, a common cause for project failures. As a project manager, it is my job to tell the sponsor what I need to do a project. So consider the most common case, in which values for P, T, and S are given. It is my job to tell the sponsor the cost to achieve those targets.

It is also true that when I do so, the sponsor may have heart failure. The response is often, "My goodness, how can it cost so much!!??" This is followed by such protests as "We can't afford it!"

> *Principle:* You can assign values to only three of the constraints. The fourth will be whatever the relationship dictates it will be.

Then my response is, "Tell me what you can afford, and I'll tell you what I can do." This means that either scope will be reduced or perhaps time will be extended. In general, it is not acceptable to reduce performance.

Notice that this is a common trade-off we make at home. We have a list of things that need to be done. The roof is leaking and needs to be repaired before it ruins the house. The car is making a strange noise. My 13-year-old daughter needs braces on her teeth, which will cost a bundle. And on and on. Trouble is, I can't afford it all.

So what am I going to do? I'm going to establish priorities for the items on the list. If the car quits, I won't be able to get to work to make the money to pay for everything, so perhaps it is number one on the list. The roof comes next. And goodness knows when I'll be able to afford braces for my daughter's teeth. Maybe she will grow up and marry someone who can afford them, but for now, they have to wait.

Interestingly, we are forced to prioritize at home, but in organizations we often try to do it all, thereby spreading our resources too thin, the result being that nothing gets done well or on time. We will return to this issue in Section 4, Managing the Project—Control. For now, the point is that you can't have it all, so choices have to be made, and my job is to help my boss or sponsor make those choices by providing the best information I can on what is needed to do the project.

The Time-Cost Trade-Off

In today's "hurry-up" world, the pressures are on to finish projects in record time. This is due in part to the pressures of competition, especially in developing products, software, or new services. If you take too long to get it done, the competition will get there first, and the first to market with a new product often captures 60 to 70 percent of the market, leaving the rest of the pack to pick up the scraps.

The pressure is on to finish projects in record time.

Time-Cost Trade-Off Curve

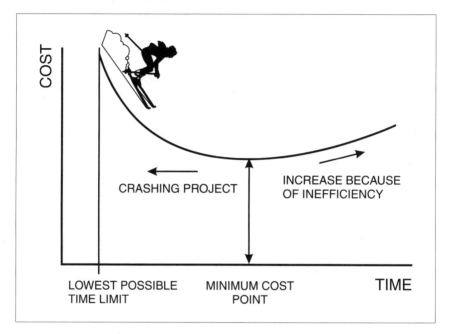

Furthermore there is pressure to reduce the cost to do the job. Again, this is partly because costs continue to rise over time, and also because if you can develop something faster and cheaper, while leaving scope and performance constant, you can recover your investment sooner and protect yourself from the dynamics of the marketplace. We will examine this in more detail in section four.

Look now at the time-cost trade-off curve shown in Figure 1.3. The best way to read this graph is to notice that there is some duration for a project in which costs are minimum. That is, there is an optimum duration. The problem is, we seldom know just what that duration is, but we aren't too concerned about it.

What is important is to note that going past that point (extending the duration) causes project costs to rise because you are being inefficient. You are taking too long to do the work.

To the left of the minimum point, we are trying to reduce the time needed for the job. The common term for this is that we are trying to "crash" the project. That doesn't mean destroy it—but that we are trying to do it faster than the optimum time.

As you can see, costs start to rise as you reduce time, and they rise very steeply. This is because we usually speed up a project by assigning more resources. In common language, we "throw bodies at it."

The difficulty is that, as we throw more bodies at a project, they begin to get in each other's way, the work can be subdivided only so far, and we then hit what is called the point of diminishing returns. One way to think of this is that, if one person can do something in 10 hours, two people won't be able to do the same job in 5 hours. It may take 6. And four people may take 4 hours. So we don't get a linear gain in time.

In addition, there is a lower limit below which you cannot go, no matter how many people you put on the job. I call this the "forbidden zone." Naturally, there is always someone who thinks that if you just put enough people on a project, you can get it done in almost zero time, but it simply is not true.

BROOKS' LAW

Adding people to an already late project may only make it later.

— Brooks

Further, there is a principle called Brooks' Law, originally specified for software projects, that says, "Adding people to an already late project will just make it later." I believe this principle applies to all kinds of projects—not just to software.

Worse than that, you can actually destroy a project by adding people at the wrong time. This is shown in Figure 1.4. If you add someone new to the project, that person must be "brought up to speed." That means that orientation and training are needed. Who is going to do the training? You, most likely, but perhaps some other member of the team.

No matter who, that person's productivity will drop. In order to keep from delaying the job, that person will have to work some

F I G U R E 1.4

The Rework Spiral

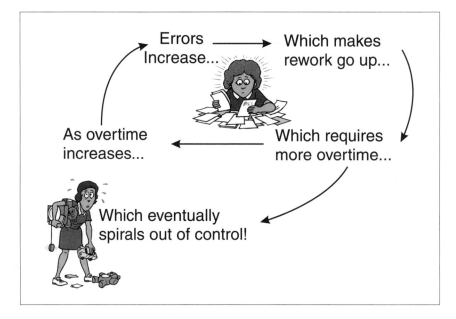

overtime. In doing so, she will get tired, thus losing more ground. She will probably also make more errors, which means she will have to correct them. This is called rework. As the rework increases, she will have to work more overtime to keep up, thus getting more tired, which causes more errors, which increases rework, which . . .

In other words, the project is likely to spiral downward, out of control. The message is, be very careful about adding people to help get the job done on time.

If You Always Do What You've Always Done

Now let's come back to the pressures that we feel to get the job done faster and cheaper at the same time. The time-cost trade-off curve shows that, if you are below the minimum point on the curve, crashing the project costs more money. Yet we are being told to reduce costs *and* time simultaneously! Are we being set up? Maybe.

There is a saying in psychology that goes, "If you always do what you've always done, you'll always get what you always got." And there is a corollary. "Insanity is continuing to do what you've always done and hope for a different result."

> If you always do what you've always done, you'll always get what you've always got.

The message is that, if what you're doing isn't working, you have to change the way you're doing it. That is, you must change the *process*. In fact, that is what formal project management is all about.

Many of you have been managing projects for a long time in an informal way. I call that "seat-of-the-pants" project management, and I know, because I did it that way for about 10 years. Why? Because I didn't know any other way. And I got the job done—usually to everyone's satisfaction.

> Insanity is continuing to do what you've always done and hope for a different result.

The trouble is, we didn't know the work could be done any better. Can formal project management (a change in process) really help you get the job done faster and cheaper at the same time?

> *Principle:* If what you are doing isn't working, you need to change the process by which it is done.

I believe so.

Estimates are that about one-third of the cost to do many projects is rework. As someone has said, that is equivalent to having one of every three people on the job working full time to just redo what the other two people did wrong in the first place. That means, of course, that the cost is extremely high.

Why all the rework?

I think it is safe to say that it is the result of taking a ready-fire-aim approach to the project. The job is ill-conceived, poorly defined, and inadequately planned. Everyone just wants to "get the job done."

There is an old saying, "Haste makes waste." It is very true. But in our hurry-up-and-get-it-done world, there is little patience with "wasting time" on all that planning. So the result is rework, which is 100 percent waste.

I would suggest that, if you find a way to measure it, you will find that the rework in your projects ranges from 5 to 40 percent. As I have heard Tom Peters say on a tape (I forget which one), this is a good-news, bad-news story. The bad news is that it can be so high. The good news is that there is lots of room for improvement!

The nice thing about measuring rework is that you can show progress fairly soon. If you try to do baseline comparisons, you often find that baseline data for previous projects do not exist. With rework, you simply plot trend graphs. Such a graph is shown in Figure 1.5.

F I G U R E 1.5

Trend Showing Rework Declining

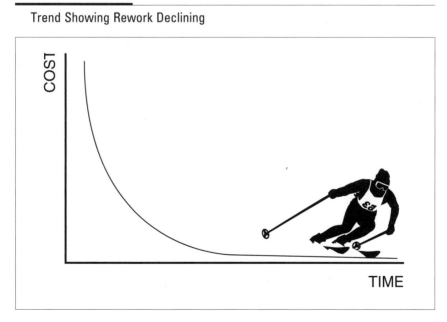

Quality

I have always considered this to be the forgotten aspect of project management. It has to do with the performance constraint. If the functional and technical requirements of the job are not met, you have done a poor quality job. So, to some extent, performance is synonymous with quality.

If you put people under pressure to get the job done really fast, and won't allow them to reduce scope, then you can almost bet that they will sacrifice quality in the process. Furthermore, as a former quality manager at ITT, I learned that, if you improve quality, you get jobs done faster and cheaper, so in addition to improving processes, we must improve quality. In fact, the two go hand in hand.

In the past, quality has been defined in two primary ways. One was that quality was conformance to specifications. Another was that quality was meeting customer requirements. Of course, specifications should be written so that, if you meet them, you meet customer requirements, so the second definition could be said to be the better of the two.

In the development of the six-sigma approach to quality at Motorola, a new definition of quality was also developed. This definition says that *quality is a state in which value entitlement is realized for the customer and provider in every aspect of the business relationship* (Harry and Schroeder, 2000, p. 6). This new definition recognizes the profit motive of every for-profit organization, whereas the old definitions focused only on the customer.

Harry and Schroeder say that most organizations are producing product and service quality levels at about three sigma. This refers to the number of errors that occur in a given number of opportunities. For 1 million opportunities, a three-sigma level will yield 66,807 errors. At six sigma, there will be only three errors in a million opportunities!

They also say that a three-sigma quality level means that of every sales dollar earned by the organization, approximately 25 to 30 percent (or 25 cents) is lost because of poor quality. This is called the cost of poor quality (COPQ). Most executives think that the COPQ is a few percent, and are horrified to learn that it is this high.

That cost comes from three factors: Prevention, Appraisal, and Failure (PAF). Prevention is anything that we do to keep errors from happening in the first place. As an example of this, Alan Mulally, director of engineering at Boeing when the 777 airplane was being designed, explains how toy company Fisher-Price foolproofs the assembly of their model airplanes, so that you can put them together on Christmas Eve without a lot of hassle. "Fisher-Price makes a little notch in their wheels so that you can only put the right wheel on the right hub and you can only put the left wheel on the left hub" (Sabbagh, 1996). This approach has been used by the Japanese in manufacturing processes for years.

Appraisal cost results from the inspection of a finished part to be sure that no errors have been made. A basic given in quality is that you cannot inspect quality into a product—it must be designed in and built in to begin with. In fact, the work with six-sigma programs has shown that "80 percent of quality problems are actually designed into the product without any conscious attempt to do so (Harry & Schroeder, 2000, p. 36). When the problem is designed into the product, you can't inspect it out.

Failure cost is incurred once the product leaves the plant and reaches the customer. It includes warranty costs, repair costs, and so on. What is almost impossible to track, but is part of failure cost, is lost customers.

The important thing to note is that an increase in money spent on prevention leads to significant reductions in inspection and failure costs. This is shown in Figure 1.6. So most of our quality costs should go into prevention so that we reap significant savings in the other two areas. If you want to see how significant these savings can be, I suggest you read Harry and Schroeder.

> *Principle:* If you improve quality, you reduce total project costs.

As for projects, if you improve your processes so that quality is improved, then you will also reduce time and cost of project

F I G U R E 1.6

Reduction in Total Cost of Quality When Prevention Is Increased

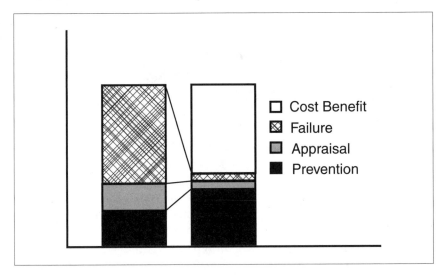

work simultaneously. Again, this is because you eliminate rework, which adds no value to the project. Large gains can be made if more attention is paid to quality improvement in projects.

How to Have Your Cake and Eat It Too

In Figure 1.2, I showed the relationship between P, C, T, and S as a triangle and said that these are the quadruple constraints of a project. There is a problem with using a triangle as an analogy. Suppose I want to hold P, C, and T constant and increase the scope of the job. On the basis of the triangle analogy, this is impossible. If I increase scope, at least one of the three sides of the triangle must get longer.

However, if I think of the triangle as being drawn on the surface of a sphere, then this is no longer true. If I change the radius of the sphere, it will change the area bounded by P, C, and T.

Figure 1.7 shows a sphere with a spherical triangle drawn on it, and inside the spherical triangle I have also drawn a plane tri-

The PCTS Relationship Shown on a Spherical Surface

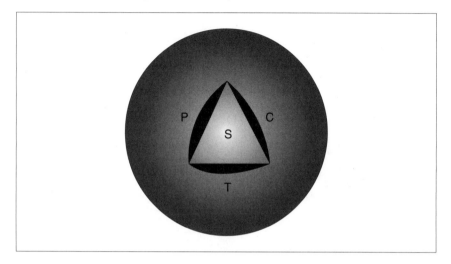

angle. If I assume that the sides of both the spherical and plane tri-angles are the same lengths, then the spherical triangle has a greater area, which represents project scope, so the scope has been increased while holding the sides of the triangle to constant lengths.[1] What does the radius of the sphere represent? I suspect it is a measure of how well the process works.

There is still another way to think of the relationship between the variables. Suppose P, C, and T are the sides of the base of a pyramid with a triangular base. This is shown in Figure 1.8. Now the scope is the entire area of the pyramid. What would be the physical meaning of the vertical sides of the pyramid? Perhaps they are factors of P, C, and T. Furthermore, it may be that the height of the pyramid represents how well the process performs. If it is a poor process, the height of the pyramid diminishes until you simply have a conventional triangle (the base of the pyramid).

---

[1]   For the mathematically inclined, the drawing is, of course, not correct, but I am trying to explain the concept in as simple terms as possible for the benefit of those readers who have no background in spherical geometry.

F I G U R E 1.8

The PCTS Relationship Shown as a Pyramid

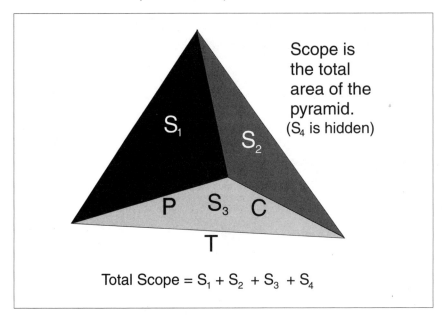

Scope is
the total
area of the
pyramid.
(S_4 is hidden)

S_1

S_2

P S_3 C

T

Total Scope = $S_1 + S_2 + S_3 + S_4$

What these figures help us understand is that by changing the process by which we do project work, we can get more for our money. We can reduce rework, increase productivity, decrease time, and so on.

Earlier I mentioned that Alan Mulally wanted the 777 airplane to be designed like a Fisher-Price toy so that it would go together easily. In addition, Boeing changed the process by which the airplane was designed. There were two aspects to this change. One was the technical and the other was the human.

The technical change was to go to complete three-dimensional computer design. When you design parts in two dimensions, it is impossible to know ahead of time that components inside the wing are going to run into each other. You have to build a model to find these problems. Then to correct them is extremely expensive. By modeling the plane in three dimensions, these interferences can be seen on the computer screen and corrected before a prototype is built. It isn't perfect, and there were still some problems in the design, but it is a vast improvement over two-dimensional methods.

The human change was expressed by the slogan *Working Together*. In most organizations, you find various teams building silos around themselves. When conflicts arise, they fall into an us-them mode and snipe at each other. The Boeing approach was to tear down those silos and create a climate in which people understood that the success of the project meant that they were totally *interdependent* on each other (Dimancescu, 1992).

They were encouraged to discuss their problems freely. Mechanics and assembly workers were involved with the design teams to produce a product that would be easy to build and easy to use. The chief test pilot for Boeing worked closely with the designers to produce a plane that would be accepted by other pilots, because this design departed from the conventional approach of using cables to move the flaps and rudder of the plane to a fly-by-wire method of controlling these components electronically. Because this causes the plane to lack the "feel" that pilots are accustomed to, it was important to make the difference as unobjectionable as possible.

Most significantly, representatives from the first customer, United Airlines, were part of the team, to make sure the plane would meet their needs when it was finished. There was ongoing dialogue between all of these parties to ensure that all interests were represented in the design of this twenty-first century jet (Sabbagh, 1996).

The ultimate result was that United Airlines accepted the 777 airplane on the first test by their own pilots! This had never happened before. It is a world-class example of what good project management can do.

Facilitation

Previously, I said project management is *facilitation* of planning, scheduling, and control. That word is very important. A project manager does not develop a project plan for a group. The general

Develop
a game
plan.

PROJECT MANAGEMENT

rule is that the people who must do the work should participate in developing the plan.

There are two reasons for this. One is that they know best how they will do their own work and how long it will take. Second, they are likely to think of everything that must be done, whereas if you plan the project by yourself you may forget something. And, because they know that your plan is likely to be flawed, if you develop it by yourself and try to "lay it on them" they will most likely reject it. So if you want to have a plan that is valid and accepted by your team, get them involved in the planning process.

> *Principle:* The people who must do the work should develop the plan.

How about one-person projects? Well, I suggest that it is very helpful to have someone else review your plan, so they can spot those things that you may have overlooked. Forgetting something is one of the top 12 causes of project failures. If you can't get someone to review it for you, then the best alternative (if you can do it) is to "sleep on it" for a few days. Then when you go back to it, you will probably see things that you missed before.

NATURE OF PROJECTS

Projects often involve many different disciplines to do the work. Consider a simple home-building project. You need carpenters, plumbers, electricians, landscaping people, roofers, and painters. These different disciplines often don't talk the same language, see the work of the other disciplines as interfering with their own work, and in the end analysis, don't cooperate very well. Furthermore, the project manager often does not understand all disciplines. This is especially true in high-tech projects. That presents problems of evaluating progress and quality of work.

Projects also have various phases. All too often, the sequence is as shown in Figure 1.9. The project is kicked off with great enthusiasm, but soon things begin to turn sour. The next thing you know, the team is in chaos and after the boiling point is reached, they sit down to define the project requirements. Naturally, this should have been done first.

> *Principle:* The nature of a project changes at each phase in its life cycle.

That is why I advocate the life-cycle model shown in Figure 1.10. My model is meant to be generic, and consists of five phases. Some models consist of only four phases: definition, initiation, execution, and closeout. Note that a project always begins as a concept, and a concept is usually a bit fuzzy. Our job as a team is to clarify the concept, to turn it into a *shared understanding* that the entire team will accept. It is failure to do this that causes many project failures.

In fact, I believe that projects almost always fail in the definition stage. They may hang around for a long time, going through

F I G U R E 1.9

The Typical Project Life Cycle

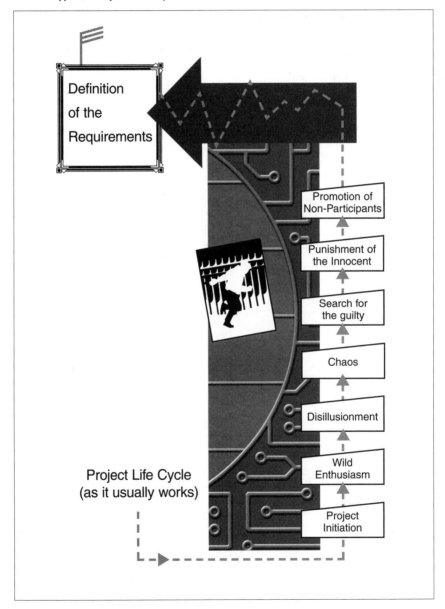

F I G U R E 1.10

Life-Cycle Model for Projects

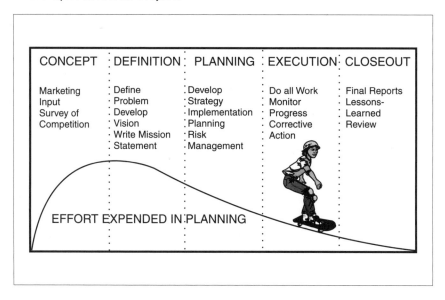

CONCEPT	DEFINITION	PLANNING	EXECUTION	CLOSEOUT
Marketing Input Survey of Competition	Define Problem Develop Vision Write Mission Statement	Develop Strategy Implementation Planning Risk Management	Do all Work Monitor Progress Corrective Action	Final Reports Lessons- Learned Review

EFFORT EXPENDED IN PLANNING

the other phases, but if the initial definition is wrong, they cannot succeed. We will return to this theme in Chapter 5.

HOW DO YOU DEFINE SUCCESS?

It seems reasonable to believe that, if you meet the P, C, T, and S targets for a project, it would be considered a success. It seems so.

Unfortunately, it doesn't always work that way. There are projects that meet all of the targets and are considered failures, and there are those that don't meet any of the targets and are considered successful.

To a person who likes to use numbers to judge outcomes, this is heresy. If you can't use the numbers to gauge success, what the heck are you going to do? Good question.

What is going on?

The answer is that part of the definition is to clarify requirements by having stakeholders tell you their expectations, understand what the results must be, and then determine what the deliverables must be to get those results and satisfy those expectations.

Consider a project in which a vendor has been chosen to provide certain equipment for a facility. One member of the staff preferred a different vendor. His expectation was that the staff would go with his recommendation, but they chose someone else. Even if that vendor meets all P, C, T, S targets, he will judge the project negatively. So the project manager needs to try to win this person over. This is the politics of project management, and will be discussed later in the book.

> *Principle:* The only truly successful project is the one that delivers what it is supposed to, gets results, and meets stakeholder expectations.

Consider Figure 1.11. The only truly successful project is one in which you can answer "yes" at each point on the tree. A truly failed project is one in which you answer "no" at each point. There are other combinations that are logically possible, but don't make any sense and are highly unlikely to happen.

THE PROJECT MANAGEMENT SYSTEM

If you are going to have good project management in an organization, there are seven components that make up a proper management system. These are shown in Figure 1.12. Note that I have arranged these to show how they interrelate.

Human Component

The human component is on the bottom. That is because dealing with people underpins the entire structure. *Projects are people!* They are not critical path schedules or Gantt charts. Those are the tools we use to manage projects.

If a project manager cannot deal effectively with people, the project is likely to have difficulty. In fact, I have never seen a pro-

F I G U R E 1.11

Expectations, Deliverables, and Results

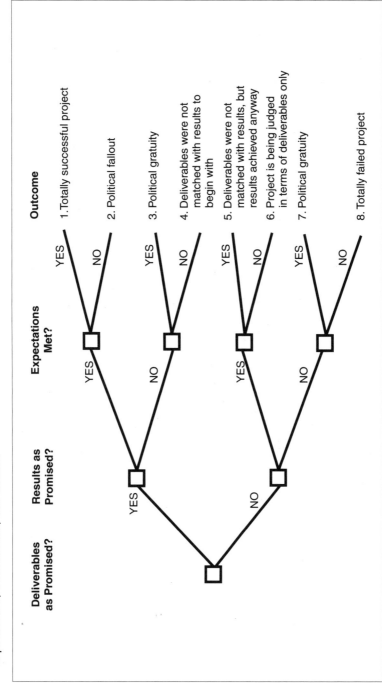

33

F I G U R E   1.12

A Project Management System

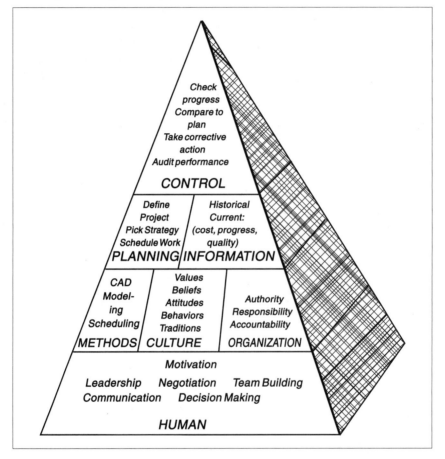

ject fail because the manager or her team didn't know how to draw a critical path schedule, but I have certainly seen a lot of them have serious difficulty because of "people problems."

As a project manager, you have to be able to do all of the things listed in the box: deal with communication, conflict, motivation, leadership, decision making, politics, and so on. The list is by no means complete.

I sometimes have technical people look at the list and say, "Oh, man, I really hate that part! Projects would be okay if you could just get people to be logical!"

I say to them, "If you really mean that, I suggest you rethink your career. Don't be a project manager—or any other kind." The reason I say this is that dealing with people is what managing is all about. If you hate people problems, you probably won't handle them very well, and they will drive you crazy to boot. In my value system, life is too short to spend doing something you hate. Choose to be a technical person instead.

> **Principle:** Projects seldom fail because of tools. They fail because of people!

On the other hand, some people say, "I'm not very good at some of the interpersonal skills, but if I could learn them I would be willing." In that case, I suggest that they set a learning objective for themselves. All of the skills identified in the model can be learned, if you want to learn them. Yes, even leadership skills. Everyone may not be equally good at all of them, but you can definitely improve.

Culture

On the next level up, we have a component that is related to the human system, but is so special that it must be considered separately. This is culture. The word culture designates the sum total of the values, attitudes, traditions, and behaviors that exist in an organization. In fact, one way to know that people are talking about their culture is when they say, "We don't do it that way here."

Cultural differences come from geographic differences within a given country, from ethnic background, race, religion, and so on. Broadly speaking, there is nothing good or bad about these differences (not everyone would agree with this). However, the differences lead to conflicts, misunderstandings, and disagreements.

Projects are becoming more global in nature.

Because projects are becoming more global in nature, and teams are often more culturally diverse than in past years, it is important that project managers learn about and value cultural differences and how to deal with them. A few examples will illustrate.

In Japanese society, it is considered impolite to say "no" directly. Furthermore, the word "hai," which we interpret to mean "yes," actually means "I am listening." So when a foreigner asks a Japanese person, "Do you agree," and he says "yes," it sounds as if an agreement has been reached. Later, when the Japanese individual seems to be violating the agreement and this is mentioned, he may say, "Well, we agreed to *this*," and it will have a shade of meaning different than what the foreigner thought it had.

Speaking as an American, we like to be very informal and are quick to call each other by first names. When I was a boy, we never called anyone over 25 by his or her first name, but our culture has changed. So, when we go to countries like Germany on business, we are quick to call managers by their first names. Many Germans find this offensive. I recently met a German engineer who has been working for his manager for eight years and still does not call him by his first name.

On one of my first trips to Malaysia, I tried to learn about their cultural taboos so that I wouldn't offend anyone. I found a book called *Understanding the Asian Manager* (Bedi, 1992) and picked up some good tips from it.

I taught for a company in Kuala Lumpur and, following the program, I had to fly over to Singapore. They arranged for a company driver to take me to the airport, and he was driving a van. As is customary in the United States, I started to get into the back seat. He looked back at me and said, "Sir, you're kind of fat. You would probably be more comfortable up here in the front seat."

It was all I could do to keep from laughing out loud. I could picture this poor fellow coming to the United States and working as a limo driver. He makes this remark to a passenger, who complains, and he is fired. "What's wrong," he protests. "I was only trying to be helpful." And he was.

What the book told me is that being fat in Asian countries is not a stigma as it is in our twiggy society. It is actually a sign of affluence, because it is believed that unless a person has a lot of wealth he or she doesn't eat a diet that is very fattening. Not knowing this, of course, it would seem insulting to an American to be referred to as fat.

One last example. A German man came to the states to work with a company in Seattle, Washington, for a couple of weeks. One day he went to the men's room, and it was being cleaned. He went inside and used the facility. The woman cleaning it was incensed. She filed a grievance, alleging that he had deliberately come in and exposed his private anatomy to her. This was sexual harassment.

Such a furor ensued that the president of the German company had to write a formal letter of apology, explaining that it is common in Europe for women to clean the men's restrooms without closing them. I have experienced this myself in Zürich and Frankfurt, as well as in Malaysia and Singapore.

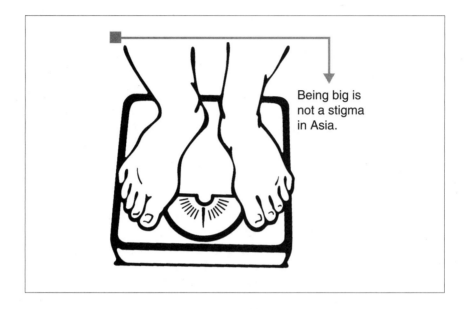

Being big is not a stigma in Asia.

All of these examples show the importance of being sensitive to cultural differences. The difficulty is that you don't know that you are violating someone else's culture until you do it, and they often don't tell you. And unfortunately, there aren't a lot of sources for training or education in such differences. You simply have to be sensitive to the cultures of other people, and if things don't seem to be going well, discuss openly what is wrong, so the problem can be corrected.

Methods

The Methods component of the model indicates the tools used to manage projects. This includes scheduling methods, earned value analysis, work breakdown structures, and so on. I don't find this to be a significant problem for most people. Tools are easily learned. The biggest struggle seems to be with scheduling software, and the reason this is such a problem is because organizations provide the software to managers without giving them training in how to use it. Even the most basic scheduling program today has considerable power, and the more power it has, the harder it is to use superficially, much less master. Giving a person a saw and hammer does not make her a carpenter. She needs training and experience in the art of carpentry. The same goes for scheduling software.

Organization

This component deals with how a project is organized, as well as how the company is organized. Every organization must delineate the limits of an individual's authority, responsibility, and accountability. A common complaint from project managers is that they have a lot of responsibility, but very little authority. I always tell people who say this that they may as well get used to it. As far as I can tell, it isn't likely to change a lot.

However, there are two kinds of authority, and we need to note the differences. One is to be able to tell people to do something and expect them to do it. This is authority over people, and this is the one that project managers won't usually have. So you have to get things done through influence, and this is true even for managers who do have authority over people. So concern about not having authority over people is an exaggerated issue, in my opinion.

The second kind of authority is to act unilaterally, without having to get one's actions blessed by 12 people in advance. This is most evident where spending is concerned. It is still one of my "pet peeves" that organizations require that project managers get approvals for purchases over $25, when they are managing projects that have million dollar budgets. This is ludicrous.

In my system of managing projects, as you will find as you read on, once a plan (which includes a budget) is developed and signed off, there should be no need for further approvals so long as the project manager is spending in accordance with the preapproved plan. Requiring such approvals simply makes work for someone, slows down the project work, and sends a clear message to the manager that he is not trusted with company money. Then why give him such a large project?

Control

Now I want to take this one out of order. I will return to planning and information later. The entire reason for managing a project is to make sure you get the results desired by the organization. This is commonly called *being in control,* and it is what is expected of a project manager.

Like many words in English, the word *control* has a couple of meanings. One is almost the same as the word *power.* Authoritarian managers attempt to control people through the use of power.

In management, the word control should have another meaning—that of guidance or an information systems definition. As you can see in the sidebar box, control is exercised by comparing where you are to where you are supposed to be, then taking steps to correct for deviations from targeted performance. This can only be done if the two components of the model in Figure 1.12 labeled Planning and Information are functioning correctly.

> **Con • trol:** the act of comparing where you are to where you are supposed to be, so corrective action can be taken when there is a deviation from the target.

Planning and Information

If you have no plan, you cannot have control, by definition, because it is your plan that tells where you are supposed to be in the first place. Further, if you don't know where you are, you can't have control. This comes from your information system. Most organizations have difficulties with both of these. They don't do a very good job of plan-

> *Principle:* If you have no plan, you have no control—by definition!

ning. In many cases, it is cultural. The company has grown from a one-person, garage-located business to be a prosperous concern with hundreds of employees. As the business grows, managers begin to realize that the old loosey-goosey way of managing is not working any more, and they try to impose some structure. This is often resisted. "We've never had to do it before, and we've been successful," people complain.

"Yes, but we can no longer continue to be successful this way," someone tries to explain. In fact, there is considerable danger for an organization that is successful, because people tend to become complacent.

As for information, most organizations do a good job of providing information systems to track inventory, payroll, orders, and other measures, but they don't have systems for tracking projects. Why? They didn't realize that they needed such a system. This means that most project managers have to track projects manually, which actually isn't too hard in most cases. Further, most scheduling software provides the capability to do earned value reporting, so generating your own progress reports is fairly simple.

Note that the information component also includes information on history. This is needed to permit estimating of project time, cost, and resource requirements. If I ask you how long it takes to clean your house or mow your lawn, you can tell me the approximate time because you have done it a million times. The same approach is used for project estimates, when history is available. This means that a database must be set up to record task durations.

This works okay on well-defined tasks, but when you try to apply it to engineering, software, or scientific research, it turns out not to work as well. The reason is simple. You seldom do the same task twice. So it is harder to develop good history for knowledge work, but such records do have some value, and we will discuss estimating in a later chapter. Additionally, alternative methods of estimating knowledge work will be presented in Chapter 7.

PROJECT MANAGEMENT AND ISO 9000

I am sometimes asked about the relationship between project management and ISO 9000. As I understand ISO, organizations are required to document their processes and procedures so that everyone does them the same way. So you need to develop a project management methodology if you want to be ISO certified. Many of my clients have taken the Lewis Method™ of project management (presented in this book) and written a methodology that requires their members to follow my method.

PROJECT MANAGEMENT AND SIX SIGMA

Another system that people ask about is the six-sigma model. This is a philosophy dealing with acceptable errors in processes or products. The idea is to reduce such errors or defects to extremely low levels.

If you draw a normal distribution curve that represents conformance of a process or product to its requirements, you find that going ± 3 standard deviations on either side of the mean will contain 99.74 percent of the population. That is, 0.26 percent of the measures you take will fall outside these limits. If you consider only one side of the mean, then 0.13 percent of measures will be

Conformance to Requirements

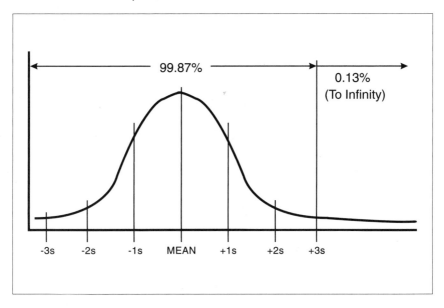

unacceptable (assuming that a product that performs better than expected is acceptable). This is shown in Figure 1.13.

If you draw the normal distribution curve to cover ± 6 standard deviations, then the percentage of nonconforming measures drops to 1 in a million. The six-sigma system requires that performance targets be set to this level.

Project management and six sigma, then, are different. Project management offers tools to help organizations achieve six-sigma performance targets.

Earlier I said that estimates place rework figures in projects at between 5 and 40 percent. That means that many projects are not even achieving three-sigma levels. If you go one standard deviation below the mean, you have 84 percent of the population conforming to requirements. That means, of course, that 16 percent of the population does not conform. So we are not even achieving three-sigma levels if we have rework that exceeds 0.13 percent.

THE LEWIS METHOD OF MANAGING PROJECTS

I attended my first seminar on project management around 1978. Since then, I have looked at project management systems of all kinds, and have developed my own model for managing projects. I call it the Lewis Method and have applied for a trademark for the term. Other models exist. Probably the best known was developed by my colleague Harold Kerzner, and is called the Kerzner Approach®. If they are valid, all methods are similar. So you may find that you want to combine characteristics from several models to arrive at one that best fits your project requirements.

Does One Size Fit All?

The question you might ask is, Does one approach work for all projects? The answer is "yes and no." The "yes" part comes from the fact that project management is a disciplined way of thinking about how a job will be done. That disciplined way of thinking is shown by my flowchart (see Figure 1.14), and it can be applied to any kind of project. It can be brain surgery, preparing a meal, developing hardware or software, or constructing a power dam. The overall approach is the same.

> *Principle:* The thought process can be applied to any project, regardless of type or size.

What differs is the tools used. I believe that there are some projects that are so small that to do a critical path schedule would be a waste of time. On the other hand, there are projects that could not possibly succeed without a good schedule. What you need to do is pick and choose what tools you use.

My Projects Are Too Small to Use This Stuff!

For some reason there are people who think that formal project management techniques are only valid on large projects. What I believe troubles them in many instances is that they are confusing documentation with the thought process. If I were preparing a meal, I would still go through the thought process outlined in my model, but I wouldn't create a lot of paperwork to do the job.

> *Principle:* The thought process is not the same thing as documentation.

I am a strong advocate of the KISS (keep it simple stupid) principle in managing projects—don't do any more than you must do to get the job done. (But don't do any less either!) I also like to call this the laziness principle, and I am lazy by nature. I don't want to spend more time or effort than needed to get the job done.

So go through the thought process, then decide how much of it should be documented, and do that. Keep it simple!

An Overview of the Lewis Method

My method contains five phases: definition, planning strategy, implementation planning, execution and control, and lessons learned (which can also be called the closeout phase). The model has been applied by thousands of project managers and forms the basis for many organization methodologies. It is a practical, no-nonsense approach that, when followed, helps managers avoid many of the pitfalls that cause projects to fail. This even includes some of the more common behavioral issues that seem to plague projects.

The model is presented in Figure 1.14 as a flowchart. This chart can be carried around and used as a memory jogger, rather than carrying the book around. Notice that there is another component of the model shown in Figure 1.15. This chart is necessary because step 6 of the model consists of a number of substeps, so rather than make one very large chart, I have broken step 6 out into a separate diagram.

To explain the model in detail would require that I write the entire book, so it will be covered in depth in the various chapters.

F I G U R E 1.14

The Lewis Method of Project Management

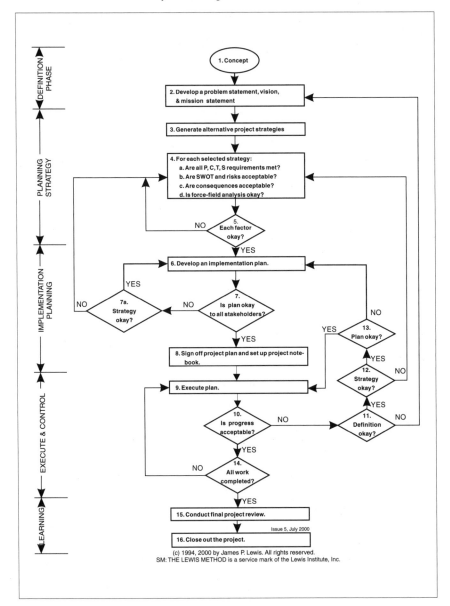

F I G U R E 1.15

Step 6 of the Lewis Method Expanded

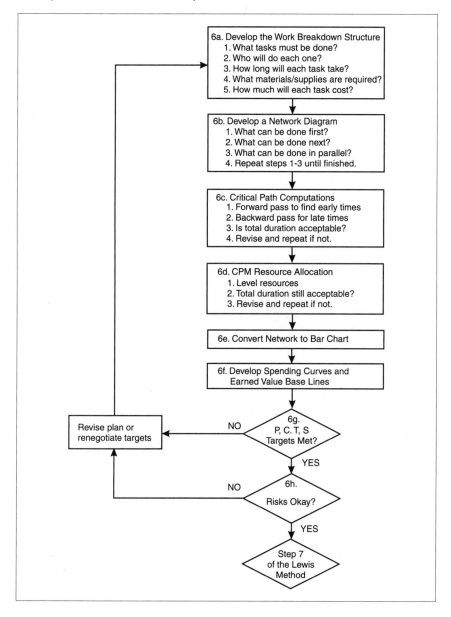

For now, I will provide just a summary of the main phases of the model.

Definition

As the model shows, a project almost always begins as a concept. We need something. Or we have a problem. The project is designed to solve that problem or meet that need. Remember the definition of projects offered by Joseph Juran? A project is a problem scheduled for solution. So we are solving a problem with a large-scale effort when we do a project.

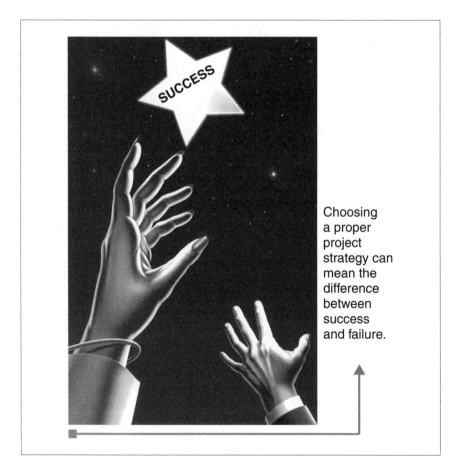

Choosing a proper project strategy can mean the difference between success and failure.

Where we get into trouble is in forgetting that the way you solve a problem depends on how it is defined. So the first stage in a project is to make sure you have correctly defined the problem being solved, that you have developed a vision for what the end result will be, and that you have stated your mission. As I will show later, failing to properly do this results in headless chicken projects. This phase is covered in Chapter 5.

Planning Strategy

The word strategy means that you have an overall approach to running a project. This step is often brushed over lightly. There is always a strategy or "game plan" implied by how a project is run, but that strategy is not chosen by comparison to other approaches. It is simply a default approach. Choosing a proper project strategy can mean the difference between success and failure, and the procedure for doing so is covered in Chapter 6.

Implementation Planning

This is what most people think of as planning. This is where you dot all your i's and cross all your t's. You work out all of the details of how the project will be done—what must be done, who will do it, how it will be done, how long the steps will take, and so on.

Execution and Control

In all too many cases, people jump directly from concept to execution. When they do this, they really have no control, because they have no plan that tells where they are supposed to be. This was discussed previously. Execution and control will be covered in Chapter 10.

Learning or Closeout

This stage is often aborted. At the Frontiers Conference on project management conducted by Boston University a few years ago, the keynote speaker asked an audience of some 400 people to raise their hands if they conducted regular end-of-project reviews for purposes of learning lessons. About 12 hands were raised. Then he asked a most compelling question.

"How many of you who put up your hands have a mandate that, before you do your next project, you must show your boss how you will avoid the mistakes you made on your last project?"

Two hands went up. And that is common. My own surveys in my seminars indicate that this response rate is pretty standard. This topic will be covered in Chapter 10.

IN SUMMARY

There you have it—a concise overview of project management. The rest of this book is aimed at expanding this overview into a complete treatment of how to manage projects. However, I should say that the word complete is an exaggeration. The subject is too big to cover in one book. But what you will get in this book are the core methods, principles, and practices of project management.

KEY POINTS FOR CHAPTER 1

- A project is a one-time job, as opposed to a repetitive activity.
- Project management is facilitation of the planning, scheduling, and controlling of all activities that must be done to meet project objectives.
- *Principle:* You can assign values to only three of the PCTS constraints. The fourth will be whatever the relationship dictates it will be.
- To crash a project is to reduce the duration below the minimum cost point.
- *Principle:* If you want to reduce both cost and time in a project, you must change the process by which you do work.
- The cost of poor quality involves prevention, appraisal, and failure.
- *Principle:* If you improve quality, you reduce project costs.
- To have good project management, you must attend to tools, people, and systems.

- *Principle:* The people who must do the work should develop the plan.
- *Principle:* The nature of a project changes at each phase in its life cycle.
- *Principle:* The only truly successful project is the one that delivers what it is supposed to, gets results, and meets stakeholder expectations.
- *Principle:* Projects seldom fail because of tools. They fail because of people!
- *Principle:* If you have no plan, you have no control—by definition!
- *Principle:* The thought process can be applied to any project, regardless of type or size.

QUESTIONS FOR REVIEW

1. Why does Juran say that a project is a problem scheduled for solution?
2. Project management is just scheduling: T   F
3. How do you define control?
4. What is meant by the scope of a project?
5. Why can you not dictate values for all four project objectives (P, C, T, and S)?
6. How can you reduce time and cost simultaneously in a project?
7. What are the three factors that contribute to the cost of poor quality?
8. Why is it not enough to define success as meeting the PCTS targets for a project?
9. Why is the human component at the base of the pyramid that shows the elements of a project management system?

CHAPTER

Getting Your Organization to Accept Project Management

This book is about how to manage projects. It is written primarily for the practicing project manager. Nevertheless, it is of value only if those of you who read it can go back to work and actually do what you have learned from it. And that is not at all certain.

Not because of you. You may find that the organization does not support you in your efforts and that your attempts to do project management are resisted. Why should this be?

There are two basic reasons. One is the paradigm problem and the other is the pain problem. And, if you can't find a way to deal with these two problems, you may as well quit reading right now.

So, before you go any further, this chapter is intended to help you get the benefits you are hoping for when you finish the book.

PARADIGMS

I am firmly convinced that the most important word in any language is *paradigm*. The word means a belief, or model of reality. A

Paradigm: A belief about what the world is like; a model of reality.

paradigm is what we believe to be true about any given situation, thing, or event. It is usually a deeply held conviction about how things actually are.

We can only deal with the world effectively if we know what it is like, so from infancy on, we are trying to understand the

A MODEL OF REALITY

PARADIGM
A belief of what the world is like.

world and the people in it. A major reason for this is to permit prediction. We want to know that, *if I do this, then that will happen.*

> *Principle:* The map is not the territory. That is, a paradigm is not necessarily congruent with reality itself.

Why should this be so important? Because all behavior is an attempt to satisfy some need of the individual. So if I am trying to satisfy a need, I want to know what I must do to get the desired outcome.

In the early stages of life, we don't yet have firm models of what the world is like. We are biologically programmed to cry when

> *Principle:* All behavior is an attempt to satisfy individual needs.

we have a need that isn't met, and if adults respond by meeting that need, we quickly learn that the world responds to crying by doing nice things for us. As we grow older, we learn that there are other things that we can do besides crying that will meet our needs, and our behavior repertoire grows.

Occasionally, a person has only learned one behavior that seems to get the outcomes she wants, and she has no choices. If crying always worked as a child, and nothing else seemed to,

> *Principle:* A person may have learned only one way to satisfy his or her needs.

then she may use the same approach to get what she wants, even as an adult. We say that her behavioral flexibility is limited.

You also see adults have temper tantrums sometimes. If it worked when they were children, then when they become adults, they may resort to the same approach—especially if more socially acceptable methods fail to get results.

> *Principle:* Paradigms determine how we will behave—we always behave consistently with them.

The reason why I say the word paradigm is so important is that we behave in accordance with paradigms. For example, if I believe that the world is a hostile, unfriendly place, then I will go around behaving as if it were true, and the important thing is that the world will most likely respond to my behavior in such a way that *it confirms my belief.*

Think about it. If I think you are a hostile person, I will approach you in a belligerent, defensive, self-protective way, and provoke in you the very hostile response that I expected. This then confirms that I was correct, and I never learn that you really are a very nice person.

> *Principle:* Paradigms become self-fulfilling prophecies. Another way to say this is that what we believe, we make real.

The paradigm, then, becomes a self-fulfilling prophecy. What we believe, we make real. Not intentionally. Not maliciously. Not even consciously. All of this operates pretty much at the unconscious level, which is why it is so hard to change.

> *Principle:* Behavior can only be changed by changing one's beliefs.

If you want to change your own or someone else's behavior, you must change fundamental beliefs about behavior. Unless this is understood, you will never succeed. In fact, it is our paradigms about behavior change that have caused us to be so very unsuccessful in changing people's behavior over the years. We believed that stored up libidinal energy caused by trauma was the reason for neuroses, psychoses, and other mental

SELF-FULFILLING PROPHECY

PROJECT NIGHTMARE #1

Behavior
can only
be changed
by changing
one's
beliefs.

aberrations, so we tried to go back into the person's history to un-
cover the trauma. The catharsis of reliving the event was supposed to relieve the person's symptomatic behavior.
Unfortunately, it seldom worked very well.

Now the trend is to believe that undesirable behavior is ge-
netically or chemically based, so the treatment is to prescribe
drugs. Nearly 30 percent of grade school children are diagnosed
as being hyperactive and are drugged with Ritalin. Does it seem
strange to you that we suddenly have an epidemic of hyperactive
children? Weren't the children in 1940 equally hyperactive?

I don't believe it. Unless there have been some significant genetic mutations in our society during the past 30 years, it seems

highly unlikely that we suddenly have so many children who are hyperactive. The problem is that we have a biological paradigm for the cause of hyperactive behavior, and that means the problem must be solved with drugs.

> *Principle:* If you believe all behavior is genetic, then the individual is not able to control negative behavior.

Of course, the drugs work. If you tranquilize the heck out of a child, he or she won't be hyperactive any more. The child won't be any good for anything, either, but that may be irrelevant if our primary concern is control in the schools.

Now I have used this example only to make you aware of the power of paradigms, and to show you that we do behave consistently with them. But what has this to do with project management?

> *Principle:* You can't make project management work in an organization that doesn't believe in it.

Easy. You can't make project management work in an organization in which nobody believes in project management. And you can train every single person in the tools and techniques and still not have anyone practicing what they have learned. You may as well throw your training money down a rathole.

Here's a case in point. For about nine years I taught two courses for the University of Wisconsin at Madison. One was my Project Planning, Scheduling, and Control seminar, and the other was How to Lead, Manage, and Facilitate Project Teams. In one of the team's classes, a fellow told me that he had attended the planning seminar several months before. When he went back to work, he said, he was eager to practice what he had learned, so he got his team together in a conference room and they started developing a plan.

His boss came by and saw them in the conference room. He called the fellow outside and asked, "What are you doing in there?"

"We're planning the project," the fellow said.

"Oh, you don't have time for that nonsense!" exclaimed his boss. "Get them out of the conference room so they can get the job done."

THEORY ESPOUSED VERSUS THEORY-IN-USE

This is a wonderful example of what Chris Argyris (1990) calls one's "theory espoused, versus theory-in-use." Argyris uses the word theory instead of paradigm. A theory is also what we believe to be true.

This fellow's manager ostensibly believed in project management, or he wouldn't have paid for him to attend the seminar. In fact, the planning and teams seminars were part of a certificate series that consisted of six programs. His boss had actually committed to spend nearly $7,000 plus travel expenses so that the fellow could get his certificate. Therefore we can say that his theory espoused was that project management is a good thing.

His theory-in-use, however, was an entirely different thing. Remember, I said that we behave consistently with our deeply held beliefs. So, no matter what we *say* we believe,

> *Principle:* You can tell what people believe by watching what they do.

it is what we actually do that tells what we *truly* believe. Therefore, you can always tell what a person really believes by watching what he or she does.

MANAGEMENT PARADIGMS

Because we behave consistently with our paradigms, let's consider just a couple of the more prevalent management paradigms that govern the management thinking in the United States. (You understand that the paradigms in Japan or India or Germany are not the same as those in the United States, so you cannot understand their management approaches in terms of U. S. beliefs.)

Perhaps one of the most prevalent of these is the lean-and-mean model. It is the outgrowth of experience we had in the 1960s. We suddenly discovered that our organizations were obese. That's right. Fat, fat, fat.

How did they get that way? Because of a previous paradigm. It was developed during the Industrial Revolu-

> It is the customary fate of new truths to begin as heresies and to end as superstitions.
> — Thomas Henry Huxley

tion (Ackoff, 1991). When factories began to spring up throughout the United States, many of the workers that were hired had just come to the United States. They spoke little or no English and many of them had virtually no education. So how could you make them productive?

Someone had to train them. Usually it was a supervisor. If a person proved that he could do several jobs really well, he was made a supervisor and told to teach new workers how to do their jobs. Furthermore, he was to supervise them closely, because they couldn't be trusted to do their jobs on their own. (Another belief in itself.)

The trouble is, you can closely supervise only about 6 to 10 workers, so a rule was developed that this was the maximum span of control for a supervisor. In turn, the supervisor's boss was supposed to keep track of what the supervisor was doing, which meant that she could only supervise six supervisors, and this continued up to the top of the organization. The result was pyramid-shaped organizational structures.

Strangely, no one noticed in the next 40 or 50 years that things changed in society, and that the pyramid was no longer necessary. The reason was education.

While our immigrant forefathers may have been uneducated, their descendants were not. Public education, child labor laws, and societal advances changed everything. For one thing, we moved from a machine-based organization to a service organization. Knowledge work grew more prevalent than manual labor. Whereas a supervisor could run almost every machine in his or her department in the 1900s, by the 1960s this was no longer true.

The result was that a supervisor could not closely supervise all of the people who reported to her, but the paradigm about span of control kept most organizations from changing.

Then the unthinkable happened. People woke up!

In one instance, a U.S. plant was bought by a Japanese company. The first thing they did was fire most of the middle managers—those between the top and the actual first-line supervisors. To everyone's amazement, the plant continued to function with

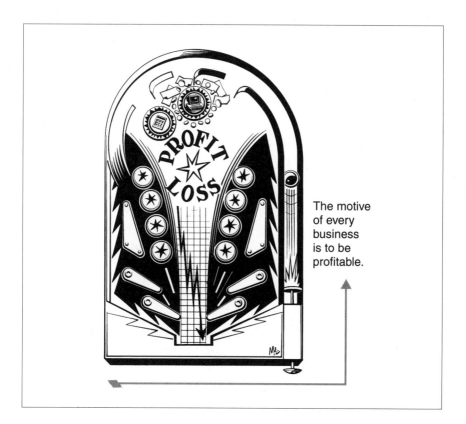

The motive of every business is to be profitable.

no serious drop in performance. There could only be one conclusion—those middle managers hadn't been contributing very much to the performance of the company.

Most important, however, their salaries now went directly to the bottom line, meaning that the company was suddenly profitable! Amazing. This is the motive of every business—to be profitable, and by the stroke of a pen, so to speak, it was accomplished. The excess fat that had made the organization sluggish and ineffective had been eliminated. The previously obese company was now thin and profitable!

The rest of the story is easy to follow. When other managers see that something has worked, they jump on the bandwagon. It didn't happen overnight. As Kuhn (1970) showed in his book about paradigms, old beliefs don't die easily. There is a period in which the new paradigm is rejected by the establishment, but as evidence for the incorrectness of the old model grows and the validity of the new model is repeated, everyone drops the old belief and adopts the new one.

> *Principle:* Things that work tend to become addictive.

The trouble is, when something works, it tends to become addictive. If cutting the excess fat improves profits, then removing all fat should make it even more profitable. This thinking has led to organizational liposuction, which is the result of anorexic thinking. "We must be thin, we must be thin," was the management mantra, but it became obsessive, which is the nature of anorexia, and now we

> *Principle:* Addictions tend to become destructive.

have organizations that have become so addicted to fat-cutting that they have continued cutting even beyond the point at which all the fat was removed. Of course, if you have already removed all the fat and you cut some more, you are now cutting muscle and bone, and in doing so, you will ultimately destroy the organization.

One writer has written a book about this. It is entitled *Corporate Executions*, and was written by a former downsizing consultant (Downs, 1995). Downs realized that the cutting had gone too far, and his book is a call for moderation.

AVOIDING PAIN

The other reason people in organizations resist the practice of project management is that they find it painful. All humans share a common tendency, which is to maximize pleasure and minimize pain. So we try to avoid the pain of planning projects.

> Good results without good planning come from good luck, not good management.
> — David Jaquith

Why is it painful? Partly because in planning a project you have to answer a lot of questions that lead to commitments. How

HOW LONG?

HOW MUCH?

We try to avoid the pain of planning projects.

> *Principle:* Human beings tend to avoid pain and maximize pleasure.

long will it take? How much will it cost? Are you willing to commit to those numbers?

Quite frankly, this scares the daylights out of a lot of people, especially engineers, scientists, and programmers. The question, "How long will it take?" can only be answered if you have a lot of history and, by definition, when you are doing science and engineering (which includes software) you don't have a lot of history. In fact, by the time you gained that much history, the thing would be obsolete. You are always trying to hit a moving target.

The consequence of trying to avoid the up-front pain of planning a project has serious long-term consequences. Instead of having pain diminish over time, it actually grows. The two pain curves are shown in Figure 2.1.

If you ever had calculus, you will remember that the total area under a curve represents the total amount of pain a person experiences. Well, there is far more area under the curve that continues to increase over time than the one that rises steeply initially and then declines. In other words, by avoiding initial pain, you actually experience more pain long-term.

OVERCOMING THE PROBLEMS

> You can't solve a problem with the same thinking that created it in the first place.
> — Albert Einstein

Einstein once said, "You can't solve a problem using the thinking that created it in the first place." If you are going to make project management work in your organization, both the paradigm must change and people must be made to understand that they will experience less pain long-term by good planning than if they avoid it.

Two Pain Curves in Project Management.

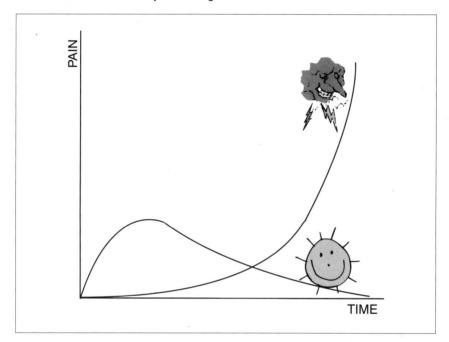

This suggests that the culture of the organization must change, and I believe that this is entirely true. However, I also know that it is not easy. My doctoral studies concentrated on organization change, teams, and leadership, and the success of organization change efforts is much like the success of psychoanalytical approaches to behavior change—very poor! As Peter Senge replied in an interview, when

> *Principle:* Getting project management to work in an organization requires a change in culture.

asked for his prognosis on organization change, "It's possible, and highly unlikely" (Senge, 1999).

It can be done, however, and I believe that it must start with a small group. For over 20 years, when I have addressed these issues, participants in my project management seminars have said to me, "You're preaching to the choir." Finally, I realized that they were not taking any responsibility for taking back to work what they had learned and trying to make it work. They saw themselves as powerless to effect change, and that is not true. Now I tell them, "I may be preaching to the choir, but the choir has to sing."

> I may be preaching to the choir, but the choir has to sing sooner or later!

You have to go back and enlighten everyone. You have to show that project management helps in the long run. You can't do it with theoretical arguments. In today's world, people are only convinced by seeing actual results.

My suggestion is that you find a sponsor who is at a high enough level in the company to have some clout, and enlist his or her support. Let this person be a champion for project management. But don't start an evangelical crusade. Go about it quietly. Pick a project and apply project management tools and techniques to it. Establish some measures to show success. Then make it happen! Do everything you can to make that project a success. If you do, you will create a bandwagon effect, because everyone wants to be successful, and when they see you do it, they will buy in quicker than they ever would from evangelizing.

> *Principle:* All of us need friends in high places to introduce lasting change into our organizations.

IN ADDITION

In addition to all of this, once you get the bandwagon rolling, get a copy of Graham and Englund's (1997) book, *Creating an Environment for Successful Projects,* and have your sponsor help you lobby with senior management to go the rest of the way. Graham and Englund have been instrumental in helping Hewlett-Packard become more effective at project management, which they see as a core competency now, and their book is packed with practical suggestions on how to make project management really work in your organization.

KEY POINTS FOR CHAPTER 2

- *Paradigm:* a belief about what the world is like; a model of reality.
- *Principle:* The map is not the territory. That is, a paradigm is not necessarily congruent with reality itself.
- *Principle:* All behavior is an attempt to satisfy individual needs.
- *Principle:* Paradigms determine how we will behave—we always behave consistently with them.
- *Principle:* Paradigms become self-fulfilling prophecies. Another way to say this is that what we believe, we make real.
- *Principle:* Behavior can only be changed by changing one's beliefs.
- *Principle:* You can't make project management work in an organization that doesn't believe in it.
- *Principle:* You can tell what people believe by watching what they do.

QUESTIONS FOR REVIEW

1. What is a paradigm?
2. People don't always behave consistently with their beliefs: T   F

3. Even if people don't believe in project management in your organization, you can still make it work: T   F
4. What is meant by *theory espoused* versus *theory-in-use?*
5. Why does the lean-mean paradigm lead to corporate anorexia?
6. Trying to avoid the up-front pain of planning only leads to greater pain later on: T   F

3

CHAPTER

The Role of the Project Manager

SO YOU WANT TO BE A PROJECT MANAGER

The first thing I think you should ask yourself is, "Do I really want to be a project manager? Or am I following a script laid on me by society?" In *Scripts People Live By*, Claude Steiner shows that we often follow a life script that was imposed on us by our parents, significant others, or society (Steiner, 1990).

In U.S. society, success is defined as having status and money. The two generally go hand in hand. Furthermore, managers have status, whereas engineers, clerks, accountants, and persons in other positions do not. Thus, these people are not successful; managers are. So, if you want to be seen as successful, you will have to be a manager.

Another factor that makes people want to be managers is the desire to be in control, rather than being controlled. The need for independence is very strong in some of us, so we think we will gain that freedom if we just become managers. It turns out to be a

Do you really want to be a project manager?

myth at midmanagement levels in most organizations, so the individual strives to reach the top—to be CEO (chief executive officer)—because then real independence will be achieved. That, too, is largely a myth as any CEO will tell you. They have more bosses than anyone—the stockholders, board of directors, and every employee in the company.

Please don't misunderstand my message—there is nothing wrong with being a CEO or a project manager. I am simply pointing out that you should want to be one for the right reasons, not the wrong ones.

There are two kinds of project managers—dedicated and accidental. If you are a dedicated project manager, you own the project from cradle to grave. Not your grave, but the project's grave. That is, it is your total responsibility from project initiation to project closeout. If that is not your situation, then you aren't a dedicated project manager, with all the rights and accolades that accrue to that position.

Also, if you are a real project manager, you are proactive, not reactive. I know, I know, you're sick of hearing about people who are proactive. You want to barf as soon as someone uses the term. But it's true, whether you like it or not. A project manager absolutely must take the project and run with it. If you aren't doing so, you need to get with it.

> *Principle:* Management is proactive, not reactive.

Proactive really means being assertive, as well as taking initiative. The difference between assertive and aggressive is important. To be assertive means to stand up for your own rights, while simultaneously respecting the rights of others. The aggressive person simply runs over others to get what he or she wants.

> *Principle:* The assertive person stands up for his or her own rights, while respecting the rights of others. The aggressive person runs over other people.

I was recently asked by someone in a seminar, "What do you do when a project is stalled?"

"Tell me what you mean by that," I said.

"Well, we refurbish buildings," he said. "One day you come in and realize that the gas needs to be turned off before some work can be done, and you have no idea how to go about getting it done. What do you do?"

I must confess that I had a hard time keeping a straight face. If you are a true project manager, wouldn't you be thinking ahead

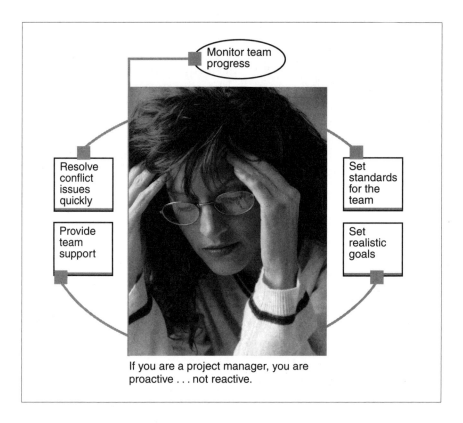

If you are a project manager, you are
proactive . . . not reactive.

about this sort of thing? This person was not being proactive, he was
totally reactive. I would say he was a project coordinator at best.

I don't mean to be condescending when I say this. He was an
accidental project manager. He may not have wanted to be a project manager in the first place, but the job was thrust upon him,
and he didn't fully understand the role. I believe this is true of
many individuals who have become project managers the same
way as this person.

The "I Don't Have Authority" Trap

One reason that project managers sometimes fail to be proactive is
that they don't have any authority granted by their position, and

they think they have to get permission before they can take an action. In fact, organizations tend to establish this as a procedure. You can't purchase anything without having it approved—often by three levels of managers above yourself.

Naturally, we can't do anything about the red tape. However, we can ask ourselves, "Where could I exercise discretion in my job?" As an example, I once worked for an absentee boss. He traveled all the time, so he was never around when I needed a decision on something. I was fortunate enough to read somewhere that the best approach was to assume the authority when it wasn't given to me, so when I couldn't reach my boss I would decide what to do and later tell him what I had done. I am convinced that this behavior contributed to my rise in the organization from an entry level position to chief engineer in about seven years. *The lesson was that you have as much authority as you are willing to assume.* If

> *Principle:* You have as much authority as you are willing to assume.

you wait for someone to give you authority, it may never happen, because you haven't demonstrated that you can handle it.

Another aspect of this was taught to me by a colleague. His favorite saying was, "It's always easier to get forgiveness than permission." I think he's right, and in those environments that are so rigidly controlled that this is not true, I would ask myself whether it is the place I really want to be.

DO YOU REALLY WANT TO MANAGE?

In the 30-plus years of my career I have observed that there are a lot of people who want to be *managers,* but a lot of them don't want to actually *manage!* Part of the reason is that managers have status,

> *Principle:* A lot of people want to be managers, but many of them don't want to *manage.*

some authority, and generally make more money than nonmanagers do. Even in technical organizations that claim to have dual career paths, the managerial path usually goes higher than the

technical path, both in terms of hierarchical level and salary. In fact, I met a fellow once who had done a study for his M.B A. degree on organizations with dual career paths, and he had found that the number of companies actually having such paths was very small, and in many cases the technical path was a dumping ground for individuals who could not make it in management.

WHAT IS MANAGEMENT?

Before you can really understand project management, you need to understand management in general. One common definition is that management is getting work done through other people.

It is easy to see why this definition is inadequate. A guard over a prison work crew gets work done through the prisoners, but would hardly be called a manager. And there are countless people who are called managers who really don't manage very well.

> One common definition is that management is getting work done through other people.

Peter Drucker, considered by many to be the "father" of modern management thinking, has written that management is making an unsolicited contribution to the organization (Drucker, 1973). That is, a manager does not wait until a situation exists that requires a reaction; rather, a manager is proactive. Furthermore, a manager is looking for ways to improve the functioning of the organization. He or she is forward-thinking.

Mintzberg (1989) has argued that very few managers whom he has shadowed fit the theoretical mold of careful, reflective planners. I agree with him. But I would argue that this is because so many managers find themselves caught in a firefighting mode that indicates they simply don't have time to do the careful, reflective thinking and planning that they really should be doing. In addition, according to Mintzberg's experience, they are being interrupted at the rate of once every 8 minutes, so they can't get their everyday jobs done.

I think of management as being very similar to the job of a pilot. The pilot's job is to get an airplane to a distant destination. She begins with a flight plan. She checks out the plane to ensure that it is functioning properly. Then she practices principles of navigation to guide the plane to that final goal. She compares where she is to where the flight plan says she should be, and makes course corrections as necessary to get the plane back on target when it has drifted because of crosswinds. The same could be said of managing.

A manager has a goal in mind. He makes a plan for how he will reach that goal. Then he sets in motion steps to reach the goal, compares progress against the plan, and takes corrective action when there are deviations from the plan.

> Control is exercised by comparing progress against planned performance, and taking steps to correct for any deviations from the proper course.

This is called control, and it is a primary function of management. Now note that, if you have no plan, you don't know where you are supposed to be, so control is—by definition—impossible!

So a manager is like a pilot, guiding his or her organization to a predetermined destination. Of course, a pilot occasionally finds that the airport at the desired destination is fogged in, and must divert to an alternate until the fog lifts. Managers must sometimes do the same thing and, occasionally, they decide that the original destination should be changed because the environment in which they operate has changed so that pursuit of the original goal would be inappropriate. So the analogy with piloting is not perfect.

The Law of Requisite Variety

An organization is like an organic system. Such systems attempt to adapt to the changing conditions in the environment so that they can survive. There is a law in systems theory that says, in any system of humans or machines, the element in the system that has the greatest variability in its behavior will control the system.

> **The Law of Requisite Variety**
>
> In any system of humans or machines, the element in the system that has the greatest variability in its behavior will control the system.

Now we have seen that managing is essentially a process of controlling the behavior of an organization so that it can reach a desired goal. Thus, the law of requisite variety suggests that a

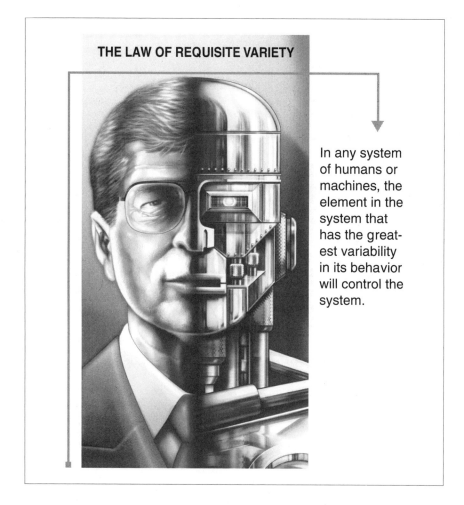

THE LAW OF REQUISITE VARIETY

In any system of humans or machines, the element in the system that has the greatest variability in its behavior will control the system.

manager must have more variability in his or her behavior than any other element in the system, or he won't be in control—some other element will be.

There are two possibilities for achieving such control. One would be to increase your flexibility to be greater than that of any element in the system. The other would be to decrease the variability of the system elements so that you can match or exceed the variation in the system.

> *Principle:* You must increase your flexibility or reduce variation in the behavior of the organization.

Any experienced manager knows how difficult it is to be flexible enough to respond to all the variations in the system. There are simply too many of them. We live in a turbulent environment, and chaos theory (Wheatley, 1992) has shown that even minute variations in some system element can lead to extremely large excursions in overall system performance. The best expression of this is that if a butterfly flaps its wings in San Francisco, a few days later the effect will be felt in the weather on the East Coast of the United States.

For this reason, some authors have argued that planning is futile, because the effects of chaos soon wipe out your efforts to control (Wheatley, 1992). I think this goes too far. A more balanced approach is recommended by Stacey (1996), who suggests that long-range planning should be tentative, a broad-brush stroke in nature, but day-to-day planning can and should be more detailed.

The Negative Approach

Because increasing one's own flexibility is so difficult, I believe that most managers resort to the second approach, which is to try and limit the variation in the system. Unfortunately, they do this in a negative way, rather than a positive one.

By this I mean that they try to limit variation with rules, regulations, and procedures that often stifle the variation the organization actually needs in order to survive in its environment. Another way to say this is that they create the ultimate bureaucracy, inasmuch as bureaucracies are known for being highly rule-governed.

The rules and regulations are essentially *thou shall nots.* Thou shall not go over budget. Thou shall not go around thy manager to his boss. Thou shall not spend more than $25 of company money without approval from three lords above you. Thou shall not pee in the elevator.

Why a rule prohibiting peeing in the elevator? Because some fool did it one time, and the management want to ensure that no one will ever do it again. I once read that they had installed pee detectors in elevators in Singapore. I wondered why, in an orderly society like that of Singapore, people were going around peeing in elevators. I finally realized that it wasn't people doing the peeing, it was their dogs.

> *Principle:* The negative approach (reducing system variation) tends to stifle the system and does not lead to real control.

Anyway, Tom Peters (Peters, 1987) has argued that these policies (as they are usually called) don't guarantee that people behave in acceptable ways. All they do is give the organization grounds to exercise sanctions over anyone who violates the rule. (Besides, did the rest of the troop need to be told not to pee in the elevator? Just because one person does it, are the rest of us going to rush out and do it? It gets a bit ridiculous, don't you think? Of course, I suppose elevator peeing could become the in-thing to do.)

The Positive Approach

A better way of reducing variation in system behavior is through proper planning. If every member of the organization knows what he or she is supposed to be doing, and how to do it, then variation in behavior is constrained by the plan, and the manager has control. And this is the only way. Unless every individual in the organization is in control of his or her own behavior, the manager won't have control.

> *Principle:* The only way you will ever have control is if every individual in the organization is in control of his or her own behavior!

This cannot be accomplished through micromanaging, either. In the end analysis, micromanaging means that you can supervise only one person, and I submit that one of you is redundant.

Rather, what is required is that conditions exist that allow every employee to be in control of his or her own behavior. How this is accomplished is covered in detail in Chapter 13.

> *Principle:* Control cannot be achieved through micromanaging.

A WORD OF CAUTION

It would be easy to conclude that, because few managers really spend a lot of time planning, this is appropriate for project managers. Every major study that I have seen on the correlates between what the project manager does and project success have shown planning to be vital. What may be important is that good project managers *facilitate* good project planning.

> Just because few managers do much planning does not mean that project managers should abandon planning. If you have no plan, you have no control!

They don't do it themselves. As I have written in all of my books, the first rule of planning is that the people who must do the work should do the planning. There are two principal reasons why this is true:

1. They have no commitment to someone else's plan, not because of ego, but because it is generally not correct—either in estimates, sequencing, or in being inclusive of everything.
2. Collectively, the team will think of things that no one individual (namely, the project manager) would think of. It is a fact that project managers are supposed to be in control,

PLANNING is not an option.

Control is defined as comparing where you are to where you are supposed to be, so you can take corrective action when there is a deviation.

in the sense of getting results from the project team. And because control is defined as comparing where you are to where you are supposed to be so that you can take corrective action when there is a deviation, it follows that if you have no plan, you cannot have control because you have nothing to compare progress against. For that reason, planning is not an option—it is a requirement! Perhaps if more general managers spent time planning, we would have fewer organizations operating in crisis mode.

THE MANAGING VERSUS DOING TRAP

Many managers have risen to their jobs after having first been technical experts in some field. In their new role as manager, they feel a bit like a fish out of water. They aren't very comfortable with it. I recently was told by a woman who was just promoted, "I sometimes wonder if what I'm doing is what I *should* be doing." Her boss is in another location, so she seldom gets to talk with her, much less receive any guidance. I assured her that most of us experience the same anxiety. The only way out of it is to be extremely clear about what you want to accomplish with your department or project team, which means you have a clear mission and vision in mind.

Even then, however, it is easy to fall into the *doing* trap. It happens when someone in your team has a technical problem that you could solve blindfolded. Or perhaps it is a bit of a challenge (that's the most dangerous kind). Next thing you know, you're spending a lot of time working on the technical issue, and you are neglecting your management job.

Or you may also have a tendency to micromanage. You don't fully trust your direct reports or team members to do the job as well as you would do it, so you resort to supervising them very closely. Either way, the managing suffers.

The Working Project Manager

One true trap that is imposed on project managers by the organization is that they are expected to do some of the work that is being done by other members of the project team. They are called *working project managers*. The problem with this setup is that, when there is a conflict between getting

> *Principle:* A working project manager almost always winds up in a double bind. Work takes precedence over managing, and the managing suffers.

work done and managing the team, the work always takes priority and the managing suffers. I would personally rather see that a person be given several small projects to manage, with no work responsibility, than have everyone try to manage the project and do work at the same time. It just never works.

MAKING YOUR CAREER DECISION

Graham and Englund (1997) have written that there will eventually be no more accidental project managers. Rather, project management will be recognized as a true profession, and we will have dedicated project managers with their own special career paths. They also observe that project management will be the proving ground and possibly the path taken to CEO status.

The reason is that project managers are exposed to almost every facet of the organization, they require exceptional political and interpersonal skills, and if they can manage projects successfully, they probably can manage the entire organization.

If, after reading this chapter, you are still undecided about whether you want to pursue project management as a career, then you should read "Career Guide" in *World-Class Project Manager*, by Bob Wysocki and me (Wysocki and Lewis, 2000). We offer a fuller treatment of the career than is possible in this book, together with diagnostics and other aids to help you make your decision.

KEY POINTS FOR CHAPTER 3

- *Principle:* Management is proactive, not reactive.
- *Principle:* You have as much authority as you are willing to assume.
- *Principle:* The only way you will ever have control is if every individual in the organization is in control of his or her own behavior!
- Managing is a set of roles.

QUESTIONS FOR REVIEW

1. Why does the author say that a lot of people want to be managers, but don't want to manage?
2. Is it safe to assume that, because most managers don't spend much time planning, the activity is a waste of time?
3. What is the "managing versus doing" trap?

CHAPTER

Whole-Brain
Project Management

No doubt there is no one who has not heard about left-brain, right-brain orientations in thinking. Left-brain thinkers are more analytical, logical, and sequential in their thinking than are right-brain thinkers, who are more parallel thinking, intuitive, and global.

THINKING STYLES

In his studies of how people think, Ned Herrmann found that the left-right dichotomy did not go far enough to explain thinking differences, and he postulated another axis based on cerebral-limbic thinking (Herrmann, 1995, 1996).

Principle: The HBDI measures one's preference for thinking in certain ways, not one's ability.

F I G U R E 4.1

HBDI Profile of Thinking Styles

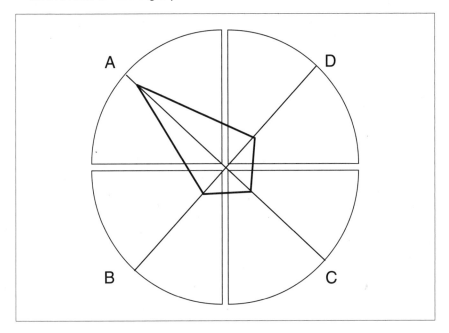

When this dimension is added, you have four pure styles that combine to yield a wide range of different thinking styles. Ned developed an instrument that measures these preferences, called the Herrmann Brain Dominance Instrument (HBDI), and the respondent receives a profile like the one shown in Figure 4.1.

In this profile, scores range from 1, which is most preferred, to 3, which is least preferred. There is no such thing as a 0 score because everyone uses all four styles to some degree. The instrument measures *preferences*, not skills or abilities. Herrmann believed that the preference for styles was based on brain chemistry or genetics, but whether this is true or not, the preferences are very real, and at this time, over 1 million people have taken the HBDI, and most find that the measures represent them fairly well. Seldom does anyone say, "That's just not me!"

The A Quadrant

The thinking associated with the A quadrant can be described as logical, analytical, technical, mathematical, and problem solving (see Figure 4.1). People with a strong preference to think in these ways are also attracted to professions that require such thinking. Examples of such careers include technical, legal and financial areas, including accounting and tax law, engineering, mathematics, and some middle-management positions.

A project manager with a single-dominant profile in quadrant A could be expected to be very logical, to be interested in technical issues affecting the project, to be inclined to analyze status reports carefully, and to be keen on problem solving. If he or she has very little preference for thinking in the other quadrants (particularly the C quadrant), this person may be seen as cold, uncaring, and interested only in the problems presented by the project.

A - quadrant
worker

The B Quadrant

The B quadrant is similar to the A quadrant, but with significant differences. Words that describe the B quadrant are organizational, administrative, conservative, controlled, and planning. This is the preferred thinking of many managers, administrators, and planners, bookkeepers, supervisors, and manufacturers. Individuals who have single-dominant profiles in the B quadrant could be expected to be concerned with the detailed plans of a project, and with keeping everything organized and controlled. Note that individuals with financial interests who are dominant in quadrant A will probably be financial managers, whereas those with dominant B quadrant profiles may be drawn to cost accounting.

If you want someone to pay attention to detail, to dot the letter "i" and cross the letter "t," then you want someone who has a

B - quadrant
worker

strong preference for this quadrant. If they have a single-dominant profile, however, they may see the trees and be unaware of the forest.

The C Quadrant

People with single-dominant profiles in the A or B quadrants probably see individuals with strong C quadrant preferences as being very "touchy-feely." Words that describe this quadrant are interpersonal, emotional, musical, spiritual, and talkative. Individuals with single-dominant C profiles would be very "feeling" and people-oriented. Such individuals are often nurses, social workers, musicians, teachers, counselors, or ministers.

A project manager with a single-dominant C profile would naturally be concerned with the interpersonal aspects of the pro-

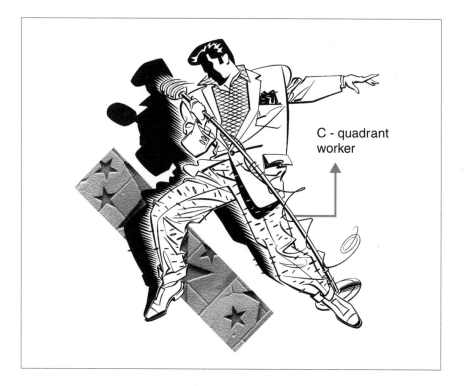

C - quadrant worker

ject, perhaps to the detriment of getting the work done. Such an individual would be drawn to the coordination of project activities with people both inside and outside the team, and would be a relationship builder. For highly political projects, this would be a good bias to have, so long as other members of the team are attending to the work itself.

In fact, you will remember that we have said several times, projects are people, and dealing with people is one aspect of project management that some individuals find distasteful. So you could expect that the person who has very low C quadrant scores on the HBDI will be bothered by this aspect of the job. Our counsel is that you can develop the skill if you have the desire, but given very low scores in the C quadrant naturally means this is not your "cup of tea." So you will have to work very hard at this aspect of the job if you want to manage projects.

There is an interesting finding about how we behave in terms of our least-preferred thinking styles. I (Jim Lewis) have a very strong D quadrant preference, with the B quadrant being least preferred. This means that I love developing concepts, and dislike doing detail work. However, if I must do detail work in order to have one of my ideas see the light of day, then I am very motivated to do so. What this means, then, is that you can be motivated to deal with the touchy-feely stuff, if it means achieving success in terms of your other thinking preferences.

The D Quadrant

Words that describe this quadrant are artistic, holistic, imaginative, synthesizer, and conceptualizer. Individuals who have single-dominant D quadrant profiles are often drawn to careers that involve entrepreneurial effort, facilitation, advising, or consulting, or being sales leaders and artists. These are the "idea" people in a team, and they enjoy synthesizing ideas from several sources to create something new from that combination.

This is the natural domain of people who are thought of as being creative. At the beginning of this chapter we discussed the need for creative thinking in projects. So you may conclude that if

D - quadrant
worker

you are primarily a left-brain thinker, having strong preferences for A or B quadrant thinking, and low preference for thinking in the D quadrant then you are out of luck. Not so. It turns out that it is easier for left-brain thinkers to learn to do conceptual or creative thinking than it is for conceptual thinkers to do analytical or detail thinking.

Project managers who have single-dominant D quadrant profiles could be expected to be very "big picture" in their thinking. They may run the risk of seeing the forest without realizing that it consists of a bunch of trees. They are generally good at thinking strategically, so in planning a project the D quadrant thinker will develop a game plan, but will need help from B quadrant thinkers to turn it into something practical.

Double, Triple, and Quadruple Profiles

In this book, we have limited space to cover thinking styles in detail, so we will have to limit our discussion about various profiles. As you can imagine, you can have a wide variety of profiles. We have discussed single-dominant profiles and what they may mean for project managers. But suppose you have strength in two quadrants. Or three. Or all four. What would that mean?

An example is shown in Figure 4.2. This individual has a double-dominant profile, but interestingly, it is across the diagonal between quadrants B and D. The person was an interior designer, and I asked her, "Do you sometimes talk yourself out of some good ideas?" She admitted that she did. The reason was that she would conceive the idea using her D quadrant thinking, and then when she tried to work out the details of how to execute the idea, she would begin to find problems and throw it out.

On the positive side, though, she did have the desire to make her designs a reality, something that a person with a single-domi-

Interior Designer's Double-Dominant Profile

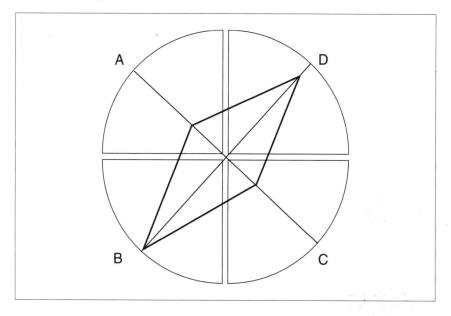

nant D quadrant profile may not otherwise do. The single-dominant person may conceive all kinds of good ideas but not implement them.

Think of this person in a project manager's role. I would guess that she would be good at seeing the big picture of the project, and at developing project strategy, but she would also be interested in doing detailed implementation planning as well. In other words, she could see both the forest *and* the trees.

Work Motivation and the HBDI

One aspect of thinking preferences that you should consider is that you probably have a least-preferred thinking style (or several). Mine is the B quadrant, which requires lots of attention to detail. I would find a project requiring such thinking to be drudgery. When I was an engineer, I disliked the detailed work involved in reviewing drawings or making sure a bill of materials was exactly right. It was vital work, but I hated it. So knowing your most-preferred and least-preferred thinking styles should help you determine when a particular kind of project is a good match for you, or what you should do when there is a mismatch.

Is There a Best Profile?

Ned Herrmann was always careful to say that individuals with almost any profile *can* do most jobs. The HBDI measures one's *preference* for thinking, not one's *ability*. There is, of course, a relationship.

> *Principle:* No single profile is "best."

When you have a strong preference for something, you tend to do it over and over, and in the process, become good at it. So we could expect that our profiles will bear some relationship to our skills, simply because we have practiced thinking in some quadrants more than in others, and have gotten good at those particular preferred modes.

Ned did postulate that there may be an ideal profile for a CEO and that was a square—a quadruple-dominant profile. The reason is easy to understand. A CEO must deal with people who think in all four quadrants, and if she prefers to think in all four, then she can translate between them for all parties involved. The HBDI group found that these profiles occur only about 3 percent of the time, so we wouldn't expect to find many individuals in this category.

I met one such individual, and sure enough, he was a turnaround CEO who specialized in saving hospitals from financial disaster. Unlike some individuals who specialize in turnarounds, this man tried to employ measures that saved as many jobs as possible. The turnaround CEO with very low C quadrant thinking is often concerned only with the bottom line, and the quickest way to improve financial performance is to eliminate jobs, regardless of the cost in human suffering. Naturally he or she will justify such action by saying that sacrificing a few jobs is better for everyone in the long run.

We did have the Herrmann group pull a composite profile for all of the project managers that they had in their database, and the overall is square. They had 1250 profiles for project managers, with the population being almost perfectly split 50-50 between men and women. These profiles are shown in Figures 4.3 and 4.4. There is a small tilt toward the A quadrant for men and a small tilt toward the C quadrant for women.

What this suggests is that project managers come in all "shapes and sizes." There has to be a fairly even distribution of profiles to get a composite square, so the distribution for project managers is not very different than for the population in general.

F I G U R E 4.3

Profile of Female Project Managers

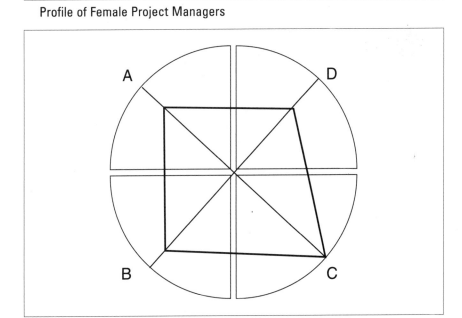

FIGURE 4.4

Profile of Male Project Managers

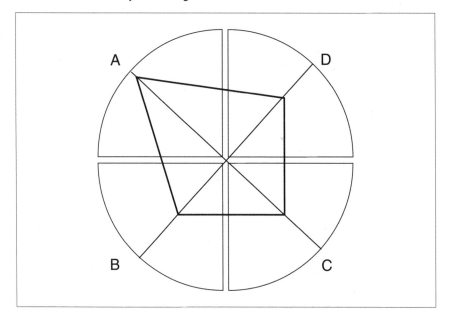

As has been stated above, what the thinking preference of an individual will do is affect her or his "style" of managing projects. The one concern we would have is with project managers who have very little preference for C quadrant thinking. The reason is that the age-old problem of project managers is that they have a lot of responsibility and very little authority, so the only way they can get anything done is through influence, negotiation, begging, and selling. Project managers with very low preference for the C quadrant are inclined to say, "I hate dealing with people problems," and to them we generally suggest that they rethink whether they truly want to manage projects. This would be the one deficit that we believe should enter into one's decision about whether to be a project manager. If you hate dealing with people, then why subject yourself to the daily agony that you are sure to experience as a project manager?

Is there a *best* profile? No.

Is there a best profile for a specific job? Perhaps.

However, the Herrmann group stresses strongly that the HBDI was not designed as a selection instrument, and they caution against using it for that purpose unless it is validated by a skilled psychometrician.

It is an excellent instrument for counseling individuals about career choices, and it is available on the Lewis Institute website (www.lewisinstitute.com). It can be administered only by a certified practitioner. The profile is accompanied by a write-up on the meaning of the results, and is best reviewed with the practitioner by phone or in person.

One application of the HBDI that is now well documented is its use in putting together teams. A team should collectively represent a "whole brain," meaning that if you overlay the profiles of all members of the team, they will form a composite profile that shows preferences in all four quadrants. Otherwise, if they have a strong aversion to one of the quadrants, you could expect that issues requiring thinking in that area may not be handled very well.

WHAT IF YOUR TEAM DOESN'T HAVE A WHOLE BRAIN?

As I said, many teams do not collectively represent a whole brain. For example, technical groups often have a profile like the one shown in Figure 4.5. They are strong in the A, B, and D quadrants and weak in C—the one having to do with interpersonal matters.

This means that they may very well attend to technical issues, are good at detail, and generate good ideas, but neglect the touchy-feely things that may undermine their team's performance. What should they do?

The important thing is that they be aware of the profile and that they know how to compensate for the low preference in quadrant C. Remember, it is not that they *can't* think in this quadrant but that they simply don't have a strong preference to do so. If they can understand that failing to deal with quadrant C issues is going to cause them problems in dealing with what they really

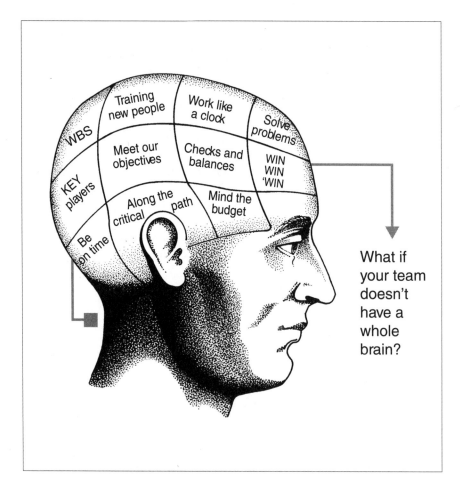

care about (namely technical things), then they are more likely to spend time working on such issues.

Here is another example (see Figure 4.6). This time we have a very creative group of people. They love ideas, they are interpersonal, even like doing analytical work, but they dislike detail. We can expect that they will generate good ideas but have trouble executing them—at least so far as the details are concerned. As one of my friends is fond of saying, "The devil is in the details," and the devil may just get this group.

F I G U R E 4.5

Profile of a Technical Team

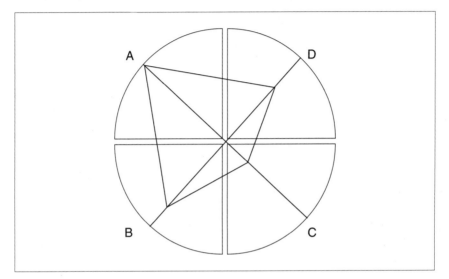

F I G U R E 4.6

Profile of a Creative Group

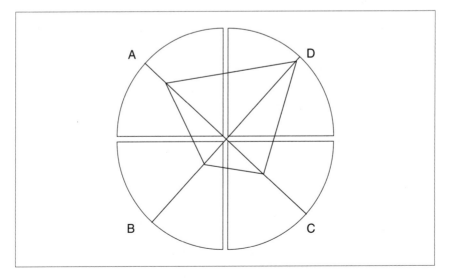

> *Principle:* We can all think in all quadrants—we just have to work harder in the least-preferred ones.

Again, however, if they are aware of the low quadrant B score for the team, they can compensate. They can work hard to ensure that details are not over-looked.

TEAM DYNAMICS

A project team is meeting to discuss an important project issue—a missed milestone. Everyone is a little apprehensive. They aren't sure how senior management is going to react to their failure to complete the project work by the scheduled time.

Wanda says, "I don't see how we could have done any better. We did everything humanly possible to complete the work on time. I feel really bummed out over the whole thing!"

"In looking at the numbers," Chuck says, "I believe we were set up to begin with. We were allocated to the project at a 95 percent rate, which is too high."

"I didn't like the concept we started with in the first place," chimes in Karen. "It was too flaky."

Don has been studying the schedule in front of him. "We should have moved these two tasks in parallel," he offers. "Then we could have finished on time."

This sets Wanda off. "You're always changing the plan, Don," she insists. "Can't you see we did everything we could to meet the deadline?"

"But the schedule is the most important part of the project plan," Don says defensively. "If we don't use the schedule prop-erly, we can't hope to complete the work on time. It's a question of being better organized."

"It doesn't matter how well organized we are if the concept is no good to begin with," Karen interjects.

At this point, the project manager, Beth, interrupts. "Okay, let's calm down for a moment," she says. "And let's look at what's going on."

They all lean back in their chairs and wait for Beth to continue.

"Wanda, you're concerned about the effort you've put into the job, and you're feeling a little guilty that it didn't pay off," Beth says. "In terms of your HBDI profile, you're thinking in the C quadrant."

Wanda nods in agreement.

"And Karen, you're in the D quadrant, thinking conceptually as usual," Beth says.

Karen smiles and nods. Beth has her pegged.

Beth continues around the table. "Naturally, Don is concerned about the schedule. He's a predominantly B quadrant thinker, and Chuck is analyzing the numbers—his normal A quadrant thinking."

Everyone laughs.

"The bad news is that each of us sees the situation from a different perspective," Beth continues. "And the good news is that each of us sees the situation from a different perspective."

She pauses to let the impact of her comment sink in.

"That's true," Karen says. "If we all saw it the same way we would probably fall into groupthink and really get into trouble."

"Exactly!" Beth says. "We need every perspective to be effective as a team, but the different thinking styles make us think the other person doesn't understand what we're talking about, and we get into conflict."

They all murmur their agreement.

"Now let's see if we can use your varying points of view to get a handle on this project," Beth suggests. "How about if we come back to Karen's contention that the concept is flawed. She's right. If it is, then the detailed plan can't be any good."

From this point on, the meeting proceeds to a solution.

By understanding the fact that each member of the team sees the project in different ways, on the basis of their individual thinking styles Beth is able to draw on those preferences to the benefit of the project. Were she unaware of thinking preferences, she would probably see the team as dysfunctional, and be tempted to disband it altogether or perhaps ask a group facilitator to come in and help her keep them in line.

Of course, this scenario has been framed somewhat unrealistically because I have treated each individual team member as though he or she had a single-dominant thinking style. Most of us think in more than one quadrant, but it is true that there may be a quadrant that does dominate our thinking, and when we communicate with others who are in different quadrants than our own, we have difficulties.

> *Principle:* Misunderstandings sometimes occur because of differences in thinking preferences.

The opposite is also true. A couple of years ago I met a fellow with whom I seemed to have almost instant rapport. We saw eye to eye on so many things it was almost scary. At that time I was aware of the HBDI, but had not yet been certified as a practitioner, so it didn't occur to me that this may be the source of our easy communication and understanding. I did know the Myers-Briggs, and found that we had similar temperaments. In any case, we became good friends.

After I became certified, I sent a survey to my friend, and to our amazement, his profile and mine are congruent to within a few points in every quadrant! No wonder we think so much alike. Naturally, we don't agree on everything. But the similarities are so striking that it is uncanny.

The danger for us, of course, is that we may too quickly agree on an issue without doing the critical thinking that might change our opinions. As Beth told her team, we need opposing points of view to achieve a balanced perspective on some issues.

Managing Conflict

If a team is to have creative capacity, it must be able to generate a lot of ideas so that a good one will emerge. These ideas must then be screened and the best one selected. During the screening pro-

CREATIVITY IN THE OFFICE

"You Think Funny."

cess, various ideas are critiqued, and it is at this point that conflict sometimes turns nasty.

There is a sense in which, if you criticize my idea, you are finding fault with me. So I respond by getting angry. Next thing you know, we are locked in an interpersonal conflict. These are often labeled *personality conflicts.* They are, in a sense. But they have a fundamental cause—we see things differently and identify with our points of view and the ideas we have.

As a project leader, you have to get people to give you ideas, and you have to manage the critiquing of these conflicting ideas so that they don't develop into interpersonal conflict. If this happens, as it will sometimes, you then have to resolve that interpersonal conflict, and if people understand the concept of thinking preferences, this is somewhat easier than it may be otherwise.

KEY POINTS FOR CHAPTER 4

- *Principle:* The HBDI measures one's preference for thinking in certain ways, not one's ability.
- Left-brain thinkers are more analytical, logical, and sequential in their thinking than are right-brain thinkers, who are more parallel thinking, intuitive, and global.
- *Principle:* We can all think in all quadrants—we just have to work harder in the least-preferred ones.
- *Principle:* Misunderstandings sometimes occur because of differences in thinking preferences.

QUESTIONS FOR REVIEW

1. The HBDI measures one's thinking ability: T   F
2. Is there a best thinking profile?
3. What do you do if your team doesn't have a "whole-brain" profile?
4. What is the advantage of knowing the thinking preferences of each member of your team?

SECTION TWO

PROJECT DEFINITION

CHAPTER

The Headless Chicken
Project (and How to Avoid It)

When I was a boy we lived in the country for a few years, and my parents kept some chickens around. In those days, if you wanted to have fried chicken for lunch on Sunday, you didn't go to a grocery store and buy a processed chicken. Instead, you caught one in the back yard, whacked its head off, and that was your lunch.

When you cut off a chicken's head, the body runs around spewing blood for a few seconds, then falls over, quivers a bit, and the chicken is officially dead. It was

> *Principle:* Projects often fail at the beginning, not the end.

actually dead when you cut off its head, but it took some time for the message to reach the rest of the body.

Projects are like that. We whack off the project's "head," and it runs around for a while spewing blood, finally falls over, quivers a bit, and becomes still.

Someone says, "I think that project is dead." It is. It was dead from the very beginning, but like the chicken, it took a while for the message to reach the body.

I call these *headless chicken projects.* No doubt you have seen one yourself. They're all around us.

They are the projects that are doomed before they get started, because we whacked off their heads at the beginning.

THE COLD, HARD STATISTICS

Every year the Standish Group (www.standishgroup.com) does a survey of software development projects in the United States. How many succeeded, failed, or were changed dramatically? Results from a survey they did in 1994 are shown in Figure 5.1. These data are on their website, so you can review them for yourself. Statistics haven't changed much in the subsequent years.

F I G U R E 5.1

Standish Group Survey Results

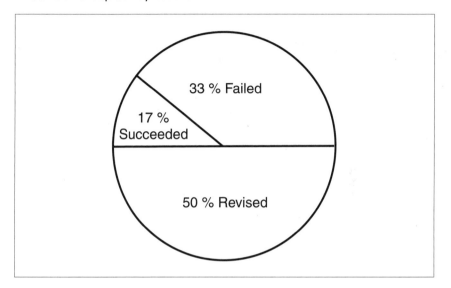

As you can see, 80 percent of all projects suffer serious problems, with nearly a third of them being bad enough to be canceled. That means that of the $250 billion spent on software development, about $80 billion is wasted.

THE CAUSES

What causes headless chicken projects? First, consider how projects are kicked off. In many cases, the project sponsor conceives the need for the project. A project manager is recruited to do the job. She is told about the sponsor's concept, which both find very exciting. Of course, the sponsor has only a half-baked idea, and is certain that the project manager can turn it into a fully baked cake that everyone will admire. The project manager is equally certain that she can do this.

She assembles a team, and in breathless enthusiasm tells them all about the project. Their mission is to create a fully baked cake, complete with icing that has been beautifully decorated. When the cake is completed, there will be a huge celebration, and guests from throughout the world will be invited to share in their revelry.

Members of the team sit in rapt attention, nodding their agreement with the project manager's words of anticipation. She is overjoyed that they have so readily "bought in" to the general concept of the job, and she sends them forth to do the work, fully confident that they are bound for glory.

They leave the room, walking side by side down the hall, going back to their desks. Unknown to the project manager, one of the chosen team members, Matthew, asks Karen, "Did you understand what Heather was talking about?"

"I don't have a clue," Karen says, shaking her head. "Something about a birthday party, I believe."

"Boy, I was hoping you understood her," Matthew says. "Because I didn't get it at all. Maybe Susan got it," he says, as he notices Susan walking ahead of them.

"Hey, Susan, can we ask you a question?" Matthew asks.

"Sure." Susan pauses to wait for them.

"We were wondering if you understood what Heather wants us to do," Karen tells her. "Neither Matthew nor I have a clue."

> *Principle:* Many people are socialized to remain silent, even when they don't understand.

Susan shakes her head, an obvious expression of dismay on her face. "I don't either," she admits. "But I was sure I was the only one in the group who was confused, so that's why I didn't say anything."

"I thought the same thing," Matthew confesses. "I guess none of us really understood, but were afraid to say so."

The Abilene Paradox

This is an example of what Jerry Harvey calls the Abilene Paradox (Harvey, 1988). Harvey made up a story about a family that lives in Texas. One hot Sunday morning, they are sitting around with nothing to do. They are bored.

So someone asks, "What do you want to do today?"

Another member of the family suggests, "How about if we go to Abilene and have lunch at the cafeteria?"

Next thing you know, they all pile into an old car with no air conditioning. It's 110 degrees in the shade, but driving 75 miles an hour with the windows down creates enough of a breeze to make the 90-mile drive bearable.

They have lunch. Not a very good lunch. A cafeteria lunch.

Following the mediocre meal, they go out onto the streets of Abilene, only to find that there is nothing to do.

Now they are bored in Abilene.

There's nothing to do now but go home, so they make the 90-mile blast-furnace trek back home.

As they walk back to the house, someone says, "Boy, that was a waste of time!"

"I thought you wanted to go," another person protests.

"No, I just went because the rest of you wanted to go," replies the first person.

They look at each other sheepishly. They take a poll.

It turns out nobody *really* wanted to go to Abilene—not even the person who first suggested it. She was only thinking out loud.

They have all made a 180-mile round-trip to Abilene, for a mediocre meal, when nobody really wanted to go at all!

Now Harvey makes a highly significant point about this. He says it appears to be a failure to manage agreement. It is not. It is a failure to manage *disagreement!*

> *Principle:* The false consensus effect is a failure to manage disagreement, because no one knows it exists.

The reason?

They never knew there was any disagreement, because no one said anything. They have fallen into the trap called "silence means consent." This is the nature of the Abilene Paradox.

Notice that the same thing happened to our project team. Because no one said anything, the project manager assumed that they were all in agreement, and that they all understood the mission.

They didn't. But they were afraid to say so. Why? Probably because they did not individually want to appear stupid to other members of the group. After all, *they could tell* from the smiling faces of their peers in the team that all of them understood. "Surely," each of them was thinking, "I must be the only team member who doesn't understand."

Overcoming the Abilene Paradox

Notice that the way a group falls into the Abilene Paradox trap is that the message is delivered in a way that allows the team members to remain passive. Furthermore, they are not yet a true team. They have been brought together to be *told* about the project, and in most cases the project manager does nothing to make them feel that they are a team. She is so excited about the project that she wants to dive right in and get them started. She is completely *task-focused.*

This is a pervasive problem. We forget that there are two aspects to all projects—the *what* and the *how*. The what is called the task to be performed. How it is to be performed is called process.

> There are two aspects to all projects—the *what* and the *how*.

But process also applies to how the team functions in total—how they communicate, interact, solve problems, deal with conflict, make decisions, make work assignments, run meetings, and every other aspect of team performance.

And the lesson that most managers have not learned is that *process will always affect task performance!* We have understood this in manufacturing for many years. We have applied statistical process control (SPC) to manufacturing to detect process problems. We have worked to improve processes, to eliminate non-value-added steps, and to reduce scrap and rework, and we have even begun to recognize that nonmanufacturing processes should be improved. This realization may have been championed by Hammer and Champy in their book *Reengineering the Organization* (1993).

For that reason, we must employ a process that will avoid the Abilene Paradox. The best approach that I know of is to get the team members actively involved in defining the project, which includes

> *Principle:* Process will *always* affect task performance!

examining the problem to be solved, then developing a mission statement that tells where the team is going and a vision for the end result they wish to achieve. I have found that the steps in Figure 5.2 meet this requirement.

In this procedure the team members are told the mission, but are then asked to put it into their own words. Each member writes out what he or she believes the mission to be. They then try to consolidate all of their individual statements into one that they can all support. This statement is then polished and published. From that point on, every time a question about the team's performance comes up, you ask how to answer the question, take the step, make a decision, or solve a problem in such a way that you support attainment of the team's mission.

Notice that this procedure makes team members active participants in drafting the statement. Furthermore, once the statement is written, it is used to keep the team on track and to give them guidance on how to address various issues as they arise. This makes the mission statement a living document that is operational. This is in sharp contrast to what usually is done. In many cases, the mission statement is drafted and then forgotten, leaving everyone wondering what all the fuss was about.

I have found that almost every team will have at least one member who is initially going the wrong way, compared to where the team is going. This is shown in Figure 5.3. Ideally, when they write out their individual statements and compare them, they will all be going in the same direction—the one represented by the big

FIGURE 5.2

The Steps in Developing a Mission Statement

Misalignment of One Team Member with the Others

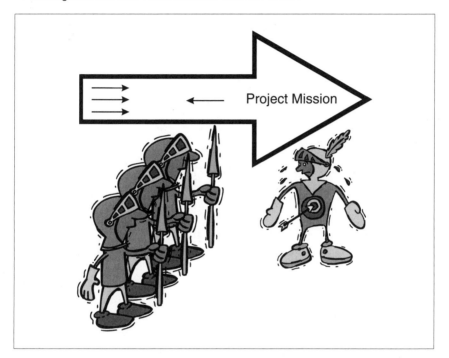

arrow. This means that they are aligned with the direction to be taken by the project. However, you usually find that someone has a different idea about what they are supposed to be doing, and unless this discrepancy is resolved, the team will not be successful.

There are only three things that can be done to resolve the disconnect. First is to convince the person to go in the same direction as the others. This may be done through discussion in which any misunderstandings of the individual are corrected. Or he may need to be convinced of the proper direction.

The second response is to change the direction of the entire team. It may well be that the "errant" person has thought of the mission in a way that everyone else missed. In this case, the team agrees to go in the direction advocated by the individual.

In the event that neither of these responses is possible, the only remaining step is to remove the person from the team. You simply cannot have a successful project when a core team member disagrees with the mission as it is seen by the other members. This may be the most difficult step

> Suffer fools gladly. They may be right.
>
> — Holbrook Jackson

you will be called on to take because you often do not get to choose core team members, but it really is necessary. And you can't kid yourself by thinking it isn't important. Ensuring that you have a shared understanding of the mission, vision, and problem is the most important action you can take as a

> *Principle:* The first objective for a project manager is to achieve a shared understanding of the team's mission.

project manager. Otherwise you are certain to have a headless chicken project.

PROBLEM, MISSION, AND VISION

I can almost hear the groans from readers when they see this section headline. As a fellow in one of my seminars said, "You aren't going to talk about mission statements are you? They've been totally discredited."

I agreed with him. Most of the mission statements written by corporations can be cloned. They say, "Our mission is to make lots of money for the stockholders." Usually they are a bit more flowery than that. But this is the essence of what they say.

I've often wondered just how many people in an organization get excited by such statements. Do you suppose the CEO wakes up in the morning eager to go to work to make money for the stockholders?

I have no doubt he may stay awake at night worrying about it. Failing to make money for the stockholders may cost him his job.

But does it excite him? Who knows. I only know that most members of the organization are not motivated by such expressions.

The thing is, can you imagine taking a team to a destination when they don't know what that destination is? I can't. You have to have some statement that tells everyone where they are going, and if you don't like the word mission, then call it goal, objective, target, or peanut butter. I don't care. I'm going to stay with the word mission, because it is the correct term. But you can take your pick. Fine. Now we have that taken care of.

> Mis • sion: the goal or objective that the team must achieve.

But what about vision? This begins to sound really flaky. You may wonder if it has anything to do with hallucinogenic mushrooms. Or with seeing Elvis sitting in your project team meeting.

I guess that's possible. But what I mean

> Where there is no vision, the people perish.
> — Old Testament, Proverbs 29:18

by vision is what will the final result of the team's efforts look like? It's that simple. If you know what the final result will look like, you will know when you're finished with the job. Otherwise, people may not be certain that the job is done. In addition, if everyone

> Vis • ion: what the final result will look like.

doesn't agree on the vision, each person will try to achieve the outcome she or he imagines, with disastrous results.

Note that this is much easier with tangible things than with projects intended to produce intangible results. For example, software projects may be harder to visualize than those that produce hardware.

Okay, we have explained the need for mission and vision. But what about a problem statement? Remember, a project is a

problem scheduled for solution. That is, we are solving a problem on a large scale when we do a project. Building a bridge solves the problem of not being able to easily get across a river or gorge. Developing an automobile solves the problem of not being able to transport people easily from one place to another.

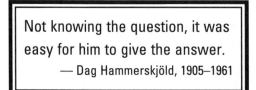

Developing an insurance package provides protection against financial ruin for people. The financial ruin would be a major problem, and that problem is solved by the insurance package.

In the same way, every project solves a problem for the organization, but we often make the mistake of assuming that we understand the problem when, in fact, we do not. As an example, let us suppose that you have a headache. You assume the cause is stress. So you take some capsules for pain and the headache goes away. The next day it returns, so you again take some pain pills. It retreats.

> The uncreative mind can spot wrong answers, but it takes a creative mind to spot wrong questions.
>
> — Anthony Jay

This is repeated for an extended period until you finally become concerned and go to the doctor. After some exhaustive tests, the doctor reports that you have a brain tumor that can only be removed by surgery.

You have been treating the *symptom*—not the cause—of the problem. The symptom is the headache itself. The cause is the tumor.

> *Principle*: The way a problem is defined determines how we attempt to solve it.

This is typical of so many attempts to solve problems. The way we define the problem always determines how we try to solve it, and if the definition is incorrect, the solution won't work.

And this is the major cause of headless chicken projects. We don't spend enough time working out the actual definition, and so we may very well develop the *right solution*

> *Principle:* If the definition is wrong, you will develop the right solution to the wrong problem.

to the wrong problem, leaving the organization with the original problem the project was intended to solve.

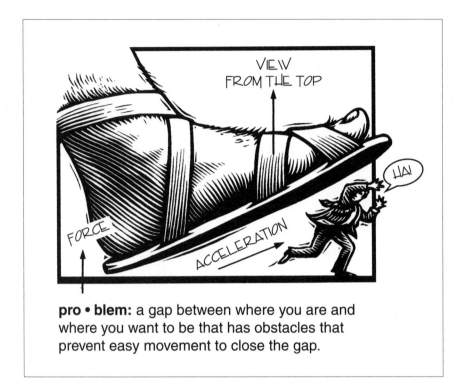

pro • blem: a gap between where you are and where you want to be that has obstacles that prevent easy movement to close the gap.

KINDS OF PROBLEMS

If we are to ensure that our projects don't solve the wrong problem, clearly we must spend more time on the definition stage. Furthermore, we need to have a clear understanding of what is meant by a problem because the word is used so loosely that it means a lot of things. We say that the headache is a problem, when it is actually a symptom of the underlying cause. We claim that the problem is that sales are down when this again is a symptom of something. So there is a tendency to equate symptoms with problems, guess at the cause, and go off on a happy hunt for the witch we think caused the symptom.

A problem is defined as a gap between where you are and where you want to be that is confronted with obstacles that make closing the gap difficult. It is actually the obstacles that make the gap a problem. As an example, if you are at the end of a long hallway and want to go to the other end, that in itself is a simple goal. If, however, someone puts a large alligator in the hall, and you know the alligator will bite off your leg if you try to pass, then you truly have a problem. The essence of all problems is having to deal with alligators. You must remove it, get around it, or momentarily neutralize it if you want to reach the other end of the hall. All problem solving is dealing with alligators!

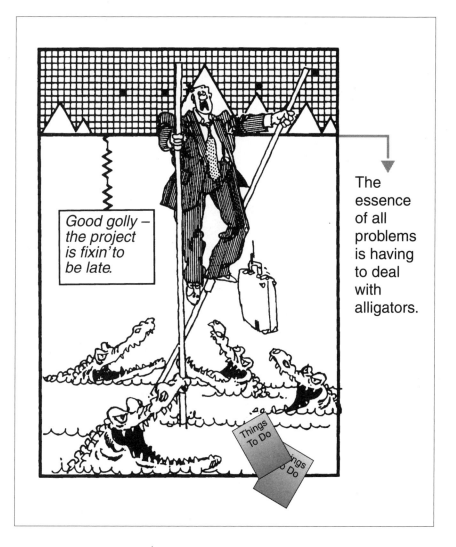

There is another alternative. It may be that you want to reach a room just off the end of the hallway, and instead of going down the hallway that contains the alligator, you detour around another path to get to the desired destination. You have avoided the alligator altogether. This is the essence of creative thinking—finding another route to the solution that can be easily navigated.

Open- and Closed-Ended Problems

Another cause of our problem-solving difficulty is that there are two categories of problems. There are those that have single solutions and those that have multiple solutions. Those with single solutions are called closed-ended problems. Those with multiple solutions are called open-ended problems.

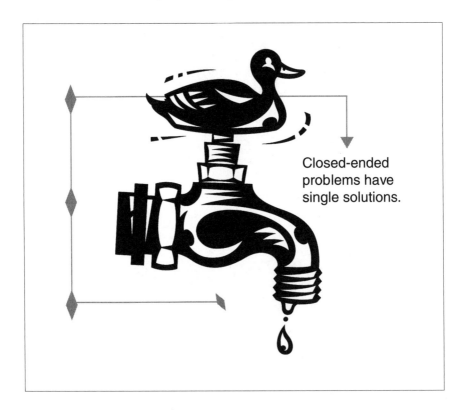

Closed-ended problems have single solutions.

Solving each category requires a different approach. Closed-ended problems are best solved using a left-brain analytical approach, whereas open-ended problems are solved by

> Closed-ended problems have single solutions.
> Open-ended problems have multiple solutions.

applying a right-brain synthesis approach. So, in terms of the Herrmann brain dominance model, we would expect quadrant A thinking to be required for solving closed-ended problems and quadrant D thinking to be required for solving open-ended ones. Remember, of course, that preference for thinking in a certain quadrant does not indicate *ability*. We all have a whole brain. However, if your preference is very strong in the A quadrant and very weak in

> *Principle:* Solving closed-ended problems requires an analytical, left-brained approach; solving open-ended ones requires a right-brained, synthetic approach.

the D quadrant, you will probably be drawn to analytical problems, and conversely.

Interestingly, most of our American education is focused on solving closed-ended problems, and very little attention is given to solving open-ended ones, yet it is clear that there are far more open-ended problems in the world than closed-ended ones. The result is that we leave school with a mindset that all problems are closed-ended, and we also have limited skills for solving open-ended problems. Of course, projects deal with both kinds of problems, so we must be able to deal with both kinds.

As an example, an environmental cleanup project is closed-ended. So is one to overhaul a piece of equipment, repair a car, or discover the cause of a disease. On the other hand, a project to develop new software or hardware is open-ended, as are pro-

> *Principle:* Closed-ended problems are oriented to the past. Open-ended problems are future-oriented.

jects to build a house, improve a process, sell a product, or develop a project-based organization. One way to think of these is that closed-ended problems are oriented to the past, whereas open-ended ones are oriented to the future.

Repairing a car is an attempt to return it to a condition that existed previously. Math problems are closed-ended. The solution exists already. We are simply trying to discover it.

Building a house, however, is open-ended. The house has not yet existed and there are several ways to build it. You may say that one approach is better than another, but that does not discount the fact that there is more than one way to go about it. The same is true for developing a new product. It does not yet exist, and there are a number of approaches to doing the design.

DEFINING CLOSED-ENDED PROBLEMS

For closed-ended problems, the best approach to defining the problem is to use what is commonly called the scientific method, which consists of the following steps:

- Ask questions.
- Develop a plan of inquiry.
- Formulate hypotheses.
- Gather data to test those hypotheses.
- Draw conclusions from hypothesis testing.
- Test the conclusions.

Constructing a Good Problem Statement

1. The problem statement should reflect shared values and a clear purpose.

2. The problem statement should not mention either causes or remedies.
3. The problem statement should define problems and processes of manageable size.
4. The problem statement should, if possible, mention measurable characteristics.
5. The problem statement should be refined (if appropriate) as knowledge is gained.

Defining Closed-Ended Problems with Problem Analysis

As was previously stated, closed-ended problems have single solutions. Something used to work and is now broken. The remedy is to determine what has broken and repair it—a single solution. To solve closed-ended problems, we use a general approach called *problem analysis*, which is presented in the following section of this chapter.

Conducting a Problem Analysis

The steps in the problem analysis process are shown by the diagram in Figure 5.4.

Identification

The first step in the problem analysis process is identification. "How do I know I have a problem?" As was previously stated, a problem is a gap between a desired state and a present state, which is confronted by an obstacle which prevents easy closure of the gap. That gap can be a *deviation* from standard performance when a process is involved. In monitoring progress in the project, when the critical ratio falls outside acceptable limits,

> *Principle:* Symptoms tell us we have a problem but the symptom is not the problem itself.

Problem Analysis Steps

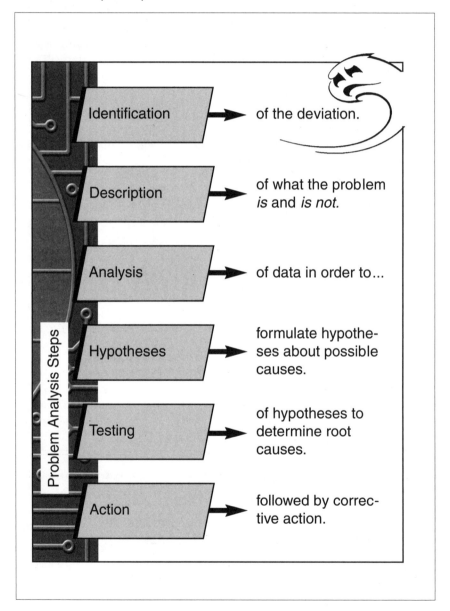

this is a signal that a potential problem exists with the task in question. This is where problem analysis begins in that situation.

When dealing with deviations, we have to know the *norm*. How is the process supposed to behave? Some project work will have a great deal more variability than others. For that reason, critical ratio limits for some tasks might be set tighter than others. Once the normal variability is known, then we can determine if the deviation is significant, whether it is positive (performance is better than the norm) or negative (performance is worse than the norm).

In a more general sense, a problem is generally recognized because the *effects* produced are different than the normal outcomes expected from the process. Those effects might be a change in scrap level, higher or lower production, or a drop in customer purchases.

In order to correct for the deviation, we need to find its *cause*. For a desirable deviation, we must know the cause so it can be replicated. For undesirable deviations, the cause must be remedied. To determine the cause of the deviation, we employ a process called *description* of the problem.

Description Using Is/Is-Not Analysis and Stratification

Stratification and is/is-not analysis are ways to localize a problem by exposing underlying patterns. This analysis is done both before collecting data (so the team will know what kind of differences to look for) and after the collection (so the team can determine which factors actually represent the root cause).

> *Stratum:* a layer.

To stratify data, examine the process to see what characteristics could lead to biases in the data. For example, could different shifts account for differences in the results? Are mistakes made by new employees very different than those made by experienced individuals? Does output from one machine have fewer defects than that from another?

Begin by making a list of the characteristics which could cause differences in results (use brainstorming here). Make data collection forms which incorporate those factors, and collect the data. Next look for patterns related to time or sequence. Then check for systematic differences between days of the week, shifts, operators, and so on.

The is/is-not matrix in Figure 5.5 is a structured form of stratification. It is based on the ideas of Charles Kepner and Benjamin Tregoe (Kepner and Tregoe, 1965).

Analysis

Once stratified data have been collected, the differences can be analyzed so that hypotheses can be formulated as to causes of the problem. The following questions are designed to help identify differences:

- What is different, distinctive, or unique between what the problem is and what it is not?
- What is different, distinctive, or unique between where the problem is and where it is not?
- What is different, distinctive, or unique between when the problem is seen and when it is not?

The focus of these questions is to help us determine what has changed about the process. If nothing had changed, there would be no problem. Our search should be limited to changes within the differences identified above. The following question is intended to help keep us focused:

- What has changed about each of these differences?

Noting the date of each change may also help us relate the start of the problem to some specific change that was made to the process.

Hypotheses

At the heart of the scientific method is the testing of hypotheses based on the foregoing steps of data collection and analysis. A hy-

F I G U R E 5.5

Is/Is Not Matrix

	Is Where, when, to what extent, or regarding whom does this situation occur?	Is Not Where does this situation NOT occur, though it reasonably might have?	Therefore What might explain the pattern of occurrence and nonoccurrence?
Where The physical or geographical location of the event or situation. Where it occurs or is noticed.			
When The hour/time of day/ day of week, month/ time of year of the event or situation. Its relationship (before, during, after) to other events.			
What Kind or How Much The type or category of event or situation. The extent, degree, dimensions, or duration of occurrence.			
Who What relationships do various individuals or groups have to the situation/event? To whom, by whom, near whom, etc., does this occur? (Do not use these questions to place blame.)			

Instructions: Identify the problem to be analyzed. Use this matrix to organize your knowledge and information. The answers will assist you in pinpointing the occurrence of the problem and in verifying conclusions or suspicions.

pothesis is a guess or conjecture about the cause of the problem. At this point *all* reasonable hypotheses should be listed.

One of the most commonly used tools for formulating hypotheses is the Ishikawa or cause-effect diagram. It can be used separately or in conjunction with is/is-not analysis to help formulate hypotheses. The group technique employed will usually be brainstorming.

Test Hypotheses

To test hypotheses, we first ask if the suspected cause can explain both sides of the description. That is, the cause must explain both the *is* and the *is-not* effects. If it cannot explain both, it is unlikely to be a real cause. It may be possible to modify the assumption of "only if" to the statement. The testing method follows:

- Test each possible cause through the description, especially the sharp contrast areas.
- Note all "only-if" assumptions.

The most likely cause will be the one that best explains the description or the one with the fewest assumptions. To be certain, you must now verify the hypothesis quickly and cheaply.

One test is whether you can make the effects come and go by manipulating the factor which is supposedly causing the deviation. If you can, you have probably found the true root cause.

Action

At this point, there are three possible actions which might be taken. These are:

Interim action	This action buys time while the root cause of the problem is sought. It is only a Band-Aid for correcting symptoms.
Adaptive action	With this action you decide to live with the problem or adapt yourself to the problem.

Corrective action   This is the only action that will truly solve the problem. It is aimed at the actual cause of the problem.

DEFINING OPEN-ENDED PROBLEMS

In solving project problems, it may be necessary to employ creative techniques to develop definitions, ideas, and so on. In particular, the problem being solved by the project itself is likely to be open-ended, requiring different methods than those presented previously for solving closed-ended problems. Even the approach used to define the problem is different. For closed-ended problems, the scientific approach to analyzing data can be used. For open-ended problems, however, we need different methods. The techniques presented in this chapter are intended to help problem solvers develop good definitions for open-ended problems and also to apply idea-generating aids which have been found useful.

I should mention here that Edward de Bono is considered by many people to be one of the leading experts on creative problem solving, and his book, *Serious Creativity* (1992), covers the subject in more detail than this chapter can possibly do. I heartily recommend that the interested reader consult de Bono's works.

REDEFINITIONAL PROCEDURES

The procedure outlined in Figure 5.6 is designed to help you develop a good definition for an open-ended problem. However, it is only one approach, and others are presented following the table. Note that you are not trying to solve the problem with this approach, even though there are questions that say, "If I could solve the problem. . . ." You are simply trying to understand what the problem is.

THE GOAL ORIENTATION TECHNIQUE

Goal orientation is an attitude, first of all, and second, it is a technique to encourage that attitude. Open-ended problems are situa-

F I G U R E 5.6

A Form for Redefinition of a Problem

PROBLEM DEFINITION AID

Project: _____

Prepared by:_____ Date: _____

---

1. Write a general description of the problem under consideration:

---

2. Now complete the following statements about the problem. If you cannot think of anything to write for a particular statement, move on to the next one.

   a. There is usually more than one way of looking at problems. You could also define this one as:

   b. ...but the main point of the problem is:

   c. What I would really like to do:

   d. If I could break all the laws/rules of reality (physical, social, organizational, etc.) I would try to solve it by:

   e. The problem, put another way, could be likened to...

   f. Another, even stranger way of looking at it might be...

---

3. Now return to your original definition (step 1). Write down whether any of the redefinitions have helped you see the problem in a different way.

GOAL orientation is an attitude

tions where the boundaries are unclear, but in which there may be fairly well-defined needs and obstacles to progress.

The goal-oriented person tries to recognize the desired end state ("what I want") and obstacles ("what's stopping me from getting the result I want").

To illustrate the goal orientation technique, consider the problem outlined in Table 5.1.

THE SUCCESSIVE ABSTRACTIONS TECHNIQUE

Suppose a company that makes lawn mowers is looking for new business ideas. Their first definition of their problem is to "de-

T A B L E 5.1

Use of the Goal Orientation Technique

Original Problem Statement

Adult illiteracy has reached alarming proportions. Ford Motor Company recently said they are having to train almost 25% of their work force in basic reading, writing, and arithmetic, at considerable cost.

Redefinitions:

1. (How to) efficiently and effectively teach adults to read.
2. (How to) keep kids from getting through school without being able to read.
3. (How to) get parents to take an interest in their kids so they will learn to read in school.
4. (How to) eliminate the influences which cause kids to take no interest in school.

---

velop a new lawn mower." A higher level of abstraction would be to define the problem as "develop new grass-cutting machines." An even higher level of abstraction yields "get rid of unwanted grass."

Another definition of the problem, of course, might be to "develop grass that grows to a height of only x inches above the ground." (See Table 5.2.)

T A B L E 5.2

Successive Abstractions

Highest level	Get rid of unwanted grass.
Intermediate level	Develop new grass-cutting machines.
Lower level	Develop new lawn mower.

ANALOGY AND METAPHOR PROCEDURES

One of the really interesting ways of describing problems is through the use of analogy or metaphor. Such definitions help increase the chances of finding creative solutions to problems. Such

methods are especially useful in group techniques, such as brainstorming. In fact, they are actually preferable to literal statements because they tend to be extremely effective in stimulating creative thinking. For example:

> "How to improve the efficiency of a factory" is a down-to-earth statement.
>
> "How to make a factory run as smoothly as a well-oiled machine" is an analogical redefinition.
>
> "How to reduce organizational friction or viscosity" is a metaphoric definition.

WISHFUL THINKING

Many left-brained, rational people do not appreciate the value of wishful thinking. However, wishful thinking can provide a rich source of new ideas. Edward de Bono, in his work on lateral thinking, talks about an "intermediate impossible"—a concept that can be used as a stepping stone between conventional thinking and realistic new insights. Wishful thinking is a great device for producing such "intermediate impossibles."

Rickards (1975) cites an example of a food technologist working on new methods of preparing artificial protein. As a fantasy, she considers the problem to be "how to build an artificial cow." Although the metaphor is wishful, it suggests that she might look closely at biological systems and perhaps look for a way of converting cellulose into protein, which is what takes place in nature.

Remember the statement from Table 5.1, "What I would *really* like to do is . . ." or try, "If I could break all constraints, I would. . . ."

NONLOGICAL STIMULI

One good way of generating ideas is through forced comparisons. This method can be used in developing ideas for solving a problem or as an aid to redefinition. Table 5.3 gives an example of the procedure, used in conjunction with a dictionary.

T A B L E   5.3

An Exercise in Nonlogical Stimuli

For this exercise, you will need paper and pencil and a dictionary.

1. Write down as many uses as you can think of for a piece of chalk.

2. When you can think of no more ideas, let your eyes wander to some object in your range of vision, which has no immediate connection to a piece of chalk.

3. Try to develop new ideas stimulated by the object.

4. Now repeat stages (2) and (3) with a second randomly selected object.

5. Open the dictionary and jot down the first three nouns or verbs that you see.

6. Try to develop new ideas stimulated by these words in turn.

7. Examine your ideas produced with and without stimuli for differences in variety (flexibility) and total numbers (fluency).

BOUNDARY EXAMINATION TECHNIQUE

When a problem is defined, the statement establishes boundaries as one sees them. If it is accepted that these are open to modification, then the definition is only a starting point. Unfortunately, many people do tend to treat boundaries as unchangeable. One way to demonstrate that they can be changed is to take a problem statement and examine it phrase by phrase for hidden assumptions. The following is an example:

> How to <u>improve</u> the performance of our <u>current engineering staff</u> in <u>managing projects</u>.

The underlined words can all be examined. Should we try to improve the performance of our staff, or should we perhaps appoint project managers who are separate from the engineering staff? Is it our staff who are not performing through some innate problem, or is the system the cause of difficulty? Should the engineering staff be managing projects at all? Is it the management of projects that is the problem or are we doing the wrong projects in the first place?

REVERSALS

Sometimes the best way to do something is to not do it. By turning a problem upside down and examining the paradox that is created, one can sometimes see new approaches. For example, if a product has a weakness, try to make it a strength, as in the case of NyQuill, which was a great cold remedy but had one drawback—it made the patient sleepy. The question—how to turn that *disadvantage* into an advantage. The answer was to sell NyQuill as a *nighttime* remedy which would actually help the cold sufferer get some sleep.

A food low in nutritive value becomes a diet food. A glue that wouldn't stick permanently was the key to making Post-it notes. (The idea was rejected initially. Who needs such a thing? It was a number of years before 3-M decided to market the product, and it is hard to imagine the world without Post-it notes now. In fact, in conjunction with a white marker board, Post-it notes are a great tool for project planning.)

LINEAR TECHNIQUES TO GENERATE IDEAS

For almost every problem, we might begin by asking, "How can we do that . . . ?" How can we, for example:

Develop a new product—or an idea for a new product?

Build the new bridge most effectively and efficiently, so we make best use of our resources and make the most money?

Put together a new training program for our lab technicians?

Linear techniques for generating ideas can be extremely useful in this area. An excellent reference is the book by William C. Miller (1986), *The Creative Edge.* Miller lists 10 so-called linear techniques for organizing known information to help you see your problem from different angles. Another good resource is Michalko's *Thinkertoys* (Michalko, 1995).

MATRIX ANALYSIS

Matrix analysis is ideal for developing new product ideas. Suppose you wanted to investigate all possibilities for marketing training programs. You might then have a grid (matrix) that looks as follows:

> Nothing is more dangerous than an idea when it is the only one you have.
>
> — Emile Chartier

Delivery method	Client groups			
	Managers	Engineers	Trainers	Retirees
Seminars				
Cassettes				
Videos				
Films				
Home study				
Workshops				
Computer				

Each box in the matrix (each intersection as it is called) represents a place to look for new innovations.

MORPHOLOGICAL ANALYSIS

If you want to consider more than one or two variables, the matrix is not a very effective approach. Morphological analysis is probably better. As Miller says, this is a fancy title for a simple way to generate solutions to problems that have many variables to consider. For example, to continue with our training programs, we might have to consider:

- Delivery method

- Course content
- Audience
- Location

Some of the topics that might fit into these categories follow:

Delivery method	Content	Audience	Location
Video	Technical	College student	Local
Audio	Behavioral	Factory workers	Foreign
Workbook	Reading	Managers	Different state
Film	Writing	Farmers	Traveling
Seminar	Coping	Housewives	Same state
Satellite	Agriculture	School children	Shipboard
Computer	Computer science	Professionals	Nationwide
Mail	Medical	Paramedics	

Once the table is prepared, a single variable in each column is circled and the possibilities are considered. For example, suppose we circled *seminar, coping, factory workers,* and *nationwide*. The immediate ideas that come to mind are seminars designed to help workers cope with being laid off during the recession. They might need help with the feelings of frustration and self-doubt which invariably accompany such situations, as well as training in how to prepare a résumé, conduct themselves in an interview, and conduct a job search.

ATTRIBUTE LISTING

If you want to improve a procedure, product, or process, you might write down all the attributes or components and see how you can improve any one or all of them. For example, suppose we want to improve the project management process itself. It has the following attributes:

- Schedule
- Overall plan
- Project team
- Form of organization
- Control system
- Project manager

If we examine each of these attributes, we might ask how something can be improved. For example, how do we improve our scheduling methodology? Is our form of organization optimum? Is the control system functioning to keep the project on track?

ALTERNATIVE SCENARIOS

The two primary ways of exploring possibilities for the future are hypothetical situations and alternative scenarios. With hypothetical situations, you make up something and develop a solution for it. "If a certain set of conditions existed, what would I do?" To which of these conditions are we most vulnerable? What can we do about those vulnerabilities? Alternative scenarios are more comprehensive than hypothetical situations. They are qualitatively different descriptions of plausible futures.

When long-range planning is based on a single forecast of trends, there is a big risk of "betting the farm" on that single forecast. Thinking through several scenarios is less risky, and frees one to take more innovative actions.

Scenarios are developed specifically for a particular problem. First, a statement is made of the specific decision that must be made. Then one identifies the major environmental forces that might impact the decision.

These forces might include technology, social values, economic growth, tariffs, and so on. Now a scenario is built on the basis of principal forces. To do so, use information available to you and identify those plausible and qualitatively different possibilities for each force. Assemble the alternatives for each force into internally consistent "stories," with both a narrative and table of forces and scenarios.

FORCED OR DIRECT ASSOCIATION

This approach is similar to nonlogical stimuli, which was introduced in the previous chapter. New ideas can be generated by putting together two concepts that seemingly have nothing in common. For example, if you were trying to understand how to improve the performance of a work group, you might ask, "How is this group like a roller coaster?" The following list might result:

Tracks	We stay on the tracks, but they just go up and down and around in a circle. All we seem to be doing is making ourselves sick.
Cars	The cars are designed to keep you from falling out. Maybe we aren't taking enough risks.
Speed	We aren't going anywhere, but we're getting there pretty fast.
Control	The person controlling the roller coaster just started it going and went on a break. Who's in control here, anyway?

With these ideas, you might identify ways to respond to the situation.

DESIGN TREE

Another word for design tree is "mind-map."[1] Mind-maps have been used by a lot of people to illustrate associations of ideas. For example, one author has a book on writing which makes use of mind-maps. You begin by writing a single word—representing the issue you want to deal with—then draw a circle around it. Next list all the ideas that come to you, connect them to the first word with lines, and continue by examining each new word in turn for the ideas it might trigger. I used the word *transportation* to illustrate the approach. See Figure 5.7.

EXPECTATIONS, DELIVERABLES, AND RESULTS

It would be nice if all we had to worry about was meeting PCTS targets in a project, but this is not the case. We also have to deal

---

[1]   The term *mind-map* is trademarked by Tony Buzan.

FIGURE 5.7

Design Tree for Transportation

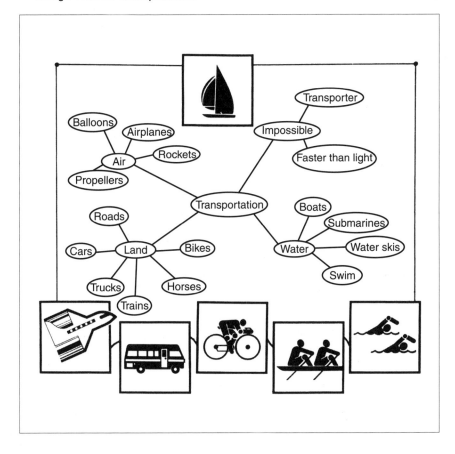

with the expectations of stakeholders, as I explained in Chapter 1. Clarifying stakeholder expectations is as much a part of project definition as anything else, and meeting those expectations is necessary for the project to be judged a success.

In addition, you must ask, "What results is this project intended to get and what must we deliver to achieve those results?" The answers to these questions should help you develop a crisp, shared mission and vision for your project.

What Happens When a Stakeholder Changes

Be aware that, if a stakeholder changes midway through the project, you will have to go through the clarification of his or her expectations all over again. You can't just assume that if you meet the expectations of the former stakeholder, everything will be okay. The new person will see the job differently than his or her predecessor, and you will have to negotiate those things that can be accommodated and those that cannot. The new stakeholder may have totally unrealistic expectations about deliverables and results, and you must bring them in line with reality.

> *Principle:* When a stakeholder changes, you must clarify his or her expectations and negotiate for those that are not in line with what you can do.

You may think of this as one of the political aspects of the project management job, and it is. Ignore it to your own risk!

THE PROJECT CHARTER

One way to ensure that the project is correctly defined and that everyone understands what is supposed to be done is to develop a project charter. The members of the team answer the questions in the document then review them with the sponsor and other stakeholders to achieve agreement, and then the charter is signed off and gives the team authority to proceed with the project. An example of a project charter is shown in Figure 5.8. A blank project charter can be downloaded free of charge from my website, www.lewisinstitute.com in Microsoft Word and pdf formats.

THE FALLACY OF PROJECT MANAGEMENT ASSUMPTIONS

Everything I have written about managing projects would be wonderful—if it could be made to work the way I have suggested.

The Project Charter

Project Charter
Project Name:
Project Mission:

Project Manager:
Project Team Members: Percent of Time Allocated to Project

Description of Project Scope (including deliverables):

F I G U R E 5.8 (Continued)

The Project Charter

Project Charter for
Customer(s):
Stakeholder(s):
Anticipated Project Outcomes (Measurable and Non-measurable):
Anticipated Start Date: Anticipated Finish Date:

F I G U R E   5.8 (Continued)

The Project Charter

Project Charter for

Project Parameters

Planning Budget:

Implementation Budget:

Kind of Decisions the Project Team and Manager Can Make:

Other Parameters for this Project:

Any other special considerations, issues, or anything else specifically pertaining to this project:

FIGURE 5.8

The Project Charter

Project Charter for

Signatures

Project Manager:	____________________	Date:	__________
Customer:	____________________	Date:	__________
Customer:	____________________	Date:	__________
Key Stakeholder:	____________________	Date:	__________
Key Stakeholder:	____________________	Date:	__________

Final Authority for this Project (Within the Organization):

____________________ Date: __________

 Issue 1, May 99 Page 4 of 4

However, there is a huge fallacy in the assumptions we make about managing projects, and that is that the world will stand still while we execute our carefully constructed project plan. This simply isn't true, and we know it.

As I discussed above, stakeholders change, and with them come new expectations, which require that we adapt our project to meet those expectations,

> Principle: The big fallacy in our assumptions is that the world will stand still while we execute our project plan.

or we will be judged negatively when the project ends. Furthermore, as projects evolve, we learn things we didn't know at the beginning. If we are developing software or hardware, we have new ideas about how the final product should function. For that reason, many products are *adaptive* in nature and cannot be planned *deterministically.*

I believe this is a major reason why software development projects have such high percentages of missed targets. Remember the Standish study that shows that only 17 percent of software projects meet the original PCTS targets? It's no wonder. The targets are constantly moving.

I can speak from experience to this. We have just about finished designing an on-line training program for my website as of this writing.

> *Principle:* Some projects are adaptive in nature and cannot be planned deterministically.

We started about a year ago, by defining what we wanted it to do. As we neared completion and started testing the program on a temporary dummy site, we began to realize that we could make the program far more effective by making some changes. We also thought of functions that never occurred to us a year ago. So the job has taken nearly twice as many programming hours as originally estimated, but we have a significantly better product as a result.

Could we have used the product in the form originally defined? Yes. But it would not have had the utility of the present version.

There has to be some caution, of course. If you continually make changes to a product in response to new ideas, you will never release it. This is the trap into which perfectionists fall. They can never finish a design because they can always make it better.

What has to be decided is whether a change is needed to make the final result as functional as it must be in the final application. If the change is not made, can it be sold? Will it be accepted by the customer? If the change is made, will it delay product introduction to the marketplace so much that competitors will seize the market share and cost you all of your profits? These are not easy questions to answer, and should never be made unilaterally by technologists. Many technologists have very little grasp of market dynamics, and will opt for technical improvements even if the product never sells.

Principle: All project plans must be flexible enough to respond to legitimate environmental changes.

I think the message here is that project planning must be done with the understanding that the plans must be flexible enough to respond to legitimate environmental forces, without going so far as to be useless. When you are doing construction projects and other fairly well-defined jobs, this is not such a big issue. Software, hardware, and scientific work (such as drug development), however, are more likely to require an adaptive, rather than deterministic management approach.

PUTTING IT ALL TOGETHER

On the following pages, you will find a step-by-step guide to getting through the definition stage of a project. By answering the questions and taking the steps shown, you should greatly increase your chances of getting this step right, and consequently of getting your project off to a good start.

Steps 1 and 2 of the Lewis Method

1. When the project is finished, what will be the outcome?

   a. What will you have—a document, thing, software product, new process, new system, new program?

   b. What will the outcome look like, how will it sound, smell, taste, function, and so on?

   c. What are the *must-have, want,* and *nice-to-have* features of the outcome?

2. Where are you now? Describe your present situation or position.

3. Because a problem is a gap between where you are and where you want to be, confronted by obstacles, list the obstacles that keep you from immediately closing the gap.

4. Has the desired outcome ever existed before? If so, you are dealing with a closed-ended problem and analytical methods of problem solving are appropriate. If you are trying to bring about an outcome that has not existed before, then the problem is open-ended, and creative methods of problem solving should be used.

5. Now write your problem statement as a negative. See the examples that follow. They should help you construct a good problem statement.

Examples of Problem Statements

1. We have no airplane that is intermediate in size between the 747 and 767. (Boeing may have written a statement of their problem in this way. This is my own construction.)

2. Our present facility is inadequate to house the 20 additional people who will be hired in the next six months.

3. Our website cannot be updated by our own staff, but must be done by the host.

4. Our building has no air conditioning, and summer temperatures cause our computers to quit.

5. Process *xyz* is only capable of producing three-sigma results, which costs us an estimated $200,000 a year in poor quality.

6. Rework in projects is running at approximately 30 percent of total budget, which costs us about $1 million a year.

7. No cure exists for AIDS.

8. Our purchasing system is incapable of qualifying vendors.

9. Our contracts have no remedies in place should a contractor default.

KEY POINTS FOR CHAPTER 5

- *Principle:* Projects often fail at the beginning, not the end.
- *Principle:* The false consensus effect is a failure to manage disagreement, because no one knows it exists.
- *Principle:* Process will *always* affect task performance!

Write the Mission Statement

A mission statement should answer the following questions:

1.   What are we going to do?

2.   For whom are we going to do it?

   Note that, if you are doing a project for yourself only, you need not state the "for whom." When there is an ultimate customer, you should designate the customer as the "for whom."

   Here are some examples, based on the problem statements just presented.

1.   Our mission is to develop an airplane (tentatively called the 777) that will be intermediate in size between the 747 and 767.

2.   Our mission is to acquire a facility that will accommodate our projected growth in personnel for the next three years.

3.   Our mission is to be able to update our website ourselves.

4.   Our mission is to install an air-conditioning system in our building.

5.   Our mission is to improve process *xyz* so that it will perform at the six-sigma level.

- *Principle:* The first objective for a project manager is to achieve a shared understanding of the team's mission.
- *Mission:* the goal or objective that the team must achieve.
- *Vision:* what the final result will look like.
- *Principle:* The way a problem is defined determines how we attempt to solve it.
- *Principle:* All problem solving is dealing with alligators!

- *Principle:* Solving closed-ended problems require an analytical, left-brained approach; solving open-ended ones requires a right-brained, synthetic approach.
- *Principle:* Closed-ended problems are oriented to the past. Open-ended problems are future-oriented.
- *Principle:* Symptoms tell us we have a problem but the symptom is not the problem itself.
- *Principle:* When a stakeholder changes, you must clarify his or her expectations and negotiate those that are not in line with what you can do.
- *Principle:* Some projects are adaptive in nature and cannot be planned deterministically.

QUESTIONS FOR REVIEW

1. What is one of the major causes of project failure?
2. What causes the Abilene Paradox?
3. How do you overcome the Abilene Paradox?
4. Why does process always affect task performance?
5. What is meant by vision?
6. What two questions should a mission statement answer?
7. What is a problem?
8. The way a problem is defined has nothing to do with how it is solved: T   F
9. What is the difference between a closed-ended problem and one that is open-ended?
10. Closed-ended problems are best solved by what approach?
11. What mode of thinking is needed to solve open-ended problems?
12. If a hypothesis can explain both sides of the equation, it is considered to be valid: T   F
13. When a stakeholder in a project changes, what should you do?

PROJECT PLANNING

CHAPTER

Project Strategy: You Can't Develop a Good Implementation Plan Unless You First Have a Proper Game Plan

In this chapter, we will discuss developing a strategy for a project. This is outlined in steps 3 to 5 of my method, and these steps are repeated in Figure 6.1 for your convenience.

As I have written in Chapter 5, there is a strong tendency for people to skip from step 1 in my model down to step 9. They want to just "get on" with it, to get the job done. In the process, they fail to properly define the problem being solved, establish a proper mission and vision for the job, and consequently have a failed project.

Another mistake is to want to jump from step 2 down to step 6. People who do this understand that they must deal with step 2, but they fail to consider project strategy. They simply want to construct a working plan—usually a schedule that is developed with some kind of software.

Steps 3 to 5 of the Lewis Method

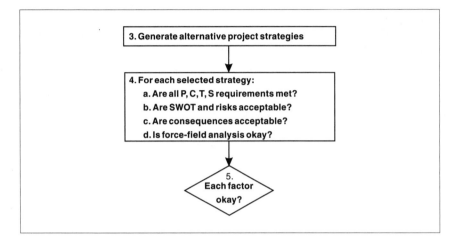

WHAT IS STRATEGY?

Strategy is an overall approach to a project. It is sometimes called a *game plan*. The difference between strategy and tactics is that tactics get you down to the "nitty-gritty" details of exactly how you are going to do the work. For example, if I decided that the best way to build a house is to use prefabricated components, then I must work out how I am going to actually make the components. Do I assemble an entire wall and send it to the job site, or do I make it in small sections that can be joined together at the site?

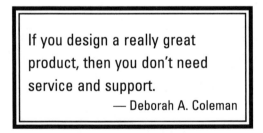

If you design a really great product, then you don't need service and support.
— Deborah A. Coleman

Logistics involves how I am going to get the prefab parts out to the site, how I will supply workers with tools and other equipment, how I will feed them, and so on. Tactics and logistics will be

"First, I'll create a diversion"

PROJECT } Develop a proper game plan.
STRATEGY }

worked out in step 6 of the flowchart when detailed implementation planning is done.

THE IMPORTANCE OF STRATEGY

A manager once told me that he could not keep engineers, because the big manufacturers in his area could pay more, and no sooner would he get a young engineer trained than the big company would steal the person. He decided to adopt a new strategy. Instead of recruiting engineers, he would hire technical school graduates and teach them to be engineers. Because the big companies generally preferred engineers with four-year degrees, he very seldom lost a tech-school graduate

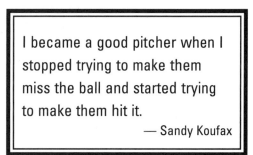

I became a good pitcher when I stopped trying to make them miss the ball and started trying to make them hit it.
— Sandy Koufax

to them. Certainly his tech-school engineers may not have been quite as qualified as those with full degrees, but they were capable enough for his needs, and the cost of constantly replacing engineers dropped dramatically.

In a similar vein, the United States has had a shortage of programmers for several years, and many companies have found that they can get programming done in India at considerably less cost than if they had local programmers do the work. The programmers in India speak good English, are well educated, and work for considerably less than an American programmer because the cost of living in India is much lower than in the United States. This strategy has been in use for a number of years to get projects done on time and at less expense than would otherwise be possible.

When the Chunnel was built to connect France with England, the strategy was to start digging from both sides. Using laser surveying methods, they met in the middle with only negligible error in position. This strategy allowed the project to be completed in about half the time it would have taken to dig from one side to another, because you can only dig so many feet per day. By going in both directions, the digging speed was essentially doubled.

> Without competitors, there would be no need for strategy.
> — Kenichi Ohmae

My first engineering job was with a very small company that designed and built land mobile communications equipment. We had only 150 employees in the company, and of course our engineering staff was very small. There was no way that we could compete directly with the big players in the game because they had far more resources than we did.

So one of our engineers conceived the idea of doing modular design of radios. Instead of having to design every new radio "from scratch," we would design some circuits that could be used in all models. Good examples are audio amplifiers and intermediate frequency (IF) strips. By employing this method, we were able to develop a family of products in relatively short time. We were leveraging our limited resources.

Air Industries has employed a similar strategy in its Airbus line of aircraft. In most cases, pilots are trained to fly a single kind of airplane. So a crew that can fly one plane can't fly one of the same design but having a slightly different configuration. Airbus has several planes with different seating capacities that can all be flown by the same crews. The cockpit layouts are the same and the planes handle so similarly that the crews don't have to be re-trained to switch from one to the other. In addition, the airline does not have to stock so many different spare parts because the planes all use the same ones. This represents a signifi-cant savings in inventory costs, pilot training, and so on.

> It is better to give away the wool than the sheep.
> — Italian proverb

PROJECT STRATEGY AND TECHNICAL STRATEGY

Suppose you had to feed a group, and you are considering how to do it. You could (1) cook the meal yourself, (2) take everyone to a restaurant, (3) have a potluck dinner, in which everyone brings something, or (4) have a caterer deliver the food. You examine the alternatives and decide that you will cook the meal yourself. This is your project strategy. But how will you cook the food?

You could (1) cook it conventionally on your stove, (2) micro-wave it, or (3) have a backyard barbecue. These three approaches would be called technical strategy. Your preference is to have a backyard barbecue, but you discover that your grill is kaput. You don't want to cook on the stove or microwave, so you decide to have the meal catered. In other words, your choice of technical strategy may determine your project strategy.

In a technological company, for example, you are considering developing a product by employing a new technology. However, no one in the company knows anything about the technology, so you may have to contract out that part of the work (a project strat-egy) or develop the capability.

> **Principle:** It is best not to employ cutting-edge technology in a project that has a very tight deadline.

A general guideline in selecting technical strategy is that you don't want to employ cutting-edge technology when you have a very tight project deadline. Of course, this rule is violated frequently in high-tech industries, but deadlines are also missed occasionally, and sometimes products are released that later have field problems. This can do serious damage to a company's reputation.

Related to this rule is that you should separate discovery from development in a project. That is, you don't want to be try-

> **Principle:** As a rule, it is best to separate discovery from development.

ing to make some technology work when you are supposed to be developing a product. The best approach is to do a feasibility study, then, based on the outcome, launch a development project. If you are trying to prove feasibility and develop a product at the same time, and you can't make the technology work, that project will be judged a failure. However, no matter what result you get with a feasibility study—yes it works or no it doesn't—that should be judged a successful project, as you have conclusively answered a question.

GENERATING AND CHOOSING THE CORRECT STRATEGY

As you can see from my model, in step 3 you generate a list of alternative project and technical strategies that may apply to your project and in step 4 you select the combination that you judge to be best. Generating the list may be as simple as looking around at existing strategies and listing them, or you may invent a new strategy. Note that what is required in this step is strategic or con-

ceptual thinking. You can expect that individuals with a strong preference for quadrant D thinking will be needed at this step. See Figure 6.2.

Inventing a Strategy

As an example of this, Charles Kepner and Benjamin Tregoe developed an approach to problem solving that was very rigorous, and convinced managers at General Motors to adopt it. In fact, GM wanted most of their employees to be trained in the new

F I G U R E 6.2

Quadrant-D Thinking Is Needed at This Step

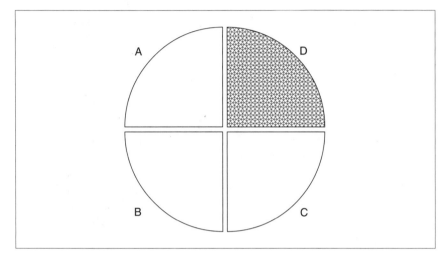

method. Kepner and Tregoe knew that they could not possibly train all of those people themselves, and they were almost destroyed by success. So they conceived a new approach. They would train individuals within GM to deliver the training. They conducted a series of train-the-trainer workshops and made GM self-sufficient in doing their own internal training. All Kepner and Tregoe had to do from that point on was sell the classroom materials to GM and that was how they made their income. This was an invented strategy at the time. It has become common since then.

> *Principle:* If no existing strategy is acceptable, you may have to invent one.

If you have to invent a strategy, you should use creative problem-solving methods. The most common one is brainstorming, in which members of a group generate as many ideas as they

One method of creative problem solving is BRAINSTORMING to generate as many ideas as possible.

can, without evaluation, then select one. There are many other approaches for developing good ideas. One good source of techniques is the book by Michael Michalko, *Thinkertoys* (Michalko, 1995). A number of idea-generating methods were presented in Chapter 5, so you may want to go back and review those.

Selecting Strategy

Sometimes it is a simple matter to choose strategy. However, if a number of issues are involved, the choice may not be so easy to make. A step-by-step procedure is presented at the end of this chapter that will guide you through the process, but you should understand why the steps are followed before applying them in a rote way.

When you were generating ideas for project strategy, you were in quadrant D of the Herrmann model. To select the best combination of project and technical strategy, quadrant A thinking is needed. Critical analysis is required to sort through the facts and details of the various choices, so if you have no one on your team who is really good at such thinking, you should bring in someone temporarily who has those skills.

Ranking the Alternatives

To select the best combination of strategies, you should rank both lists (project and technical strategies). The easiest way to do this is to use the priority matrix, as shown in Figure 6.3. There are several ways to go about this. One is to make each choice binary. Suppose, for example, that I have four strategies. If I had some way to quantitatively rank them, it would be easy to make a choice, but there may be a number of factors involved that affect the "measure" that each one would yield, and it gets too complicated to work out, so I simply ask myself if one strategy is better than another. If the answer is "yes," you put a 1 in the cell, and if it is "no," you put a 0 (zero). If I proceed across row 1 and ask this question for strategy 1 compared to each of the others, I get the result shown in Figure 6.3. This technique is called *paired comparisons*.

F I G U R E 6.3

Priority Matrix for Four Strategies with Row 1 Filled in

STRATEGY	1	2	3	4	TOTAL	RANK
1	X	1	0	1		
2		X				
3			X			
4				X		

Next, I ask if strategy 2 is better than each of the others. However, you will note that when I ask if strategy 2 is better than 1, I have already asked that question in row 1, but in reverse. So whatever I put in row 1 under strategy 2 must now be the inverse in row 2, column 1. This is shown in Figure 6.4.

Priority Matrix with Row 2, Column 1 Filled in

STRATEGY	1	2	3	4	TOTAL	RANK
1	X	1	0	1		
2	0	X	1	1		
3	1		X			
4	0			X		

In fact, it turns out that, as you continue with the matrix, you will find that every entry in column 1 is going to be the inverse of what is in row 1, so you can save time by simply filling in the rows of the matrix above the diagonal and then filling in the columns with the inverse of their rows. The final result is shown in Figure 6.5.

Priority Matrix with All Entries Filled in

STRATEGY	1	2	3	4	TOTAL	RANK
1	X	1	0	1		
2	0	X	1	1		
3	1	0	X	0		
4	0	0	1	X		

Next you total each row, and the row with the highest total will be your first choice, next-highest total will be choice two, and so on. If you find that two rows add to the same total, just look in the matrix to see which of the two choices outranks the other because that decision has already been made. The final result for this matrix is shown in Figure 6.6.

Priority Matrix with Totals and ranks Filled in

STRATEGY	1	2	3	4	TOTAL	RANK
1	X	1	0	1	2	1
2	0	X	1	1	2	2
3	1	0	X	0	1	4
4	0	0	1	X	1	3

This ranking should ideally be done by a team. When this is the case, you can still deal with the strategies in a binary fashion, but now you ask your team members how many think strategy 1 is better than strategy 2, and you count the votes. Suppose, for example that you have six team members, counting yourself, and you ask for a comparison of strategy 1 versus 2. When you enter the votes, you put the votes *for* strategy 1 in row 1 and the votes for strategy 2 in row 2. This is shown in Figure 6.7.

Matrix with Votes Tallied for Strategy 1 versus Strategy 2

STRATEGY	1	2	3	4	TOTAL	RANK
1	X	8	6	1		
2	2	X				
3	4		X			
4	9			X		

Continue in this manner until you have completed all voting, then total the votes in each row. This gives the result shown in Figure 6.8. This is a more "fine-tuned" approach than using 1s and 0s as you did previously.

F I G U R E 6.8

Matrix Completely Filled in and Totaled

STRATEGY	1	2	3	4	TOTAL	RANK
1	X	8	6	1	15	2
2	2	X	5	1	8	4
3	4	5	X	2	11	3
4	9	9	8	X	26	1

The Analytical Hierarchy

The priority matrix can be enhanced by evaluating various attributes of each choice. As you can see in step 4 of the Lewis Method, the first question is whether a given strategy can meet our PCTS targets. It may be that one choice will meet the CTS targets, but is not as good as another choice in meeting the performance objective. But are PCT and S of equal importance to the project?

It could be that performance is most important and time is second. Graham and Englund (1997) have written that *mind share* is what you want to achieve with a product in order to capture *market share*. For example, when someone mentions laser jet printers, Hewlett-Packard wants everyone to think of their units as the best available. So performance may be the foremost requirement to be met, and time may be second. Then may come scope and cost. If weights are assigned to these, you would then have a more complicated situation to analyze.

Now you would have to ask the question, "Is strategy 1 better than strategy 2 in terms of performance? In terms of cost?

Time? Scope?" And you would tally the votes for all four criteria for each paired comparison. To arrive at a numerical weight for each choice involves matrix algebra, which I long ago forgot, and which is best done with a software program called Expert Choice®. The program allows comparisons between quantitative and qualitative facets of a choice, making it an extremely powerful way of arriving at a correct decision. To find out more about the software, check out their website at www.expertchoice.com.

Conducting SWOT and Risk Analysis

In choosing the best project strategy, it is a good idea to do a SWOT and risk analysis. The acronym SWOT stands for *strengths, weaknesses, opportunities,* and *threats.* It is an analysis originally used in marketing analysis. Before entering a new market, it is useful to ask the following questions:

1. What are our strengths? and
    How can we take advantage of them?
2. What weaknesses do we have? and
    How do we minimize the effect of them?
3. What opportunities does this market offer us? and
    How can we capitalize on them?
4. What threats exist that may impact our success? and
    How can we deal effectively with these?

The best way to do a SWOT analysis is to simply fill in the form shown in Figure 6.9. I do suggest that you identify all the strengths you can think of, then answer the question, "How do we take advantage of them?" next, rather than identify a strength followed by how to deal with it. This procedure goes faster as a rule. The same goes for the other three concerns.

Threats versus Risks

Notice that the second question in step 4 asks if SWOT and risks are okay. The difference between risks and threats is that a **risk** is something that can simply happen—an accident, act of nature, or

A SWOT Analysis Form

SWOT Analysis Form

Project:	Prepared by:
Date:	Strategy, goal, or objective being considered:

List strengths of your team	How can you best take advantage of these?	List weaknesses of your team	How can you minimize the impact of these?

What opportunities does this project/strategy/goal present?	How can you best take advantage of them?	List those threats that might keep you from succeeding	How can you deal with each identified threat?

missed deadline—whereas a threat is something that may be done by another entity. It may be a competitor who beats you to market, for example.

Principle: Threats are usually done by other entities, whereas risks are things that can just happen.

For practical purposes, it is okay to combine threats and risks because, either way you look at it, they both cause the project to be in jeopardy if they happen.

Furthermore, it is not enough to simply identify risks and threats. The question is, what are you going to do about them? The essential point is that threats and risks should be managed, so that they do not cause the

project to fail. There are two points in planning a project where risks should be analyzed and managed. First is risks to the strategy itself.

For example, to employ cutting-edge technology in a product development project is more risky than using proven technology. Unless the benefits to be

> *Principle:* In practice, it is okay to lump threats and risks together for analysis.

gained far exceed the cost of failure, the cutting-edge approach would be undesirable. Even if the cutting-edge strategy is chosen, it is a good idea to have a contingency plan in place in case the strategy proves to be unworkable.

You also need to manage risks during implementation planning. There are a lot of things that can go wrong in the execution of a project plan, and if these are identified ahead of time, plans can be developed to deal with them. In the first place, you can sometimes eliminate a risk altogether with a small change in your approach to the project. As my colleague, Harvey Levine, says, it is better to avoid risks than to have to deal with them.

Risk management is covered in detail in Chapter 8. For now, suffice it to say that there are three responses to risk. They are:

1. *Mitigation.* Something is done to correct for the damage done by the event.
2. *Avoidance.* You attempt to avoid the risk in the first place.
3. *Transfer.* You transfer the risk to someone else. Insurance is an example of risk transfer. Contracting work to another party is also risk transfer.

Unintended Consequences

An unintended consequence is something that happens because of the action you have taken to solve one problem. For example, you decide to contract work to an outside vendor, and the consequence is that you lose control of that part of the project. Or you push everyone to complete a project by a certain date, and they unintentionally sacrifice quality (performance) in the process.

Unintended consequences are all around us. Someone has said that most of today's environmental problems are the consequence of solutions to yesterday's problems. I also believe that many organizational problems are consequences of actions and decisions made previously to solve problems. For that reason, it is important to ask yourself if your chosen project strategy is going to lead to serious consequences that may actually be worse than the problem you were trying to solve when you selected it.

> *Principle:* Many of today's problems are the consequences of solutions to problems we had yesterday.

As an example, I recently decided to change our way of doing seminar workbooks. In the past, I typed the text on my computer, left space for illustrations, and my wife pasted the art into the empty space. These masters were then copied and used to make quantity duplications of workbooks. The problem is that the workbook is a second-generation copy and loses some quality. It is also difficult to revise the copy. If a change is significant, it can cause page numbers to change, requiring that new pasteups be done. This is time-consuming.

To remedy this, we decided to do full desktop publishing of our workbooks. In doing so, we found that some of the art wouldn't scan without degrading. Also, the computer would occasionally crash for some reason, costing time to redo the file. To make a long story short, there were times when I questioned the wisdom of our decision. In the long run, of course, I am convinced that it was the right strategy.

Force-Field Analysis

Organizations and projects are, by nature, political. The basic nature of politics is that people try to gain and keep power, and they choose up sides on various issues and then try to have their side "win." The way this can affect a project is that a certain strategy may not be acceptable to certain individuals or groups. As an example, a facilities engineer once told me about an experience he had refurbishing an office.

He arranged to do the job over the plant shutdown that occurred for about a week around Christmas. He convinced some people from the plant to help move furniture, lay carpet, and paint walls, and paid them triple time because they were working during a holiday period. They completely overhauled the office and it was ready for occupancy when the plant resumed its normal operation.

To his chagrin, when he walked into the office on the first day, the union steward was talking with the engineer's boss. He was outraged. "We would normally have taken several months to do that job," he snarled. "Now management knows it can be done in less time."

I asked him what his boss's response was.

"You should have known better," his boss told him.

This is a good example of a strategy that would have been rejected if it had been suggested to the union steward before the fact.

Force-field analysis is a process by which you consider all of the forces in the environment that may cause your strategy to succeed or fail because of the acceptance or rejection by the parties involved. It is essentially attention to the politics of the project, and is sometimes overlooked by project managers.

The solution is to identify the parties that may accept or reject a strategy, try to assess the strength of their support or resistance, and ask if your strategy can succeed. The basic idea is that the sum of the supporting forces must exceed the strength of the sum of the resisting forces, or you can't make your strategy work. Such an analysis is shown in Figure 6.10.

The difficulty with this approach is in trying to quantify the forces. I consider it very iffy. On top of that, we assume that all resistance is the same, and we sum the resisting forces to get a total. This may not be valid. You may be adding apples and oranges. So my suggestion is that you forget about trying to quantify the forces, and concentrate instead on managing resistance. After all,

F I G U R E 6.10

Force-Field Analysis

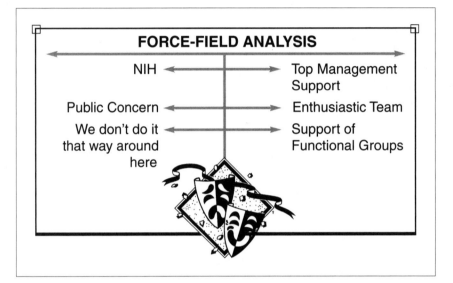

the positive forces are going to help you. You may, of course, try to bolster them or add to them.

There are four approaches to dealing with resistance. They are:

1. Ignore it.
2. Overcome it.
3. Go around it.
4. Neutralize it.

Ignore

There are times when you should ignore resistance. If you pay attention to it, you may simply make it grow. This is valid when the resistance is of low level, or the person is in no position to do you any harm, regardless of his resistance. The danger is that you may underestimate the resistance. In any case, if you later find that you should not have ignored someone's resistance, you can always adopt one of the next three approaches.

Overcome

This is one of the most common approaches to resistance. You try to counter the person's resistance by arguing against it. Suppose, for example, that a person objects to the strategy for reasons of safety. You try to convince her that her concerns are unwarranted. She counters your argument with expressions of strong fear that someone will be injured and cause the company to be sued. You go back and forth, offering argument and counterargument, until you are convinced that she is a stubborn opponent who will never "see the light." Of course, she thinks the same thing about you. What has happened is that the strength of your opposing arguments has simply grown, and neither of you has been able to convince the other of the correctness of your position.

The nature of this conflict is a move-countermove exchange, which is called a *game without end*. What this means is that there is almost no way that the game can end, because there are no rules within the system for changing its own behavior. (For more on this, see Watzlawick, Weakland, and Fisch, 1974.)

When you see that you are getting into a game-without-end interaction, I suggest that you try another approach. Otherwise, you may simply strengthen your opponent. In addition, even if you were able to convince her of your position, she has invested so much energy in her own point of view that to change now would make her lose face, which she may be very reluctant to do.

Go Around

To go around someone would mean that you go to his or her boss and ask that the boss have a "heart-to-heart" talk with your opponent. It may work, but you may very well regret your action over the long run. So it is generally not considered a very good thing to do. The only exception may be when some serious safety issue is involved and you have made no headway with other tactics. However, you should probably do this as a last resort.

Neutralize

The name suggests that you are going to blast your opponent off the face of the earth, and you may well wish you could do so, but that is not the meaning of the word neutralize in this case. What we mean is that you try to find a way to make the person's resistance go away.

The simplest approach for doing this is to ask the individual, "What would I have to do to convince you that this is a good strategy?"

The person has two possible responses. One is to tell you to forget about trying to convince him. He is never going to accept this strategy.

When I get this very negative response, I ask, "Really? There's absolutely nothing I can do to convince you?"

If the person is willing to meet you even part way, you will usually get the second response, which is, "Oh, I suppose if you could do (whatever it is) I would be convinced." The nice thing about this is that you no longer try to find out how to convince the individual, because he has told you.

I suggest that you ask one more question, even if you are able to do what the person suggests. Ask if there is anything else you need to do. The reason is that you may do what was originally suggested, only to have the person say, "Well, I still have this concern. . . ." By taking care of all his concerns at one time, you avoid the sense of playing games later on.

People Problems and Projects

I find that very few people take force-field analysis seriously. I'm not sure why. Perhaps they don't think that they have the skills to deal with resistance. Maybe they think it will go away, once the person sees the *logic* of the strategy. Or it could be that they are simply underestimating the importance of it.

This is a serious error of judgment. Just yesterday I had a meeting with a company that sells heavy equipment. They have developed some software that allows the user to get maximum advantage from the machine. The user sees this almost immediately and is eager to purchase the software.

The difficulty is with their own sales force. For years they have sold heavy equipment. They don't know anything about software or computers. One of them is sure she can do everything the computer can do, so she sees no need for it. In short, she is resisting the new system.

This is a good example of a paradigm shift. The old paradigm is that they sell equipment. The new one is that they sell a system in which the software makes the equipment more useful.

The initial response to all paradigm shifts is rejection. For example, when Henry Ford invented the automobile, people thought it was very impractical. After all, they argued, where was anyone going to get gasoline for it? Indeed, the infrastructure needed to support the auto did not exist at that time.

In the same way, when the Swiss invented the digital watch, they were unimpressed. It had no springs and gears. Anyone could see that it wasn't a *real* watch. So they didn't even bother to patent it.

However, they showed it at the annual watch congress and Seiko and Texas Instruments noticed that it had not been patented, so they could make digital watches. Over the next few years, the Swiss lost tens of thousands of watch makers as the sales of digital watches skyrocketed (Barker, 1992). This is another example of a paradigm shift.

And how many people ignored the impact of the personal computer, believing that they could never replace mainframe units?

Trying to overcome resistance to a paradigm shift is very difficult. What usually happens is that evidence of the validity of the new paradigm grows to the point that people can no longer reject it, and then there is a landslide of acceptance. This is shown in Figure 6.11.

What some organizations have had to accept is that there will be a few employees who will not accept the new paradigm, and these people become casualties of the changing direction of the business. This is unfortunate, but given the strength of resistance that can be shown to the change, it may be unavoidable.

However, it is always worth trying the strategy that I have outlined above, which is to ask the person what you must do to convince him or her of the soundness of the new paradigm. If you are unable to get a positive response, then you can resort to some other action.

The important point of all this is that projects often get into far more trouble because of these "people" issues than they do because the schedule was incorrect or someone didn't know how to do a proper plan. As I said at the beginning of the book, successful projects can only be achieved when tools, people, and systems are jointly optimized. Unfortunately, the people side of the equation is more often overlooked than the other two.

Growth of Acceptance of a Paradigm Over Time

PUTTING IT ALL TOGETHER

Following is a step-by-step procedure for developing and selecting project strategy.

Steps 3 to 5 of
the Lewis Method

Project strategy is the overall "how" the job will be done. It is sometimes called a game plan. You should consider both overall project strategy and technical strategies (when appropriate). Because these may interact, the choice of technical strategy may affect your project strategy and vice versa.

1. Brainstorm a list of alternative project and technical strategies. Remember, in brainstorming, there is no evaluation or criticism until after all ideas have been listed.

2. Once the strategies have been listed, rank the project strategies using the priority matrix presented in Figures 6.3 to 6.8. Do the same for technical strategies.

3. Is the number one technical strategy compatible with the number one project strategy? If not, decide which pair of the two will be compatible before continuing.

Step 4

4. For the chosen strategies, can you meet your performance, cost, time, and scope targets? If "yes," continue to step 5. If "no" then select another strategy to evaluate, until the answer is "yes."

5. Now fill in a SWOT form, in which you combine threats and risks. Don't bother to fill in the right panel of the Threat portion of the form at this time. Note that you are doing this for strategy only, not for implementation steps.

6. Next fill in a risk analysis form in which you calculate RPNs for all threats and risks. You will have to read Chapter 8 to do this.

7. For all risks that have severities of 8 to 10 points, you *must* find a contingency to deal with the risk. Remember, you can avoid, mitigate, or transfer risk.

8. For all risks that have high products (regardless of severity), you should identify ways that these RPNs can be reduced, either by reducing probability or severity, or improving detection.

9. Are any risks serious enough that the strategy may not work? If so, you may have to select the next strategy in your priority matrix.

10. Are any identified weaknesses serious enough to jeopardize the strategy? Can they be overcome? If not, then you may need to select the next strategy in your matrix.

11. Now consider consequences. Will the chosen strategy lead to unacceptable consequences? If so, the strategy may have to be rejected.

12. Finally, you should conduct a force-field analysis, in which you identify those positive forces in the environment that will help your strategy succeed and the negative forces that may do the opposite. These forces can be political, social, or paradigm issues. Then ask yourself:

Continued on the next page.

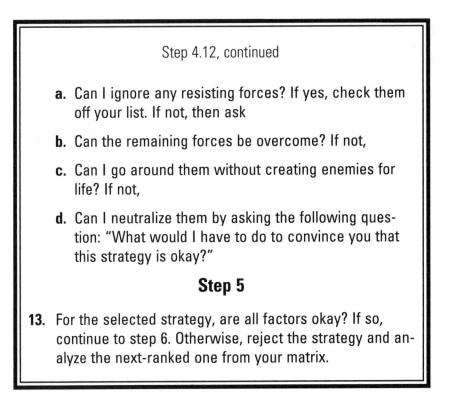

Step 4.12, continued

a. Can I ignore any resisting forces? If yes, check them off your list. If not, then ask

b. Can the remaining forces be overcome? If not,

c. Can I go around them without creating enemies for life? If not,

d. Can I neutralize them by asking the following question: "What would I have to do to convince you that this strategy is okay?"

Step 5

13. For the selected strategy, are all factors okay? If so, continue to step 6. Otherwise, reject the strategy and analyze the next-ranked one from your matrix.

KEY POINTS FOR CHAPTER 6

- Strategy is an overall approach to a project. It is sometimes called a *game plan.*
- *Principle:* It is best not to employ cutting-edge technology in a project that has a very tight deadline.
- *Principle:* As a rule, it is best to separate discovery from development.
- *Principle:* Threats are usually done by other entities, whereas risks are things that can just happen.

QUESTIONS FOR REVIEW

1. What is the difference between strategy, tactics, and logistics?
2. What is the importance of strategy?
3. What is a technical strategy?
4. What kind of thinking is needed to make a list of possible project strategies?
5. What is the difference between threats and risks?
6. What does SWOT stand for?

CHAPTER

Developing an Implementation Plan

We are now ready to discuss detailed implementation planning, which is steps 6 to 8 of the Lewis Method. These steps are shown in Figure 7.1.

In Chapter 6 I wrote that people are inclined to jump from step 1 of my model down to step 9. When I am able to convince them not to skip the definition phase, they then want to jump from step 2 to step 6. They tend to think of planning as detailed planning, omitting strategy from their thinking altogether.

In fact, I still find many individuals thinking about detailed planning while they are trying to define the project. The inclination to do detailed planning seems to be another of those genetic things. No doubt the researchers will find a gene one day that explains it.

In any case, we are finally there! You can now concentrate on how to get the job done. In terms of the HBDI, this is the place for a lot of quadrant B thinking. You want people to work out exactly how to execute the strategy chosen in steps 4 and 5. In case you

F I G U R E 7.1

Steps 6 to 8 of the Lewis Method

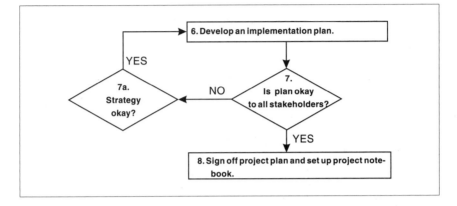

have forgotten where the B quadrant is, the model is shown in Figure 7.2, with the B quadrant highlighted.

Please note that, even though a lot of B quadrant thinking is required in this step, it does not mean that you don't need the other quadrants. It is just that planning is a particularly B quadrant activity. Nevertheless, you may need creative thinking (the D quadrant) and, especially, you should consider the C quadrant, which deals with interpersonal issues, in putting together a plan. So again, whole-brain thinking would be very helpful at this stage of the project.

In any case, you are now ready to work out the details of how a job will be done. For example, if you were building the Chunnel, knowing that you will go in both directions and meet in the middle, you must now determine all of the steps that will get you there. Because there are

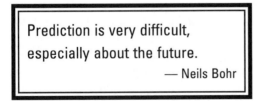

Prediction is very difficult, especially about the future.

— Neils Bohr

many contractors performing various parts of the project, you must decide *who* does what, *when* it will be done, *how much* each step will cost, *what* will be needed, and so on. In fact, this illus-

F I G U R E 7.2

Quadrant B Highlighted

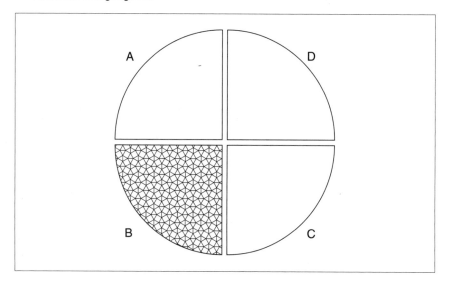

trates the definition of planning. It is answering all of the who, what, when, and how questions, much as a reporter asks when doing an article.

This is not to say that planning is easy. In fact, I believe it is some of the hardest work we ever do. One reason is that estimating is involved. How long will a step take? Who knows? As one of my engineers once told me

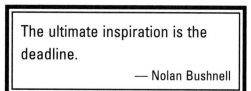

> The ultimate inspiration is the deadline.
>
> — Nolan Bushnell

when I asked how long some work would take, "You can't schedule creativity."

I agreed with him at the time, but as I told him, "We have to pretend we can, because they won't fund the project unless we tell them how long it will take."

Since then I have changed my mind. You can schedule creativity (within reason, of course). In fact, the most motivating fac-

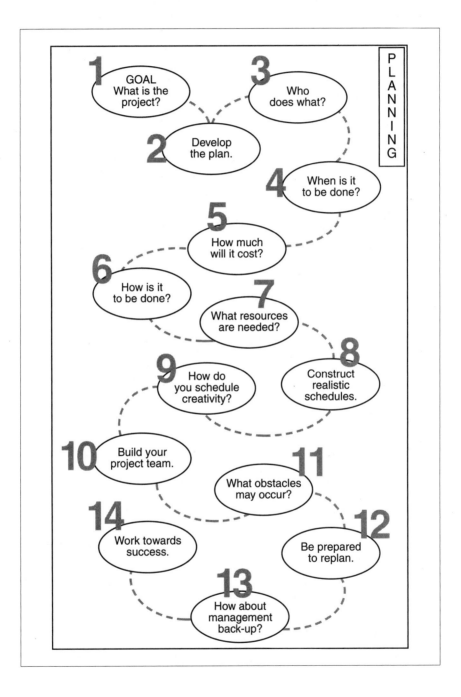

tor in creative thinking is a deadline. Ad agencies live with this all the time. So do the writers of daily "soaps." And so do engineers and programmers.

Edward de Bono, one of the world's leading gurus on creative thinking, has written that when he teaches creative thinking to children, if he gives them a deadline, they produce great results. Otherwise, if they have no time limit, they just mess around.

I know a creativity consultant who took an engineering group to the mountains for a weekend to develop a design for a new device. They started on Friday afternoon, and by Sunday afternoon they had developed a device that was patented. Using a structured approach to creativity enabled them to do this.

MISTAKES IN PLANNING

Before we go any further, it may be helpful to discuss the more common mistakes that people make in planning so that you can avoid them. There are five fairly common ones.

Unilateral Planning

This mistake is made when the project manager plans a project for the group and turns it over to them to execute. The major reason this is a mistake is that no one individual can possibly think of everything in a project. Even a one-person project can benefit from the thinking of other individuals.

> *Mistake 1:* Not involving in the planning process the people who must do the work.

Furthermore, you must estimate task durations yourself when you plan the project by yourself, and your estimates are likely to be wrong. Specifically, your estimate is very likely to be optimistic, because you forget about all of the detail that consumes most of the time. For this reason, the person who eventually must do the work is likely not to be very committed to the time you have specified. If he misses the mark, he is likely to

No one individual can possibly think of everything in a project. Even a one-person project can benefit from the thinking of others.

say, "It was your number, not mine. I knew it couldn't be done that fast."

No project can succeed when the team members have no commitment to the plan, so the first rule of project planning is that the people who must do the work should help plan that part of the project. You will not only gain their commitment to the plan, but also most likely cover all of the important issues that you may individually have forgotten.

I want to point out that one reason for this mistake (or trap) is that we confuse the thought process with documentation. I explained in Chapter 1 that my flowchart shows the *thought process* you must follow to manage a project. Even for a project to prepare a meal (it is a small project, after all), you should go through every step in my flowchart. If you don't believe it, try it out. You will find that all of the steps apply.

For example, when you get to step 6, where you would do a schedule in a large pro-
ject, do you develop a critical path schedule? No. Do you consider the order in which various steps must be done? You bet. Otherwise the meal will not come to-gether properly. You

> *Principle:* The first rule of planning is that the people who must do the work should participate in the planning.

will have your steak done and be sitting around for a half hour waiting for the baked potatoes to get done.

The Ready-Fire-Aim Mistake

One reason people don't plan projects is that they are convinced that they could have gotten the work done by the time they com-pleted the plan. The complaint is, "We don't have time to plan, we
have to get the job done." I had a fellow tell me that his boss told him exactly that. He had

> *Mistake 2:* Ready-fire-aim.

taken his team into the conference room to plan his project, and his boss came by, saw them in the room, and called him outside.

"What are you doing?" his boss asked.

"Planning my project," replied the project manager.

"You don't have time for that," said his boss. "Get them out of the conference room so you can get the job done."

If you read Chapter 1, you will remember that you can tell what people believe by watching what they do. So can you tell what this manager believes about planning? He doesn't think it is of value. You could be getting work done while you're sitting around planning, he thinks.

However, this is a counterintuitive situation. Does it seem reasonable that, if you have forever to get something done, you can afford to just mess around? On the other hand, if you have a really critical deadline, you need a good plan.

As a simple example, suppose I have flown to Chicago for a meeting and, because of bad weather, my plane lands very late. I have never been to Chicago before. I rush off the plane, dash to the rental car counter, and get my car. The agent asks, "Mr. Lewis, do you need a map?"

> *Principle:* The more important a project deadline, the more important the plan becomes.

"I don't have time for that," I say. "I have to get to my meeting. I'm already late!"

Now you can see the fault in that logic, but why can't we see the same fault in the logic that says we don't have time to plan projects?

Here's a final example. In 1983, the San Diego Home Builder's Association sponsored a contest to see how fast one could build a 2000-square-foot (approximately 225-square-meter) single-story house, sitting on a cement slab. This was not a prefabricated house. They started with raw materials and had to pour the cement slab. They had marked it out and had leveled the building site. Furthermore, they had a limited amount of building materials. If a piece of wallboard were damaged and they didn't have enough to complete the job, the competition ended.

The week before the competition, they built two houses for practice. They did an after-action review, learned from the practice session, and tweaked their plan. According to their estimates, they should be able to get the house built in about 3 hours and 40 minutes, using 350 workers on each site.

They actually completed one house in 2 hours and 45 minutes!

It was fully wired, plumbing installed, appliances installed, landscaped with sod and bushes, ready to move into.

I know it sounds incredible. Even impossible. How can you get cement to harden that fast? They put exothermic chemicals in the mortar so that it would cure in 45 minutes. You could see steam coming off the concrete. The joke was that, if the foundation hardened too fast, they would have a worker permanently cemented into the house.

No doubt one of the first thoughts that came to mind was, "I wouldn't want to live in it."

Of the four constraints (P, C, T, S) the one you are concerned with is quality (performance). They must surely have done shoddy work to get it finished so fast. Good thought.

They covered that concern by having regular San Diego building inspectors on the site, inspecting the work as it progressed. If it didn't meet building code (which is fairly rigorous in the earthquake-prone area), they made the crew do it over.

You probably have to see it to believe it, so if you are interested, you can get a video of the competition by calling the building association at 619-450-1221.

The reason I like this example is that it illustrates a project in which the planning time far exceeded the execution time.

Planning in Too Little Detail

One of the major causes of project failures is that ballpark estimates become targets. For the benefit of my readers outside the United States who may not understand the idiom "ballpark estimate,"

> *Mistake 3:* Broad-brush planning.

the expression comes from baseball. If the ball is hit over the wall, it is out of the ballpark. If it does not go over the wall, then it is in the ballpark. So we use the term ballpark estimate to mean that it is approximately correct. (It is within acceptable boundaries or limits.)

> *Principle:* If you aren't careful, ballpark estimates become targets.

The problem is that a ballpark estimate is done by comparing one project to another similar one, adding a bit for this, taking off a bit for that, then inserting some money for unknowns (called contingencies). The tolerances on ballpark estimates can be extremely large. Imagine being asked what it would cost to develop a vaccine for AIDS, as an example. The person would only be able to give a huge range on the number. There are simply too many unknown factors to be able to give a precise number.

This is an example of planning a project in too little detail. If a better estimate is desired, then you must identify the major tasks to be performed, and probably some of the subtasks as well.

I once worked with a company that did defense contracting. Their projects were bid at a fixed price. To estimate the cost to do the job, the person preparing the bid would go around to various individuals and ask each how much his or her part would cost. Each person would do a ballpark estimate. They would then be awarded the bid (based on being the low bidder) and would lose money on the job.

I explained that they were planning in too little detail. They had to actually plan the project in more detail to do a realistic estimate.

Three years later, in a follow-up interview, I asked, "How are your projects going now." The response was very positive. "We don't get as many jobs as we used to," said my contact, "but when we get one, we make money on it." Isn't that the name of the game?

As a way of indicating the level of detail that you should incorporate into a final project plan, I worked with a client who had never done much project planning. Most of their planning was on the backs of envelopes. Nevertheless, they had been very successful.

A new manager inherited the company and explained to everyone that they had to do a better job of planning. The reason was survival. A Japanese competitor had just entered their market. They were selling their product at a lower price than my client. The new manager explained that he didn't know the cost to develop his product, so in order to ensure that the company would make a profit, he had to sell at a higher margin than the Japanese company, who had a fairly accurate measure of their development costs. That being the case, they could charge a lower profit margin because they knew how many units they had to sell to reach breakeven, and therefore at what point they became profitable. His point was that good project management could give them a competitive advantage in the marketplace.

His proposal was met with considerable resistance. The engineers had never had to do this "administrative stuff" before and saw no need for it now. In part, they were afraid of being held accountable for estimates that may not be correct. This seemed like "policing" to them.

The frustrated manager told them he at least wanted them to give him a bar chart schedule. They responded by giving him a schedule that had bars 26 weeks long for individual tasks. His response was that they would never complete a 26-week task on time. They would back-end load it and ultimately fail.

His reasoning was that they would delay starting on time, fully convinced that they could always make up one day. After all, they had 26 Saturdays to make up the lost day. Next day, still busy, they would convince themselves that they could always make up two days, then three days, and so on, until they had slipped an entire week. It is incredibly hard to make up a week of lost work.

The term back-end loading means that they were going to push their work out toward the end of the task, and then if they encountered technical problems, they would ultimately fail.

He suggested that they should always follow the rule that no task ever have a duration greater than 4 to 6 weeks. So a 26-week

---

Rules for Planning

♦ No task should have a duration greater than 4 to 6 weeks.

♦ Engineering and software tasks should have durations no greater than 1 to 3 weeks.

♦ All tasks must have markers that enable everyone to tell that the work is actually complete.

task should be subdivided or "chunked down" to increments of about 4 weeks. Furthermore, they must have a marker that tells you they are actually complete, and this can be difficult with knowledge work. Another term is *exit criteria,* some way of knowing that the work is complete.

Had I known then what I know now, I would have told him that engineering and programming work should be chunked down even further so that durations fall in the range of 1 to 3 weeks. Otherwise you find that such work gets to 90 percent complete and stays there forever.

Planning in Too Much Detail

Unfortunately, the reverse of too little detail causes problems. Some people get carried away and microplan. I know. I did it myself once, and lived to regret it.

> *Mistake 4:* Microplanning.

The basic principle is that you should never plan in more detail than you can actually control. In engineering and software, that means no more than the nearest day. You simply can't control much better than that.

However, people who do maintenance work can sometimes control the work to the nearest hour. It is common practice to schedule jobs to refuel nuclear reactors or overhaul a power generator to the nearest hour. The schedules will be revised at the end

> *Principle:* Never plan in more detail than you can control.

of the shift, or once a day when they need to be. These jobs would not be scheduled to the nearest 15 minutes, however, because they can't be controlled that closely. If you make the mistake of scheduling in too much detail, you will spend all of your time keeping your schedule up to date, and that is a waste of time.

Apparently people sometimes fall into the microplanning trap because the scheduling software available permits them to plan down to minutes. So, if you can do it, then maybe you should, goes the thinking.

Failing to Plan for Risks

A "can-do" attitude is far preferable to a "can't do" attitude—up to a point. That point is when the person ignores probable risks. I once had a manager tell me he didn't want me to suggest that his people pad their schedules. He wanted their schedules

Mistake 5: Failing to plan for risks.

to be *aggressive*. I appreciate his concern, but there is a difference between aggressive and foolhardy.

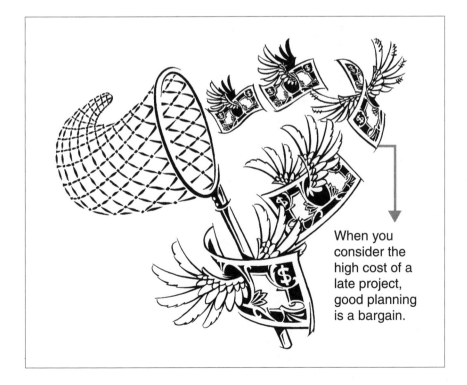

When you consider the high cost of a late project, good planning is a bargain.

> *Principle:* To ignore probable risks is not a "can-do" attitude but a foolhardy approach to project management.

If you are doing construction work, and that work may be delayed by weather, it is common risk management practice to allow for weather delays by padding your schedule. If the weather delay doesn't happen, you get ahead. If more delay occurs than you anticipated, you will have to work hard to recover. But to ignore the possibility of weather delays altogether is foolhardy.

Murphy's Law says that whatever can go wrong will go wrong. Stated in terms of probability, it says, there is a higher probability that things will accidentally go wrong than that they will accidentally go right. And, of course, we know that even Murphy was an optimist.

> *Principle:* There is a higher probability that things will accidentally go wrong than that they will accidentally go right.

Risk management is an integral part of good project management, and will be discussed in Chapter 8.

DEVELOPING THE WORK BREAKDOWN STRUCTURE

At the beginning of this chapter, I showed that we are now down to step 6 of my overall flowchart. Step 6 actually consists of a number of substeps, and these are shown in Figure 7.3.

As we saw earlier, implementation planning answers the questions shown in step 6a of Figure 7.3, and is repeated here:

1. What must be done?
2. Who will do each task?
3. How long will each task take?
4. What materials, supplies, and equipment are required?
5. How much will each task cost?

Notice that we don't worry about the order in which tasks will be done until we get to step 6b. This is the scheduling problem, and will be fully covered in Chapter 9.

For now, we will concentrate on the first question: What must be done? The tool of choice for doing this is the work breakdown struc-

> The first step in implementation planning is to answer the question, "What must be done?"

ture (WBS), which is constructed in step 6a. An example of a very

F I G U R E 7.3

Step 6 of the Lewis Method Expanded

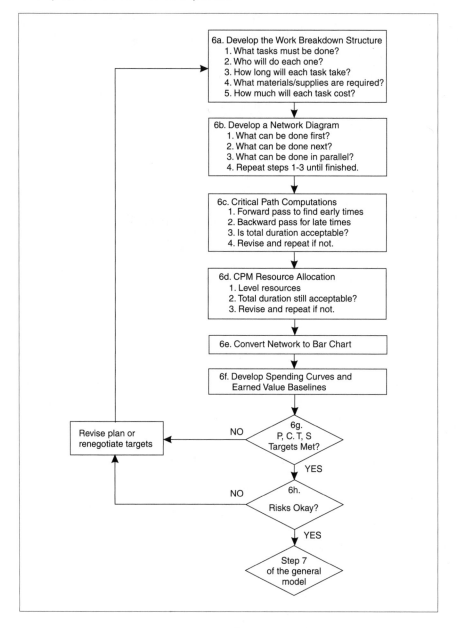

simple WBS is shown in Figure 7.4. This is a small project to do work in your yard.

As you can see, there are five major tasks to be done: Cut the grass, do trim work, and so on. Some of these tasks also have subtasks underneath. The terminology will be explained shortly.

But what use is this? First, one of the major causes of project failure is that something is forgotten until the project is underway, and then it is discovered. The forgotten work has a serious impact to the project—either in terms of schedule or cost. The WBS is one device that helps us ensure that nothing significant has been forgotten.

As a matter of fact, I consider the WBS to be the most valuable tool of project management because it ties the entire project together. This position is contrary to popular belief that project management is just scheduling. There are some projects so small

FIGURE 7.4

Work Breakdown Structure for Yard Project

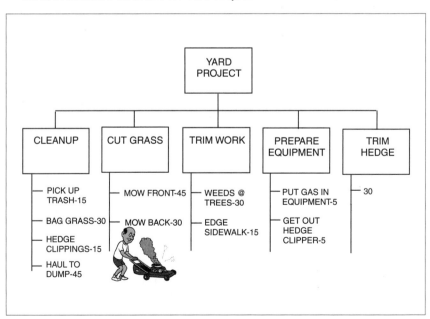

that developing a schedule would be a waste of time, but a WBS is *always* useful. Here's why:

1. It identifies all work to be done in the project graphically, so it can be reviewed by all stakeholders to ensure that nothing has been forgotten.
2. It provides a graphic representation of the scope (or magnitude) of the job. This is important because people are sometimes surprised at the cost estimates you give them, and this helps them see why the job is going to cost as much as you have said.
3. The WBS provides the basis for which resource assignments can be made.
4. This allows you to estimate working times for each task.
5. Knowing the working time then allows you to calculate labor costs for all work so that you develop a *labor budget* for the project. The times also provide the basis for developing a schedule.
6. You can also identify material, capital equipment, and other costs associated with each activity (such as insurance costs).

Now let's see about the terminology. In Figure 7.5 you will see that each level of the WBS is given a name. The first level is called *program* and the next is called *project*. This explains the difference between program management and project management. A program is a very large job that consists of a number of projects. A good example is a program to develop a new airplane. A partial WBS for such a job is shown in Figure 7.6.

The engine design is a project in its own right, with a project manager and project team. The wing design, avionics design, and so on, are also large projects. In fact, the wing design would probably be done by the aircraft company and the engine and avionics would be contracted to other companies such as General Electric, Rolls Royce, and Collins Radio.

The program manager has responsibility over the entire job. The project managers do not report to him or her on a solid line

F I G U R E 7.5

Names of Levels in a WBS

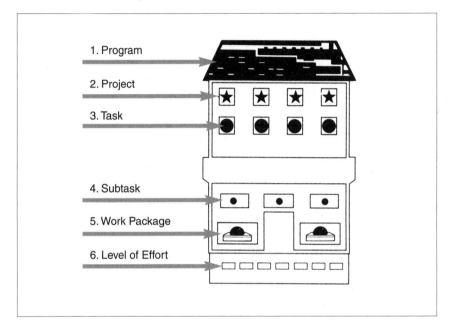

F I G U R E 7.6

WBS for an Airplane Development Program

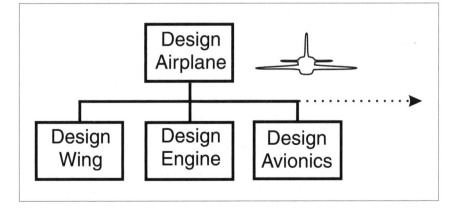

basis, but do report on a dotted line. Note that an airplane such as Boeing's 777 or an Airbus 319 has wing-mounted engines. Somewhere in the engine design project will be a task to design the mountings for connecting the engine to the wing. And in the wing design there will be a task to design the corresponding engine mounts.

Clearly these tasks will be interactive in nature, and will have to be coordinated between the two project teams. The program manager must see that this is done. However, when the WBS is drawn, we do not worry about the sequence in which these tasks are done. This will be worked out when the schedule is developed.

> *Principle:* You don't worry about the sequence of tasks while constructing the WBS.

I make this point because there is a strong tendency for people to think about sequence while constructing the WBS. "You can't do that until you have done this," they say. No doubt scientists will find a gene one day that explains this behavior. A sequencing gene. In any case, you have to keep telling people, "That's true, you can't do this until that is done, but we're not trying to work that out yet."

What the Names Mean

What exactly does work package mean? It is simply a label or name that identifies what level you are at in the structure. It is used in the same way that Jim and Bob are used. If I say Bob, and there is a fellow named Bob in the room, he responds. If there are two Bobs, they will both answer and I then have to specify the last name.

So if I ask you about a work package in the engine project for the airplane, you would know it is something at level 5 in the structure. Most people don't get concerned with names, although people often ask how you know whether something goes at level 5 or 6 or whatever. You only know where things go by breaking work down in progressive steps until you reach a point of diminishing returns. And wherever an activity falls, it falls. It is not a matter of something absolutely being a level 3 subtask. It is a function of how the work is actually structured. You will see this in the example that follows later in Figure 7.7.

The Steps in the Process

So just how do you go about developing a WBS? I'm going to use a simple example. We're planning a family camping trip. It is a family of four—two adults, and a boy who is 12 years old and a girl who is 8. They have set aside a 2-week period for the trip, and have already arranged with their employers to be away during that time. Furthermore, they have a budget. They don't want to spend more than a certain amount for this trip.

Now notice what has been specified so far in terms of the PCTS constraints. We have specified time and cost. Scope and performance are undefined.

What would scope mean in a camping trip? Things like what you want to do while you're away, that is, a list of activities you want to engage in. It may also involve whether you are doing tent camping or using a motor home. As for performance, remember this is the quality of work done. In the camping example, it means the quality of the experience the family has. If they try to cram too much into the trip, as people sometimes do when they go abroad and want to see 12 cities in 3 days, they will sacrifice quality in the process.

So suppose they make a list of everything they want to do. It doesn't appear that quality will be sacrificed, but when they add up the costs, they realize that they will exceed their budget. What do they do?

Two possibilities exist. First, they can decide that this is a once-in-a-lifetime trip, and they will just put a little more on the credit card than they had intended. Or they may decide that the budget is very important and delete some activities from the list.

The importance of this is that you can never escape the PCTS constraints in *any* project—not even a simple thing like a family camping trip. Trade-offs are always being made to balance project requirements.

First Pass on a WBS for a Camping Trip

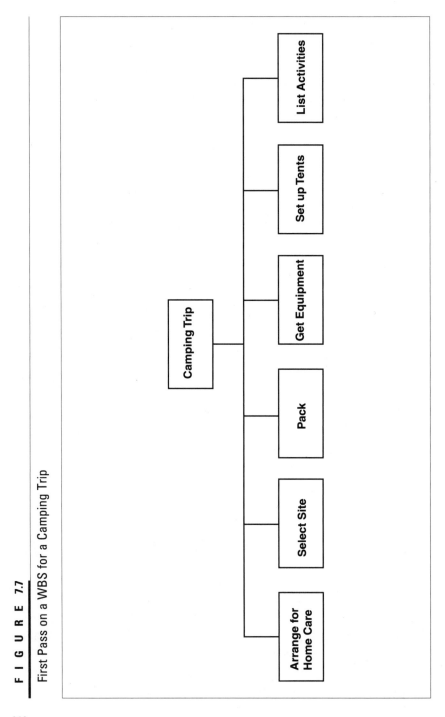

The First Step

When I draw a WBS, I begin by identifying major tasks. My first pass would look like the one shown in Figure 7.7. As I continue, this may change. For that reason, it is convenient to do this on a white board or to use Post-it notes so that things can be easily moved around.

Once I have all of the tasks, I begin breaking them down. For example, Select Site can be broken down as shown in Figure 7.8.

Now note that the task to list the activities we want to do during the trip can be a stand-alone task, or it may be part of the family meeting. That is, if I am going to make the list during the family meeting, I can remove it as a task and put it there as a subtask. This is shown in Figure 7.9.

Now I can expand the subtask called Research, as shown in Figure 7.10. This process would continue with all tasks and subtasks until I have reached a point where I think everything has been covered. When this is done with a team, you are likely to think of everything. If you do it by yourself, you may miss something, so if it is a one-person project you are planning it is a good idea to have someone else review your WBS before you go any further.

If you complete the WBS, you may have something like the one shown in Figure 7.11. This is by no means the only possible solution. Most projects are open-ended problems, in that there is no single way to go about the work.

I suggest that you pause at this point and draw a WBS for something you are currently doing. It can be a home project or work activity. Just sketch it out to satisfy yourself that you have done it correctly. If you have any questions about the procedure, you can send me an e-mail at jlewis@lewisinstitute.com, and I'll try to help you.

Some Things to Notice

If you compare the camping trip WBS with the one for the airplane, you will notice a significant difference. All the projects in the airplane program produce tangible deliverables. In the camping trip, however, very few tasks produce deliverables. Get Equip-

F I G U R E 7.8

WBS with Select Site Broken Down

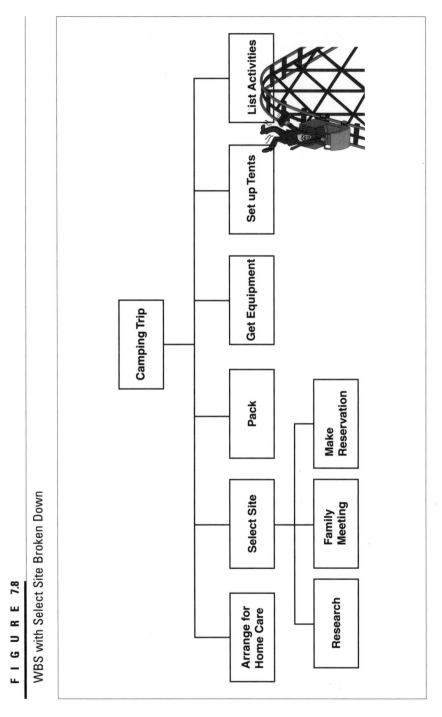

WBS with List Activities Moved under Family Meeting

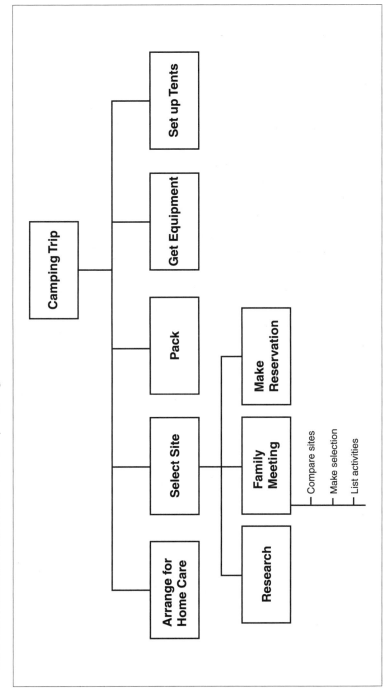

WBS with Research Expanded

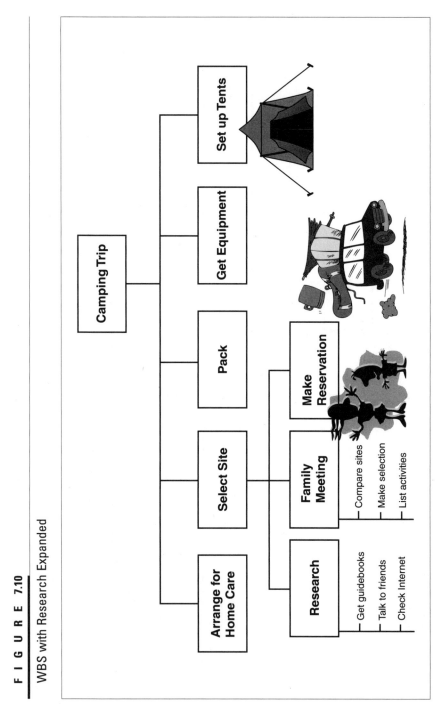

Completed WBS for Camping Trip

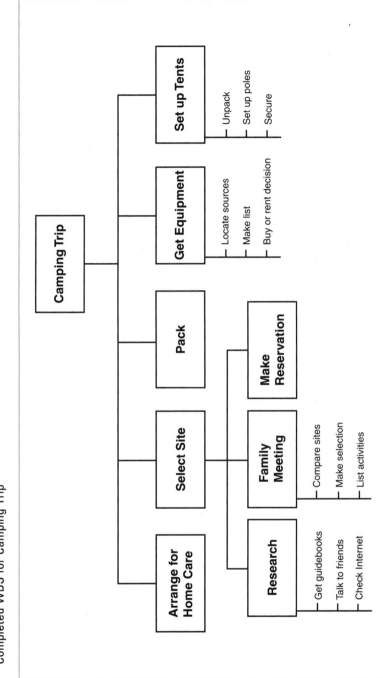

ment is one that does. Arrange for Home Care does not. You have cut off the newspaper, asked the post office to hold your mail, and arranged for someone to come over and water your plants. There are no deliverables here, so how would you know that activities have been taken care of? The simplest way is to use a checklist for things that have no deliverables.

I consider this WBS to be primarily process-oriented. The airplane WBS is things-oriented at the top level. However, as you get further down into the structure, you will find a number of activities that are process-oriented. As an example, you will have to test the engine. What is the deliverable? There is no hardware deliverable, but you will produce a test report. That is your deliverable, and it is evidence that the test has been conducted.

In many cases, you don't even produce reports, so how do you know the work has been done? You use *exit criteria*. As a simple example, if you change the oil in your car, and I ask if you are sure you've done it correctly, you could show me the dip stick which would register FULL and show clean oil, rather than dirty oil. One of these is *quantitative* and the other is *qualitative*. I would also look under the car and inspect to see whether any oil is dripping from the drain, which would mean that the plug has not been correctly reinstalled. Another qualitative exit criteria.

I heard of a situation where a company produced a prototype product and called one of the vice presidents out to look at it. He didn't like a major feature of the product and insisted that it be redesigned. The prototype had been built with tooling, which had to be scrapped. The total cost to redesign the product was huge.

In this case, the exit criteria was that the vice president approved the product. Knowing that, it would have been best to get him to look at preliminary drawings, rather than wait so late. In fact, I wouldn't be surprised if they tried to do so and were unable to get him to review the design because he had a heavy schedule and believed that he couldn't afford the time. The lesson is that corrections should always be made as early in a process as possible, because each succeeding step magnifies the cost to correct an error by about 10 times. So the progression goes 1, 10, 100, 1000, and so on.

Suggestions on How to Proceed

When you develop a project plan, you are determining the who, what, when, and how, as I previously explained. It may be helpful to approach a WBS by answering questions in this order:

1. What must be done? Example: The house must be cleaned. This would be the project.
2. What must be done to clean the house? Wash the windows. Clean the floors. Put everything in its proper place. Dust the furniture. Carry out the garbage. These would be major tasks in the project.
3. Who will do each one? Mom will clean the floors. Tommy will put everything in its place. Sue will dust the furniture. Dad will carry out the garbage. Donnie will wash the windows. This assigns roles and responsibilities.

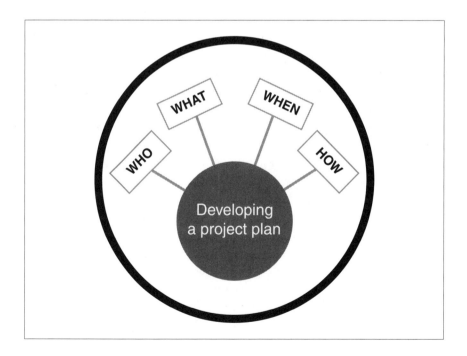

4. How will each task be done? Mom will clean the floors by vacuuming the carpets and mopping the tile floors. Sue will dust the furniture using furniture polish, and so forth. These will be subtasks.

5. What is needed to do each subtask? A vacuum cleaner. Furniture polish. Rags. Paper towels. Garbage bags. Identifying these allows you to develop costs for equipment and materials. This is a major part of the budget.

6. How long will each subtask take? These estimates provide the basis for the labor budget (see step 8) and for developing the schedule.

7. What is required for each subtask to be considered complete? This will constitute exit criteria for each activity.

8. In a normal work project, how much will each subtask cost for labor? This gives you the labor budget, which, when combined with the equipment and materials budget, yields the total project budget.

Guidelines to Follow

Following are some guidelines that you should follow in developing a WBS:

- Up to 20 levels can be used. More than 20 is considered overkill.
- All paths on a WBS do not have to go down to the same level. One path may go down five levels and another only three levels. When you have reached a point that allows you to manage the work, you stop. Don't force the structure to be symmetrical.
- The WBS does not show sequencing of work except in the sense that all level 5 work packages hanging below a given subtask must be complete for the subtask to be complete, and so on. However, work packages below that subtask might be performed in series or parallel. Sequencing is determined when schedules are developed.

- A WBS should be developed before scheduling and re-source allocation are done. Just identify the tasks first, then come back and decide who will do them and esti-mate how long they will take.
- The WBS should be developed by individuals knowledgeable about the work. Well duh, you say? Of course that must be true. The practi-cal meaning, however, is that

> Principle: A work breakdown structure *does not show the sequence in which work is performed!* Such sequencing is determined when a schedule is developed.

different parts of the WBS will be developed by various groups and then the separate parts combined. Remember, the first rule of project planning is that the people who will ultimately do the work should develop the plan.
- Break down a project only to a level sufficient to produce an estimate of the required accuracy. This should be ex-plained. One of the big advantages you get with a WBS is greater accuracy of cost and time estimates than you would get by simply comparing one project to another. A project-to-project estimate is called a ballpark estimate, as was mentioned previously, and we saw that the accuracy is not very good.

If you break a project down to a level that can be controlled, you can then develop a working estimate. But what does this mean? Ask yourself what level of detail you can control in your work. Can you predict to the nearest hour when a task will be fin-ished? The nearest day? Nearest week? If you break work down into such small units that they take hours to perform but you can't control the work to that degree, you will spend all of your time updating your schedule and you won't get any work done!

I know. I've done it. It isn't any fun.

So when you reach a level that you can control, you stop there.

Now it may be that an estimate is needed to decide if a project should be done. It may be possible to make that decision if the accuracy of the estimate is +50 percent. You may only have to break the project down two levels to achieve that accuracy.

> *Principle:* A WBS is a list of activities. It is not a grocery list.

Going further at this point would be a waste of time if the decision is to not do the work.

- A WBS is a list of activities. It is not a grocery list. Here's what this means. Imagine that I am doing a home project. I plan to do some yard work, some repairs, and buy groceries. So I draw a WBS like the one in Figure 7.12.

As you can see, I have put my grocery list on the WBS. That is not what you do. You identify the activities that must be performed to have bought groceries. It would look like the WBS in Figure 7.13.

This is a very easy trap to fall into. Here is a test to help you decide if you have made the mistake. In Figure 7.13, if I have done all of the activities listed, the task to buy groceries will be complete. In Figure 7.12, however, if I have bought eggs, milk, and bread, I am still standing in the grocery store. The activities in Figure 7.12 are not predecessor to Buy Groceries—they *are* the components of that task listed in detail. So when they are all done, the task above is complete. This is your test.

ESTIMATING TIME, COST, AND RESOURCE REQUIREMENTS

Once you have your WBS complete, you are ready to use it for estimating. This is the step that scares the daylights out of a lot of people. They don't know how long something will take, but they know if they give their manager a number, they will be held to it. So they try to waffle or avoid committing to a number altogether.

WBS for Home Project

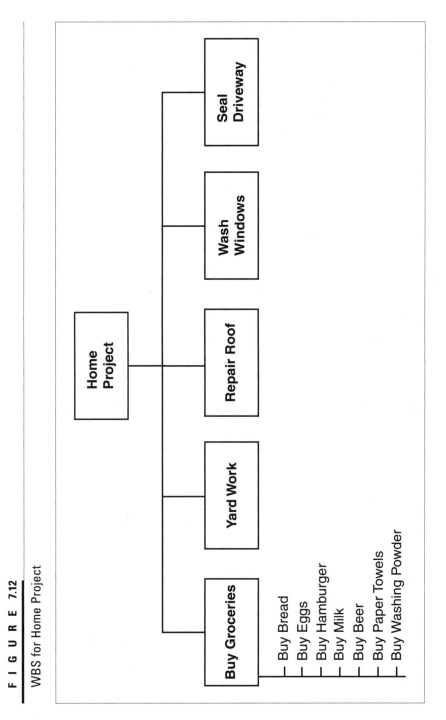

WBS with Proper Activities Shown for Buying Groceries

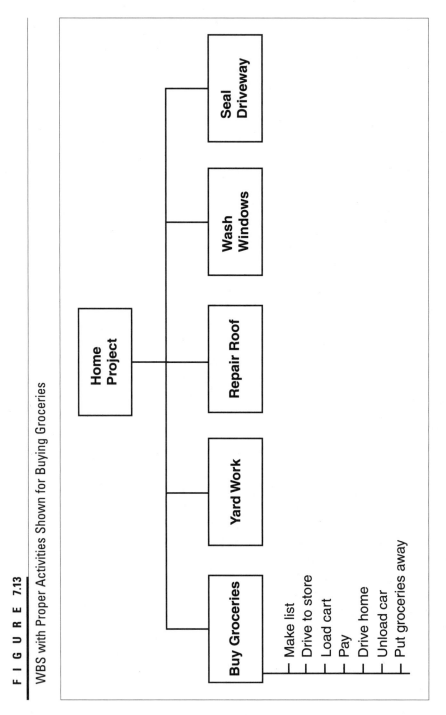

As I pointed out earlier in this chapter, people think you can't schedule creative tasks, but you can.

You *cannot*, however, schedule pure discovery work, and you should always separate discovery from development, in a product development environment. As an example, the CFO at Merck Pharmaceuticals wrote an article in *Harvard Business Review* saying that they examine approximately 10,000 compounds before one makes it as a drug. There's no way you can schedule such work.

That does not mean that you can't plan research projects, however. I've been told that by a number of scientists. What confuses them is that research projects have conditional branches. You do

> *Principle:* You cannot schedule discovery work.

a series of studies or experiments and, depending on the results you get, you go in one direction or another. This is shown in Figure 7.14.

You may not know which branch you will ultimately take at the beginning of the project, but you can plan everything up to

F I G U R E 7.14

A Project with a Conditional Branch

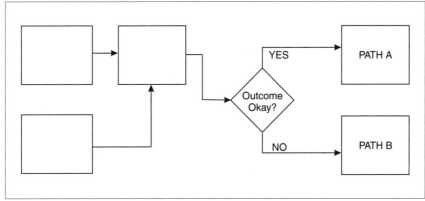

that point. Furthermore, as you get near that branch, you begin considering what you will do once the outcome is known. If you don't, you will waste a lot of time deciding later on. (And you may not have any idea what to do next—it isn't a simple thing.)

What Is Estimating?

In pure and simple words, estimating is *guessing!* Yes, there are kinder, gentler words for it, such as forecasting or predicting. But the truth is that an estimate is a guess based on something. It is best when it is based on experience. But what if you have no experience—it's the first time something is to be done?

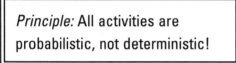

Principle: Estimating is *guessing!*

Under that condition, you have to use another approach, and there are two primary ones that we will discuss later. However, it should be clear that, no matter how much experience you have, estimating is guessing. Why? Because *all activities are probabilistic, not deterministic!* There is a probability that a task can be completed in a certain time, given a fixed level of effort. If you want to guarantee that the task is finished in a fixed time period, then you must vary effort, reduce scope, or sacrifice quality. You can't have it all. Therefore, an exact estimate is an oxymoron.

Principle: All activities are probabilistic, not deterministic!

Now I said that estimating is best done when you have experience—or history—with an activity. So let's see what that means. You have history on an activity that you perform regularly—namely, driving to work. If I ask how long it takes, you can give me three (and possibly four) numbers. One is the typical driving time. It happens most frequently. Another is the best case. You have never been able to get to work any faster. And finally, there is the worst case, where traffic tie-ups delay you. This worst-case time happens often enough so that you are well aware of it.

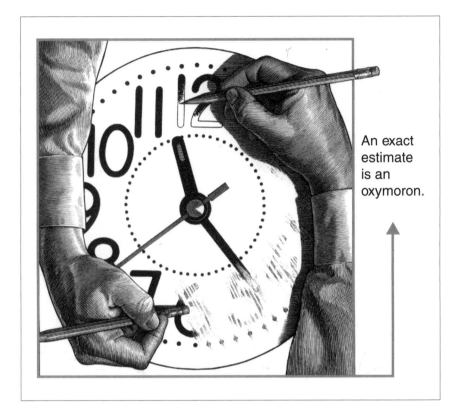

An exact estimate is an oxymoron.

There may also be a "worst-worst" case. Just once you got caught in a traffic tie-up that caused you to take 3 hours to get to work. However, it only happened once, and you don't expect it to happen again. The "normal" worst-case time does happen fairly often, so it is the one you should use.

"It's a poor sort of memory, that only works backwards," the Queen remarked.

— Lewis Carrol
Alice's Adventures in Wonderland

When I ask people for their driving times, I usually get numbers like the ones shown in Table 7.1. Notice that the worst-case time is skewed upward.

T A B L E 7.1

Driving Times Reported by Metropolitan Workers

Typical time	45 minutes
Shortest time	30 minutes
Longest time	60 minutes

The driving time is not normally distributed. A normal distribution is shown in Figure 7.15 and a skewed distribution is shown in Figure 7.16.

F I G U R E 7.15

Normal Distribution

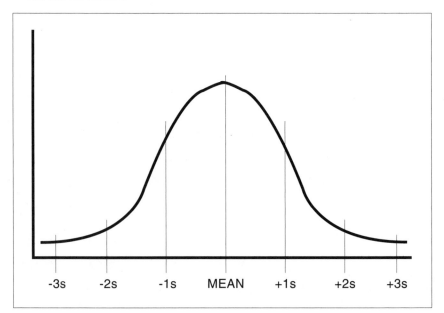

-3s   -2s   -1s   MEAN   +1s   +2s   +3s

Skewed Distribution

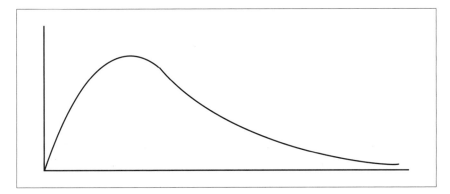

Okay. The question is, What do we do with historical data when we have it? To illustrate, write down your own driving times, and then answer this question: If I ask you how long you estimate it will take you to get to work on a random day (you don't know what day of week or what the weather is doing), what will you tell me? Most people give me the typical time. Now if you have a very skewed distribution, this is probably the modal time. If the distribution is a normal distribution, then the typical time would be an average. For an average, the probability that you could get to work in that time or less would be 50 percent. This is shown in Figure 7.17.

Most people don't feel uncomfortable with a 50 percent probability of driving to work, but they do feel uneasy if the probability of completing project work is that low. So they tend to pad the number to increase the probability of success. As you can see in Figure 7.17, if you go only 1 standard deviation above the mean, you increase the probability to 84 percent.

I often ask people, "If the president of your company wanted to have a meeting with you first thing in the morning, and it was career suicide to be late, how much time would you allow yourself to get to work?" Most of them go to the worst-case time—or higher—and raise their probability to 99.9 percent.

226

Normal Distribution with Probabilities Shown

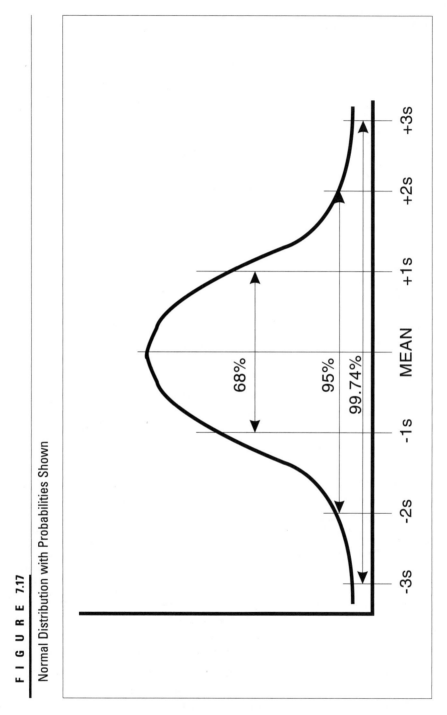

Because there is a significant penalty for being late, they reduce their risk by padding the schedule. They will do the same thing with projects. And when they do, the cost of the project goes sky high, and it will most likely not be funded.

> *Principle:* As the probability of project success goes toward 100 percent, the probability of funding goes to zero.

I can promise you, however, that if it gets funded, it will cost what we have budgeted—and possibly more. This is based on Parkinson's Law, which says that the work will always expand to take as long as has been allowed. The project will never finish early.

> *Parkinson's Law:* Work will expand to take the time allowed.

Why? Because if you finish early, everyone will think you padded the schedule, and next time they will cut your time and budget accordingly.

Now this is organizational insanity. A sample of one has created an expectation for all future work! That's crazy.

I am convinced that everyone should have to take statistics because they would then understand that all processes vary. Your driving time varies. The amount of time you need to get dressed in the morning varies. The time it takes to write a 10-page document varies. Why? Random noise.

There are all kinds of things that affect driving time, for example. The exact time that you leave home. The weather. Road construction. School buses. You name it. These are factors outside your control, and they must be accepted.

Can we reduce variation? Yes, up to a point. That is what all process improvement is aimed at doing.

Can you eliminate variation altogether? Absolutely not.

Yet we have two rules in organizations that show that we don't understand this. One is, "Thou shalt not go over budget." The other is, "Thou shalt not come in under budget."

This is plain stupid. It is insisting that people violate a law of nature—namely, to achieve zero variance in their spending to budget. This is possible only if you finagle and so everyone plays games to achieve the impossible.

The problem is, this is easier to do with a department than with a project. You budget a department on the basis of head count. You can control spending to a much tighter tolerance than you can a project, because a project is budgeted based on a bunch of guesses.

We simply must reach a point where everyone understands that variation is a fact of life, and it must be accepted. We waste millions of dollars every year playing games to make variances approach zero, when it is counterproductive to do so.

What If You Finished a Task Early?

Imagine that you finished a task ahead of schedule and passed it on to the person who is next in line. What would happen? Would she start work on it immediately? Of course not. She doesn't have to start until a few days later—according to the schedule—so she won't.

Goldratt (1997) calls this the *Student Effect*.

Remember when you were in school, and the teacher announced on Monday that there would be a test on Friday? Everyone moaned and groaned. "I already have three tests this week," says one student. "This is going to kill me." So the teacher relents and says, "Okay,

> *Goldratt's Principle:* A project will accumulate delays but will never accumulate gains.

we will have the test Friday of next week, instead of this week. Everyone gives a sigh of relief.

When will the students start studying for the test? You guessed it. They will start studying on Thursday night the following week! They won't have any more study time than they would have had if the test had been given this Friday.

So Goldratt concludes that, when you combine Parkinson's Law with the Student Effect, a project will accumulate delays but will never accumulate gains. This means that they almost always cost more than necessary and take longer than they should. There is a lot of room for improvement.

How do you solve this problem? We must change our thinking. We must accept variation and, in doing so, get rid of penalties for being either early or late on a task-by-task basis. As Goldratt argues, it doesn't matter that there is some variation

> You can't solve a problem with the same thinking that created it in the first place.
>
> — Albert Einstein

on task completion. What matters is that the project finish on time.

If you allow task completions to vary, some will finish early, some will finish a bit late, and the variations will average out. Otherwise, you will always finish late.

What this means, then, is that estimates should be based on that typical driving time, rather than the worst case.

Consensual Estimating

Earlier I said that we sometimes have no history. What do you do then? You could hold a wet string up and see how long it takes to dry, multiply the result by 33 and divide by 6. That is called an estimating algorithm.

Of course, I'm joking.

What a lot of people are doing now is to use consensual estimating. It works like this. You ask several individuals who know something about a task to each estimate how long it will take—independently of each other. You do this for all of the tasks in your WBS. Then you have a meeting in which you compare estimates. Suppose for a single task you had a result like that shown in Figure 7.18.

Notice that there are three individuals in fairly close agreement, and one whose number is considerably lower. It would be

F I G U R E 7.18

The Distribution of Several Estimates for a Single Task

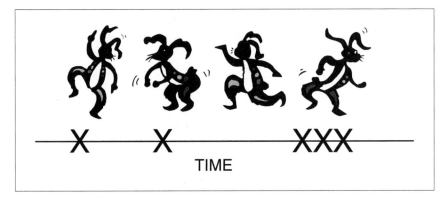

tempting to throw out the low number and go with the majority. But that's not a good idea. What you want to do is understand why the difference exists, so you discuss the issues affecting the task. In doing so, the person who estimated low may revise his estimate upward. Conversely, the majority may realize that they missed something the other individual thought of, and they may revise their estimates downward.

Whatever the case, they ultimately are asked to choose a number that they can all support. Notice they aren't asked to totally agree with the number. You almost never get total agreement in a group. What you want is that they will all support a single estimate. This is the practical meaning of the word consensus.

There are four major advantages of using this approach:

1. No one person is "on the hook" for the estimate. If it turns out to be significantly off, no individual will get chastised for it.
2. Inexperienced members of the team learn from the others, and their ability to estimate improves.
3. Collectively, they are more likely to think of all the factors that may affect the time required to do the task than would be true of any individual.

4. You will have higher commitment to the estimate than would be true if an individual produced it.

The seeming downside is that this will take a lot longer than if an individual did each estimate. But it isn't true. The cost of taking more time to refine the estimates will be more than paid for by a successful project. When you consider the high cost of a late project, you find that good planning is a bargain.

Calendar-Time Estimates

I have suggested that you use working-time estimates to plan a project. However, if you ask a person, "How long will it take you to do a report for me?" the person will most likely tell you, "Oh, I should be able to do that in about a week."

She knows it is about 2 hours of actual work, but because she has a lot of work to do, it will take her a week to get to it. So she gives you a calendar-time estimate. Do you really care about the actual working time? After all, isn't it the calendar time that is really important?

Actually, you need both. You need the actual working time to work out labor costs, and you need calendar time to predict project completion. In fact, if she tells you the report will be done in a week, and you need it sooner, you will ask if she can give it a higher priority so that she can do it in a couple of days. You are always juggling trade-offs between working time and calendar time. You just have to be sure to ask both questions when you ask for estimates.

Clarifying Roles and Responsibilities

Please note that you can't estimate task durations unless you begin with the assumption of a resource—either by name or at least by skill level. Once you have assigned resources to all activities, you may want to fill out a responsibility chart, like the one in Figure 7.19 so that everyone can tell at a glance who is responsible for each task.

F I G U R E 7.19

Responsibility Chart

Linear Responsibility Chart

Project:	Date Issued:	Sheet Number:	of
Manager:	Date Revised:	Revision No.	File: LRCFORM.61

Project Contributors

Task Descriptions													

CODES: 1 = ACTUAL RESPONSIBILITY; 2 = SUPPORT; 3 = MUST BE NOTIFIED; BLANK = NOT INVOLVED

Making Sure You Have Commitment from Resource Providers

In many projects, you don't own your resources—they are provided by functional managers on a temporary basis. Once your implementation plan is complete, you should get it signed off in step 8 of the Lewis Method model. These signatures should be obtained in a project plan sign-off meeting, if possible. Circulating the plan through the interoffice mail to be signed almost always leads to problems, because people tend to skim instead of actually reading and then their commitments won't hold up later on. They should be clear that their signatures indicate their commitment to provide resources *when* they say, in the *quantities* they say.

KEY POINTS FOR CHAPTER 7

- *Principle:* The more important a project deadline, the more important the plan becomes.
- *Principle:* Never plan in more detail than you can control.
- *Principle:* To ignore probable risks is not a "can-do" attitude but a foolhardy approach to project management.
- *Principle:* There is a higher probability that things will accidentally go wrong than that they will accidentally go right.
- *Principle:* You don't worry about the sequence of tasks while constructing the WBS.
- A work breakdown structure *does not show the sequence in which work is performed!* Such sequencing is determined when a schedule is developed.
- *Principle:* A WBS is a list of activities. It is not a grocery list.
- *Principle:* All activities are probabilistic, not deterministic!
- *Parkinson's Law:* Work will expand to take the time allowed.

QUESTIONS FOR REVIEW

1. What is the dominant kind of thinking needed for implementation planning?
2. What is planning?
3. Why is unilateral planning a mistake?
4. Why is the ready-fire-aim mistake counterintuitive?
5. What is the maximum duration you should allow for a task?
6. What are the primary outcomes of doing a work breakdown structure?
7. What is the Student Effect?

8
CHAPTER

Managing Project Risk

In step 4 of the Lewis Method, you are asked if SWOT and risks are okay. This was discussed briefly in Chapter 6. You will also note that step 6 also asks if risks are okay. So there are two places in a project where it is important to do risk management—in planning strategy and in implementation planning.

One of the single most important things you can do to ensure a successful project is to

> A risk is anything that may happen that could create an adverse effect on your schedule, costs, quality, or scope.

manage risks. A risk is anything that may happen that could create an adverse effect to your schedule, costs, quality, or scope. That is, a risk may impact your PCTS targets. Simply put, you either manage risks or they will manage you.

Be realistic about risks.

Manage risks and threats or they will manage you.

There is a supermacho mentality that doesn't understand this. Sometimes we call it a "can-do" attitude. I certainly prefer that people have a can-do attitude to a "can't-do" one, but there is such a thing as being realistic about risks and there is foolhardiness, which ignores them. A "damn the torpedoes, full speed ahead" approach sounds glamorous, but it can wreck your project.

I once had a manager tell me that he didn't want me to suggest to his people that they pad their schedules. "I want them to be aggressive," he asserted.

Again, there is a difference between an aggressive schedule and a foolish one. If you are doing construction work, and are certain that weather may delay your project, you would be derelict in your duty as a project manager to not account for the delays. You do so by allowing a bit longer for work to be completed than it would take if there were no weather delays. This is called padding the schedule, and is proper risk management in construction.

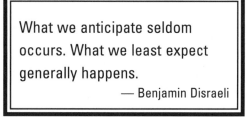

What we anticipate seldom occurs. What we least expect generally happens.
— Benjamin Disraeli

THREATS VERSUS RISKS

In Chapter 6, on planning strategy, I pointed out that there is a difference between threats and risks. A risk is something that you can do yourself, such as having an accident, or that can happen to

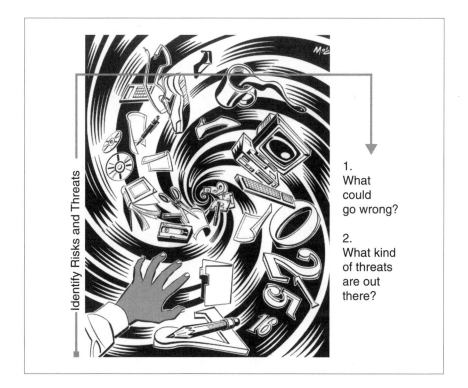

Identify Risks and Threats

1. What could go wrong?

2. What kind of threats are out there?

you in an impersonal way, such as bad weather. A threat, on the other hand, is something that will usually be done to you by some entity—whether a person or an organization. As an example, a threat to project success occurs when a competitor beats you to market with a new product. In practice, it is okay to lump the two together for the purpose of analysis and contingency planning.

THE RISK MANAGEMENT PROCESS

There are three steps in the risk management process:

1. Identify risks and threats by asking, "What could go wrong?" or "What kind of threats are there?"
2. Quantify threats and risks by assigning a risk priority number (RPN) to them.
3. Develop contingency plans to deal with risks that cannot be ignored.

Risk Identification

As I said above, you need to identify risks that may impact your strategy and your implementation plan. For example, if you are developing a new product using cutting-edge technology, there is a possibility that you can't get it to work. The more unproven the technology, the higher the probability that you will have difficulty. One way to manage such risk is to do a feasibility study to see if you can make the new technology work before you launch a full-scale development effort. Then, if you can't get the results you want, you can fall back on more proven technology.

If you launch a development program using unproven technology and can't make it work, the consequences are far more serious than if you do a feasibility study and reject the new approach. For one thing, it is obvious to everyone that a feasibility study is a success regardless of the outcome. If you say, "Yes, we can make it work," that is a success and so is the negative result, because it will save you a lot of grief from trying to make something work which can't be done.

When you get to the implementation planning stage of your project, you again want to identify things that can cause implementation problems. In this case, the WBS can be used to guide your thinking. Consider this very simple example. I previously used a yard project as an example of developing a WBS. That WBS is repeated here in Figure 8.1.

Now suppose I want to do risk management. For each task in the WBS I ask, "What could go wrong?" Here are some examples for each task.

1. *Clean up:* The dump may be closed when we get there, so we have wasted time driving over there. The contingency would be to call and see if the dump is open.

2. *Cut grass:* It might rain while we are cutting grass. The contingency would be to check the weather forecast and schedule the activity on a day when the forecast is for good weather.

3. *Trim work:* You run out of string for your string trimmer. Contingency: Keep a supply of string on hand.

4. *Prepare equipment:* Your mower runs out of gas. Contingency would be to make sure you have plenty of gas before you start.

5. *Trim hedge:* You could trim it unevenly so it looks bad. Contingency: Have someone do the trimming who has a good eye for balance.

I have listed only one risk for each task. Clearly, there could be more than one thing that could go wrong for complex tasks, so you list all of them, then quantify them, and deal with the more serious ones.

The thing you have to be careful of at this stage in planning is that people don't go into analysis paralysis. You are likely to identify the most likely risks fairly quickly. Trying to find every single thing that could go wrong is unproductive. However, you should be careful not to reject a risk simply because you consider it highly unlikely to occur. As you will see in a subsequent section of this chapter, there are low-probability events that have a very severe impact on the project if they do occur, and these should never be ignored.

240

F I G U R E   8.1

WBS for a Yard Project

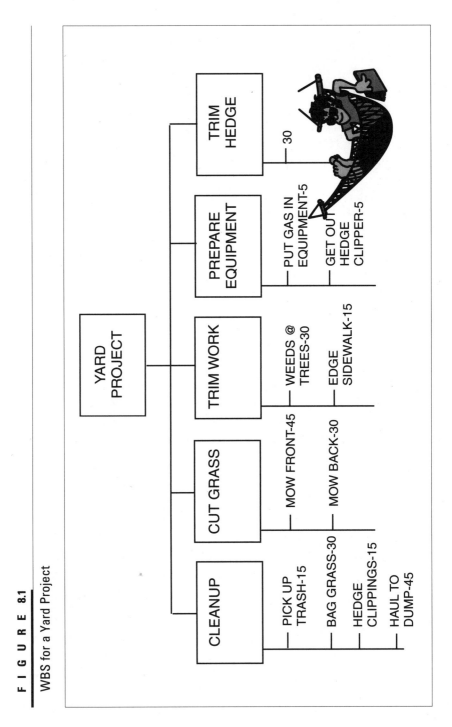

Risk Quantification

We know that all risks are not equal in their impact to a project. The question is, how would you decide which ones you can ignore and which ones you should manage? The desired approach would be to find some way to prioritize the risks, and this can be done by calculating risk priority numbers to them.

There are three factors that contribute to the RPN. First, you have the *probability* that the risk may occur. Second, there is the *severity* of the effect to the project if it should occur. And third, there is a question of whether you can *detect* the risk before it hits you.

This risk management methodology was worked out in an engineering discipline called Failure Mode Effects Analysis (FMEA). In designing a product, an engineer is supposed to identify possible modes of failure for various components, ask what the severity of that failure may be, and whether it can be detected. As an example, your dome light may burn out in your car, and you could have your transmission seize up. The probability of both occurrences may be very low. However, the severity of a dome light burning out is far lower than if the transmission seizes. Further, you will know immediately if your transmission seizes, but you may not know until you open your door at night that your dome light has burned out because you may not have noticed it in the daylight.

To calculate RPNs, we use three tables. Table 8.1 is used to quantify risk probability and assigns a rank of 1 to 10 to probability, which is based on a logarithmic probability scale. Table 8.2 assigns a similar rank to severity and Table 8.3 does the same for detection.

In the original FMEA approach, detection means that you may or may not be able to tell a failure has occurred in a product. For example, if you have manufactured a car that has a crack inside the engine block, you may not be able to detect that crack before the car leaves the factory. On the other hand, if a tire goes flat, that is easy to spot and correct before the car is shipped. If a fault can be detected with certainty, the number assigned is 1. If it absolutely can't be detected, it gets a rank of 10.

T A B L E 8.1

Probability of Occurrence

Probability of occurrence	Possible occurrence rates	Rank
Very high: occurrence is almost certain	≥ 1 in 2	10
	1 in 3	9
High: repeated occurrences possible	1 in 8	8
	1 in 20	7
Moderate: occasional occurrences	1 in 80	6
	1 in 400	5
	1 in 2,000	4
Low: relatively few occurrences	1 in 15,000	3
	1 in 150,000	2
Remote: occurrence is unlikely	≤ 1 in 1,500,000	1

The problem with this meaning of detection is that it usually gives you a 1 when used in project risk analysis, and so it loses its utility. I think a more helpful way to consider detection is to ask whether a failure mode can be detected *before* it happens.

Examples of RPN Calculation

An example that I find helpful for illustrating risk management is to assume that you are riding a bicycle from the east coast to the west coast of the United States. You identify several risks that could affect your trip, and estimate numbers as shown in Table 8.4.

Principle: Regardless of the value of the RPN, when severity is high, you must do something to manage the associated risk.

T A B L E 8.2

Severity of the Effect

Effect	Criteria: severity of effect	Rank
Hazardous—without warning	Project severely impacted, possible cancellation, with no warning.	10
Hazardous—with warning	Project severely impacted, possible cancellation, with warning.	9
Very high	Major impact on project schedule, budget, or performance; may cause severe delays, overruns, or degradation of performance.	8
High	Project schedule, budget, or performance impacted significantly; job can be completed, but customer will be very dissatisfied.	7
Moderate	Project schedule, budget, or performance impacted some; customer will be dissatisfied.	6
Low	Project schedule, budget, or performance impacted slightly; customer will be mildly dissatisfied.	5
Very low	Some impact to project; customer will be aware of impact.	4
Minor	Small impact to project; average customer will be aware of impact.	3
Very minor	Impact so small that it would be noticed only by a very discriminating customer.	2
None	No effect.	1

Now you will see that both having a flat tire and being hit by a car have RPNs of 200 points, which would imply that they are equal in importance. However, they are *qualitatively* very different. The RPN for having a flat tire is 200 points because the probability is high and detection capability is poor, giving a high number as well. Getting hit by a car has a very low probability, but high severity and poor detection. These two risks demand very different responses. This is why we talk about *risk management*, not just risk identification.

T A B L E 8.3

Detection Capability

Detection	Rank
Absolute uncertainty	10
Very remote	9
Remote	8
Very low	7
Low	6
Moderate	5
Moderately high	4
High	3
Very high	2
Almost certain	1

T A B L E 8.4

RPNs for a Bike Trip

Identified Risk	P	S	D	RPN
Flat tire	10	2	10	200
Get hit by a car	2	10	10	200
Bad weather	10	2	2	40

As a general rule, *any time severity is in the range of 8 to 10 points,* you should require that some step be taken to deal with the risk. This is especially important to consider when probability is low. People tend to ignore risks when they think there is a very low likelihood of occurrence.

The *Challenger* space shuttle disaster is a good example of this. Many of the members of the team responsible for the launch believed that the probability of failure of the O-ring seals was very low. Perhaps it was. Nevertheless, the severity of failure was a 10, as demonstrated by the fact that the explosion killed all of the astronauts aboard. Had the team considered severity and followed the rule, they would have delayed the launch until the temperature rose.

That particular disaster is also a good example of groupthink, and CRM films (see resources list at back of book) has a video that discusses what happened. Groups are particularly prone to ignore risks when they are under pressure to get a job done, as was the case here. If you don't remember the history, Christa McAuliffe was supposed to address Congress from space. This was a big political event, so the team felt pressured to launch on schedule. For more on groupthink and how to avoid it, see Chapter 15.

DEVELOPING CONTINGENCY PLANS

As I stated earlier, it is not enough to identify and quantify risks. The idea is to manage them. This might be done in three ways:

> The mouse that hath but one hole is quickly taken.
>
> — George Herbert

1. Risk avoidance
2. Mitigation (reduction, such as using air bags)
3. Transfer (such as in loss prevention through insurance)

Risk Avoidance

As my colleague, Harvey Levine, says, it is better to avoid a risk than to have to manage it. Delaying the *Challenger* launch would have been risk avoidance. This is a trap for the obsessive "can-do" manager. He drives on in the face of a risk and pays the consequences later on.

Risk *prevention* is a special case of risk avoidance. Japanese manufacturing has for many years employed "foolproofing" as a risk avoidance strategy. The idea is to set up the assembly process so that it cannot be done incorrectly. One example was that they occasionally would start to install a gas tank in a car, only to find that one of the four mounting brackets had not been welded onto the tank. The solution was to set up a fixture to hold the tank while the brackets were being welded onto it. Feelers were attached to detect the presence of the brackets. If all four brackets were not in place, the welding machine would not weld any of them.

> It seems reasonable to say that it is always better to avoid risk than it is to manage it.
>
> — Harvey Levine

In construction projects, we pad the schedule with rain delay days, based on weather history for the area and time of year. This way, we avoid the risk that we will be delayed by bad weather. In engineering design, I mentioned using parallel design strategies to avoid the possibility that the deadline might be missed because one strategy proves difficult to implement. In any project, risk aversion or avoidance might be the most preferable strategy to follow.

Mitigation or Risk Reduction

If we can think of contingencies in the event that a risk takes place, we can mitigate the effect. Placing air bags in cars is an attempt to reduce the severity of an accident, should one occur. Stafford Beer (1981) argued that seat belts and air bags in cars actually give drivers a false sense of security. We have defined the problem as protecting the driver from being harmed if he is in an accident. Beer argues that it would perhaps be better to redefine the problem as how to keep a driver from having an accident in the first place (risk avoidance). He suggests that if we lined the dashboard of the car with spikes, making it very clear that an accident has serious consequences, we might give drivers incentive to be more careful. His suggestion is not without merit.

In projects that involve procurement, sole-sourcing is a risk to consider. The alternative is to second-source all procured parts or equipment. That way, if a supplier can't deliver on time or at the specified price, the second supplier might be able to. This can be thought of as either risk avoidance or mitigation.

Temporary workers are used as backups for critical personnel who become ill or are injured. Overtime is used as a contingency when tasks take longer than estimated. This is one reason why overtime should not be planned into a project to meet original targets, if possible. Rather, it should be kept in reserve as a contingency.

Another possible contingency is to reduce scope to permit the team to meet the original target date, then come back later and incorporate deferred work to finish the job.

Having a fire evacuation plan in a building can be thought of as a contingency and also a loss-prevention plan.

Loss Prevention

Insurance is one way of protecting against loss in the event that a risk manifests. Having alternative sites available into which a group can move in the event of a disaster is a loss-prevention strategy. Backup personnel can also be thought of as loss avoidance. If someone else can do the work, then when a key person is ill, there will be no loss to the project. Of course, this is difficult to do with highly skilled personnel.

Cost Contingency

Cost contingency is also called management reserve. Unfortunately, it is misunderstood. Too often it is believed that management reserve is there to cover poor performance. This is incorrect. Management reserve is a fund that is part of a project budget to cover the cost of unidentified work. All projects should have a work budget to cover the cost of identified work and a management reserve to cover work not yet identified. In addition, on projects that are paid for by a customer, there will be a component of the total job cost called *margin*. This is the intended profit for the job. Poor performance eats into margin, not management reserve.

The management reserve account is not touched unless we identify new work to be done. This is a change in scope, of course. At that point, money is transferred from the management reserve account into the work budget, and performance is subsequently tracked against the revised budget. A log should be maintained of all scope changes and their effect on the work budget, management reserve, and margin (if the change has such an effect). In customer-funded projects, the customer may be required to pay for scope changes so that there is no impact to the management reserve account.

Buying fire insurance is risk management.

CONCLUSION

Risk management makes good business sense. Failing to account for things that may sink a project is not aggressive management, it is being derelict in one's duty as a project manager. Banks won't insure homes or cars unless the buyer carries insurance to protect against loss from fires or accidents. Risk management is an important aspect of being an effective project manager.

KEY POINTS FOR CHAPTER 8

- A risk is anything that may happen that could create an adverse effect on your schedule, costs, quality, or scope.
- Principle: Regardless of the value of the RPN, when severity is high, you must do something to manage the associated risk.

QUESTIONS FOR REVIEW

1. How is risk defined?
2. What are the three steps in risk management?
3. What are the three factors that are used to quantify risks?
4. At what level of severity *must* a contingency plan be developed?

C H A P T E R

Practical Project Scheduling

In previous editions of this book, I have shown how to do network computations in the main body of the book. However, with the ready availability of cost-effective scheduling software, almost nobody does such calculations manually any more. I do believe that you should understand how they are done, or else you won't understand what the software is telling you. For those readers who need to know how to find a critical path and float, there

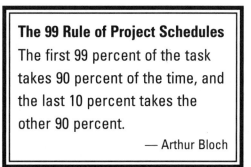

The 99 Rule of Project Schedules
The first 99 percent of the task takes 90 percent of the time, and the last 10 percent takes the other 90 percent.

— Arthur Bloch

is an appendix covering this topic. This chapter will concentrate on the practical creation of a schedule using software, and on managing resources, which is the major problem you will encounter in developing your schedule.

JUST THE BASICS OF SCHEDULING

Before we go any further, let's make sure you are familiar with all of the terms and concepts of scheduling. If you are absolutely sure you know this material, you can feel free to skip to the next section. Otherwise, read on.

> How does a project get to be a year behind schedule? One day at a time.
>
> — Fred Brooks
> System 360 Chief Designer, IBM

Until about 1960, the way projects were scheduled was to use bar charts. Henry Gantt worked out a system of notation for creating such charts and using them to report progress, so they are commonly called **Gantt charts**. A simple example is shown in Figure 9.1.

This is the way Gantt charts were drawn before 1960. You notice that the chart gives no indication of whether activities B and C depend on the completion of activity A or whether they just coincidentally start when A is completed. This means that if activity A slips, we can't tell what impact it will have on subsequent tasks.

For that reason, a method of showing such dependencies was developed in the late 1950s. The relationships among tasks was shown using arrow diagrams. Two different forms were developed. One was called Critical Path Method (**CPM**) and the other was called Performance Evaluation and Review Technique (**PERT**). The difference between the two systems was that PERT makes use of a calculated task duration and allows you to estimate probabilities of completing work, whereas CPM just makes use of estimated task durations with no regard for probabilities.

Both systems allow you to determine which series of activities (or path) in a project will take the longest time to complete. When the project is scheduled to end at the point where the critical path ends, it will have no latitude. Shorter paths, however, will

F I G U R E 9.1

A Simple Gantt Chart

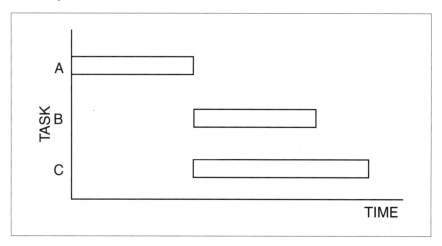

have latitude, which is called either slack or float. The slack or float provides some protection from unexpected events or from inaccurate estimates. You never want to have a schedule that has no float, because the risk is extremely high that you won't meet your completion date.

In addition to having two systems, there are two forms of notation. One is called **activity-on-arrow** (AOA) and the other is **activity-on-node** (AON). In AOA notation, the arrow represents the work to be done and the circle represents an event—either the beginning of another activity or the completion of a previous one. This is shown in Figure 9.2.

> **Critical path:** a path that has no float, and is the longest path through the project
> **Float or slack:** any path shorter than the critical path will have latitude that is commonly called either float or slack.

Activity-On-Arrow Notation

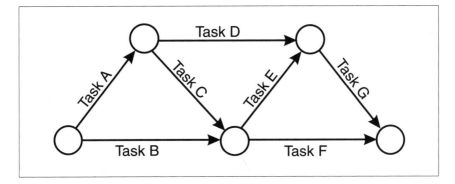

For AON notation, a box (or node) is used to show the task it-self and the arrows simply show the sequence in which work is done. This is shown in Figure 9.3.

Because both systems get the same schedule results, it makes no difference which one is used. However, most software pro-duces only one of them, and it is usually AON. A few programs, such as Primavera, allow you to choose the system you prefer.

The point of using arrow diagrams is that you can tell whether it is possible for a task to start at a certain time. When you create a large schedule using bar charting, you may inad-vertently show tasks starting before a prede-cessor is finished, and if this isn't possible then your schedule won't work. This was one of the main reasons why CPM and PERT were created in the first place. So, if you want to create a schedule that will work, you should always work out the interdependencies among all of the activities in a project.

> Be careful not to enter too many "must start on" and "must end on" dates into your schedule or you will create a schedule that simply won't work.

F I G U R E 9.3

Activity-On-Node Notation

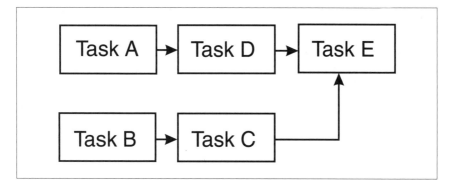

However, you don't want to give an arrow diagram to people to use as a working tool. They are too hard to read. The bar chart is a much better working tool, as it is simple to read. Fortunately, all software will produce a bar chart for you. Be careful, though. One of the common errors people make is to tell the software that every task must start on certain dates and must end on certain dates, and if these conflict with what is naturally going to happen on the basis of task dependencies, the software will just regurgitate what you have told it, and you may have a useless schedule.

> *Principle:* You *must* enter dependencies in order for your software to work out where your critical path and float are.

The software itself is designed to tell you when tasks will start and end on the basis of their durations, resource allocations, and interdependencies, so if you tamper too much with dates, you will have a garbage-in–garbage-out situation.

Furthermore, if you don't enter predecessor or successor information into your software, then it cannot work out where your critical path is and determine how much slack or float you have on non-critical paths. This approach relegates the software to a presentation tool at best, and only allows you to document your failures.

THE REAL ADVANTAGE OF CPM AND PERT

Both CPM and PERT find the critical path and float in a project, and the emphasis has always been on the critical path. However, in today's world, the objective of project management is universally to complete a project in the minimum possible time, and this is a primary advantage of using arrow diagrams. The shortest possible schedule will be the one in which as many tasks are done in parallel as possible. This is only possible to work out using a computer, because the resource allocation problem becomes formidable and manual methods are nearly impossible for all but the most trivial of networks.

> *Principle:* The real advantage of network diagramming is to help you find all the places where work can be done in parallel, thus creating the shortest possible schedule.

WHAT TO DO BEFORE YOU USE SOFTWARE

There is a great temptation to sit down at a computer and create a schedule by entering data into the templates provided by the software. There is a major flaw in this approach. First, you can see only a small segment of a large project schedule on the screen, and if activities have predecessors or successors that are off the screen, it can be almost impossible to determine what they are.

A better approach is to either sketch the network on paper or use Post-it notes on a whiteboard to work out the logic. A major advantage of this method is that a group can participate, and members can see possibilities that you may miss if you do the

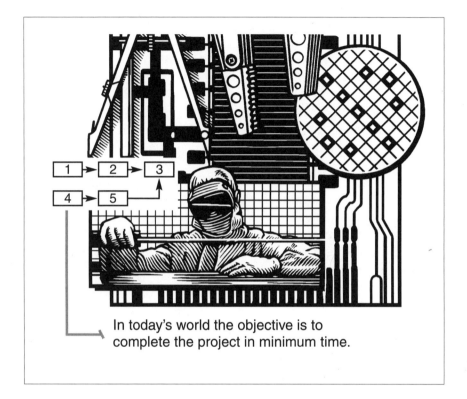

In today's world the objective is to complete the project in minimum time.

schedule individually. Then, once the logic is worked out to everyone's satisfaction, you can have someone transcribe the network into your scheduling software and let the computer tell you dates for activities.

In creating a schedule this way, the guideline you should follow

> **Principle:** You should construct the schedule on paper before entering it into your computer.

is that, if two tasks can be done in parallel from a logical standpoint, you draw them that way. It is tempting to consider resource limitations while constructing a schedule, but if you do, it takes forever to work out the network, and you may have unnecessarily tied your hands.

For example, suppose I assign Mary to two tasks that can logically be done in parallel. When I start constructing my schedule, I decide that it won't be possible to do the work in parallel, because Mary can't do two things at the same time. So I draw them in series instead.

But just who says that Mary *must* do them both? Perhaps Jane can do one of them and Mary can do the other. That will produce a shorter schedule than if the two tasks are done in series.

In addition, suppose one task has a duration of 10 days and the second has a duration of 5 days. They are in parallel with each other, but the 10-day task also has 5 days of float. Then these two tasks can be done in series without impacting project completion, and Mary can do both of them. This is shown in Figure 9.4.

A little thought reveals that following this rule means that you are adopting a hidden assumption that you have unlimited resources—which, naturally, you don't. So you find that you have double- and triple-scheduled members of your team.

Not a good rule, you say.

True, but think about it this way. An unlimited resource schedule will produce the shortest possible schedule. Because

F I G U R E 9.4

Schedule with Mary on Both Tasks

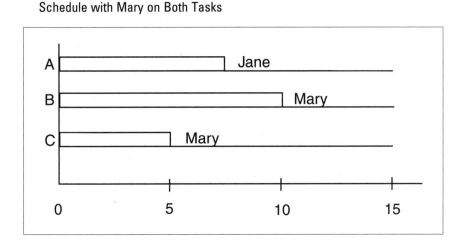

most projects are assigned an end date from the beginning, if you create an unlimited resource schedule and it won't meet the imposed end date, then you are in trouble before you do any work, and you may as well know it. You know it will only get worse when you factor in your limited fund of resources.

What is important is that the software enables everyone to see what possibilities exist for a project, and to make informed decisions about trade-offs. Remember, you are always constrained by PCTS, and if you can't meet the required time with the resources you have available (this equates to cost), then you will have to find more help, reduce scope, or—heaven help you—reduce performance (quality of work). The latter is generally unacceptable, but it is what your team may do if you don't give them relief from time or scope.

WHAT THE SOFTWARE CAN AND CAN'T DO

I have mentioned elsewhere that there are a lot of people who think that project management is just scheduling, so if they provide you with a software program, they have made you into an instant project manager—or at the very least, into a scheduler. Of course, this couldn't be further from the truth.

> Giving a person a powerful scheduling software program, when he knows nothing about project management, just allows him to document his failures with great precision!

The software can't work out dependencies for you. That is something you must do yourself. Nor can it tell you how long a task will take. All it can do is computations. It is a tool, and unless you know how to deal with the various issues in a project, all the tool can do is help you document your failures with great precision.

In fact, we have given thousands of individuals powerful scheduling software without giving them any training in how to

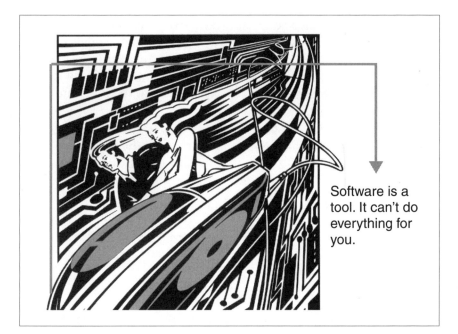

Software is a tool. It can't do everything for you.

manage. This is like giving people a fantastic accounting program when they don't know the difference between a debit and a credit and expecting the software to turn them into a skilled accountant.

A huge advantage of using software is that it will drop out weekends, holidays, and vacation periods for employees, and tell you the actual dates on which activities should start and finish. Doing calendar computations manually is an onerous task, and the software is worth its weight in gold just for this alone.

Resource Leveling

As I have said above, a schedule is initially developed under the assumption of unlimited resources. Once this is done, the software can also show you where you have overloaded your resources, and if there is enough float in your schedule, it can make use of that float to schedule tasks so that resources are no longer over-loaded and the end date can be met. This is called *time-critical* resource allocation. The software is instructed to level resources without slipping the already determined end date. It will then make use of task float to delay activities until resources become available, but it will only delay a task to the point at which it runs out of float. To delay it any further would cause the end date to be missed.

However, if there is insufficient float in the schedule to level resources completely, the software can be instructed to relieve the overloads, even if it means sliding out the end date. This is called *resource-critical* allocation. Under this condition, you may find that a schedule which was going to end in December 2000 under the unlimited resource assumption is now going to end in the year 2013, because it is starved for resources.

Clearly, this is an unacceptable solution. Nobody is going to accept a schedule that is going to take so long to complete. So what good is the resource-critical method?

Simple. It creates a *moment of truth*. It alerts everyone to what is going to happen to a project if something isn't done. Either more help is needed, scope must be reduced, or performance requirements must be relaxed. Otherwise the project will take forever.

The advantage is partly psychological. In the days before software (DaBS), when we had this problem, we had no credibility with our managers when we told them about the problem.

"I need more help," you would tell your boss.

"Quit whining and get the job done," the boss would snarl. And all too often, you pulled it off. And shot yourself in the foot in the process.

Why? Because they expected you to pull it off the next time. After all, you've just proved that you didn't need all the help that you claimed you needed. You were just whining.

Now please don't misunderstand me. I have no objection to pulling off a miracle—once in a while. But I don't want it to become the expectation for all time to come. After all, how did I pull it off this time? Through blood, sweat, and tears. Every member of the team put in extraordinary effort to meet the end date. You don't want them to have to do that on every project, because it may not work next time. So if I get shot in the foot, my company may be set up for a fall next time around.

The beauty of using software to do a what-if schedule is that you have more credibility. We all know that computers simply produce garbage out when we put garbage in, but it is *calculated garbage,* and that is more believable than whine!

So there is a psychological advantage that you never had in the DaBS.

Guidelines for Major and Minor Increments in a Schedule

One trap that you may fall into is to schedule work in more detail than you can manage. This is especially tempting when you are using scheduling software. After all, the software can compute virtually any kind of network you create. Sure, but can you do the work as scheduled?

I know about this trap. I have made most of the mistakes you can make in managing projects. I got carried away and scheduled work in increments of days. The only problem was, we couldn't control the work that accurately, so before I could get the schedule published, it was off, and my boss was on my back because I had already missed a scheduled date. The net result was that I spent all my time managing the schedule rather than letting the schedule help me manage the project.

The first guideline, then, is to never schedule work in more detail than you can control.

Principle: Never schedule in more detail than you can control

---

For some people, this means you can schedule to the nearest hour. Projects to overhaul power generators are sometimes scheduled to this level of detail because they have enough history to know how long each step will take, and also because getting the generator back on line as quickly as possible is very important.

For others, scheduling to the nearest day is all that they can control, and in some cases, the nearest week is adequate. In very large projects that last several years, you may find work being scheduled to the nearest month.

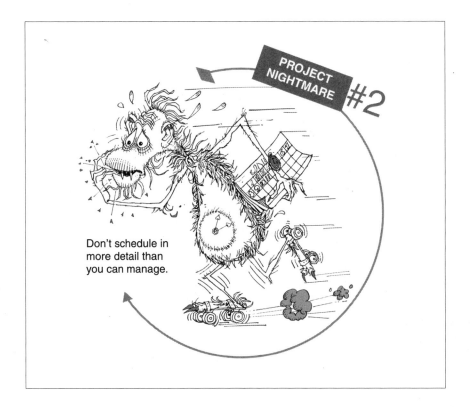

PROJECT NIGHTMARE #2

Don't schedule in more detail than you can manage.

The opposite of minor increments is the major durations that tasks should have. The first rule is that no task should have a duration greater than 4 to 6 weeks. Furthermore, you must have a marker that tells whether the task is actually complete, and this can be very difficult with nontangible tasks, that is, those that have no tangible deliverables. When there is no specification or deliverable that indicates task completion, you must use some kind of *exit criteria*. As an example, the work is examined and a "pass-fail" judgment is made. This is totally qualitative, but it is the only thing you have where aesthetics are involved.

The rule about 4- to 6-week increments applies to long-duration tasks. It is especially useful to apply to outside vendor projects, such as long-lead capital equipment. It is a good idea to require your vendors to report progress on their projects in minimum increments of 4 to 6 weeks, and the progress report must go

beyond an affirmation that the work is on schedule. You must require that they report progress using some such method as earned
value tracking (see Chapter 10 on project control) or, if this is not
possible, then they should use exit criteria to ensure that progress
is really what they say it is.

The next rule applies to engineering, programming, and
other knowledge work, in which there may be no tangible deliverables. For such work, the rule is that work should be scheduled in
maximum increments of 1 to 3 weeks. This is very important, or
you can bet that such work will reach 90 percent complete and
stay there forever. The
progress report for
knowledge work invari-
ably looks like the graph
shown in Figure 9.5.

> *Principles:* No task should have a
> duration greater than 4 to 6
> weeks. For knowledge work, the
> maximum duration should be 1 to
> 3 weeks.

This is actually a
universal graph. Here's
how it is generated.
Let's suppose the work
is supposed to take 10
weeks to complete. This is by agreement with the person doing
the work. At the end of the first week, you check on progress.

"How's your project work going?" you ask.

"Fine," says the person.

"I can't plot 'fine,'" you say, "I need to know what percent
complete the job is."

Now what do you think she will tell you? You guessed it. It's
the end of the first week on a 10-week job, so she must be 10 percent complete.

And at the end of the second week? Right again. It will be 20
percent complete.

This is called *reverse-inferential* progress reporting, and is a
method used when people can't tell exactly how much they have
actually done.

Now you notice that when the work reaches around 80 or 90
percent complete, something happens, and the graph turns horizontal.

Progress Graph for Knowledge Work

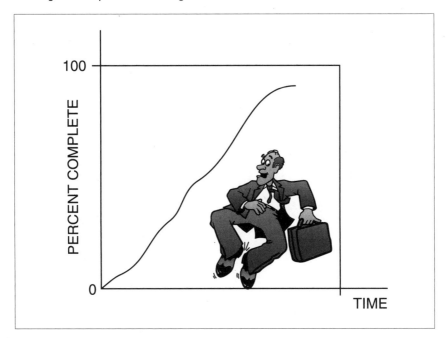

One of two things happens. Either the person has an existential crisis, which means that she discovers the part of the iceberg that's underneath the water (that is, all the work she has to do that she has forgotten), or she is in the debugging phase of her design work. If it is an iceberg problem, she would have to show that she is really only perhaps 50 percent complete, which would mean that she would have to report negative progress. This is shown in Figure 9.6.

Now there must be a gene that makes us understand that we can't report negative progress. Senior managers get very excited if we do this. So the best alternative is to just report that progress is stalled.

In the situation where the debugging has started, it is common to go past the deadline and then find the solution to the

Graph Showing Negative Progress

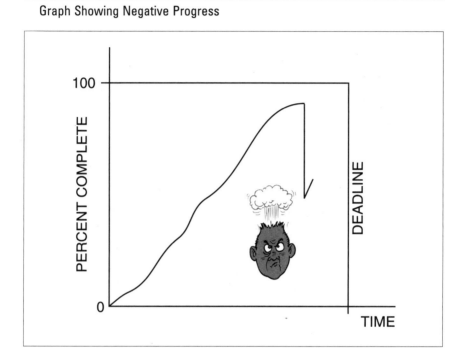

problem so that the work is completed in one simple step. This is shown in Figure 9.7.

RESOURCE ALLOCATION

If you are going to manage resources in a project, you have to tell the software who is working on each task, and at what allocation level. When you do this, you have to be careful. Microsoft Project (now called Project 2000, as of this writing) behaves differently than other scheduling software in how it treats the allocation level and task duration.

In most software, if you specify a task duration as 10 working days and tell the program that Ron is working on the task half-time (50 percent would be what you specify), the software

Graph Showing Progress Being Completed in One Step

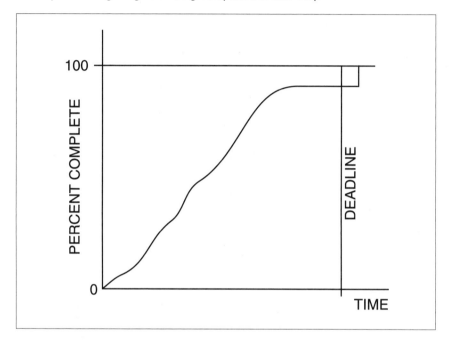

will leave the task duration at 10 days. It treats the calendar duration as *fixed*—or as being the same as the working time minus any
weekends or holidays that may intervene. With MS Project, however, you get a different result. Project will change the duration to
20 calendar days. The assumption is that the duration of the task
is *variable,* meaning that the calendar duration depends on the rate
at which the person works on the task. You can change the default
so that Project works like other programs, treating task duration
as fixed. However, there is a certain logic to the Project default.
Ideally, you should always estimate working time and convert to
calendar time in exactly the way that Project does it.

In any case, you have to be careful that you assign the correct
resource availability, or you will get an invalid result. For example, I had a fellow tell me that his company had always assigned

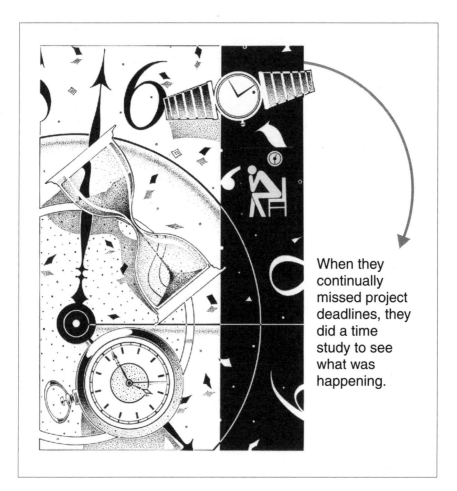

When they continually missed project deadlines, they did a time study to see what was happening.

people to tasks on the assumption that they were working about 80 percent of the time on projects. When they continuously missed project deadlines, they did a time study to determine what was really happening. To do this, people logged their time once an hour for 2 weeks, and then analyzed the logs. To their surprise, they found that people were only working on projects 25 percent of the time, not the 80 percent that they had assumed! This meant that their schedules were off by a factor of 3, because of their incorrect allocation assumption.

This is common in projects, and is a common cause of problems. The only time you ever get 80 percent availability from people is when they are tied to their work station, and the only people for whom this is true are factory workers. You may get close to 80 percent availability from them, but for knowledge workers—who aren't tied to their work stations—you never get such a high level. It is more likely to be around 50 or 60 percent.

The thing is, you have to know what that number is if you are going to correctly schedule work. So it helps to do a time study, as was described above, to determine that level. Have people log their time once an hour—it need not be more often—and find out what the true availability is. And if the number seems too low, then you have to remove the causes.

Major Causes of Reduced Availability

There are two major causes of reduced resource availability. One is having people work on too many projects at the same time and the other is overallocation of people to their work. When people have to work on more than one project at the same time, they are constantly having to shift back and forth between the projects. This is called multitasking. The trouble is, every time a person "shifts gears," to use the normal expression, it takes time for them to remember where they were, get their work in place, and so on. This added time is called *setup time* in manufacturing, and we learned years ago that setup time is total waste—no value is added to the "product" by setup time. So in manufacturing, an effort has been made to reduce setup time as much as possible, or to even eliminate it altogether by running a process continuously.

Think about it this way. Suppose you are sitting at your desk working and the phone rings. You answer it. The person says, "Sorry, I have the wrong number," and you hang up.

"Now where was I?" You think.

You have completely lost your train of thought. The time management experts say that you will typically lose 10 to 15 minutes every time you get interrupted, so if you get four phone calls in an hour, you may easily lose the entire hour!

F I G U R E 9.8

Eight-Hour Task Performed in One-Hour Increments

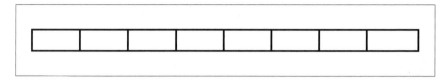

So let's assume that each time you switch from one project to another you add 15 minutes setup time to each task. As an example, suppose you had planned to work on a single project task all day. You could finish the task in that single 8-hour day if you could just work on it continuously.

However, if you are working on several projects, you will be expected to share your time between them, and if you get no more than 1 hour of uninterrupted work at a time, your 8-hour task will take at least 9 hours and 45 minutes. This is shown in Figure 9.8.

We assume that all tasks have some setup time built in, so we add only 15 minutes for each time the task is stopped and restarted. That is seven increments above the single 8-hour block, so it adds 1 hour and 45 minutes of setup time, rather than 2 hours.

I can almost guarantee you that this task will actually take 10 to 12 hours to complete, rather than the original 8 hours. The 15 minutes of setup time is a very conservative number.

QUEUING AND RESOURCE AVAILABILITY

The second major cause of reduced availability is from over-allocation of people to their work. To understand this, we need to understand the basics of queuing theory. Now you may never have studied queuing theory, but I can assure you that you have experienced it. Every time you try to get onto a busy highway at rush hour, you have experienced the effects of queuing.

As an example, Raleigh, North Carolina, has a beltway around the city. At rush hour, you can bet that the beltway is packed with cars, all doing 60 to 70 miles an hour. In fact, let's as-

Over-allocation of people
to their work is tough on
the schedule.

sume that the cars are packed so tightly that you couldn't put another car on the road if your life depended on it.

No problem. Everyone is happy. How can this be? No one wants to get on the beltway and no one wants to get off.

Of course, you realize that this is a fictitious condition which could only exist in a steady-state universe. One that may have been approximated about 1800, when people weren't in as much of a hurry as they are today.

Today, we live in a turbulent universe. Everyone wants to be where they are going 10 minutes ago. So suppose someone wants to get on this bumper-to-bumper beltway. If no one gets off, how long will it take this interloper to get onto the beltway? You guessed it. It will take forever!

Queuing theory shows how long you must wait to get access to a system as a function of how fully it is already loaded. The curves look something like the one in Figure 9.9. Notice that, by

F I G U R E   9.9

Waiting Time as a Function of System Loading

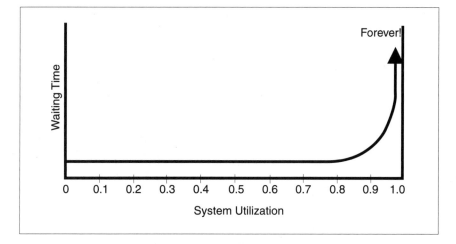

definition, a system can't be loaded beyond 100 percent. It doesn't matter. At 100 percent, you have to wait forever to get access to the system—just like our driver has to wait to get onto the beltway.

Okay, what does this have to do with projects? First, let's think about a practical application of queuing theory. Manufacturing people have known for a long time that you shouldn't load a factory more than about 85 percent on the average. You may exceed that level occasionally, but if you consistently stay higher than 85 percent, you are asking for big trouble.

Why? Because if anything happens out of the ordinary—a machine breaks down or someone is out sick, or a supplier is late delivering materials—you are already so high on the curve that your waiting time goes to forever in a heart beat.

Well and good, but this has nothing to do with projects, does it? Of course not. We don't load people to 85 percent. We load them to 120 percent. We know that if we loaded them to only 85 percent, they would sit around and do nothing during that 15 percent free time, and that would be costly, so we make certain that they have no free time. (This is commonly called being *lean and mean*, and is a biological metaphor. The question is, do you want to get rid of all of your body fat? No way. You want some for reserve energy. Same is true of an organization.)

Carrying lean and mean too far is dumb, dumb, dumb. When you have no reserve capacity, you can't respond to surprises, glitches, or even opportunities. And because Murphy's law guarantees that there will be some hitches in every project, you can also be sure that there will be delays caused by queuing, and that the result will be a late project.

> *Principle:* No system should be loaded beyond 85 percent capacity for very long.

Every organization should have some reserve capacity if it is going to respond to turbulence. But tell that to senior management, who believe that lean and mean is the correct way to fly!

A few people are beginning to realize that the lean-and-mean paradigm has gone too far. Downs (1995) was a downsizing consultant until he realized this. His book *Corporate Executions* goes into far greater detail about the insanity of going too far with cutting fat from an organization than is possible in this chapter.

And what do you do about setup time? Reduce it. How? By prioritizing projects. As a general rule, no one should be working on more than two or three projects. Ideally, a person would be on a single project until it is completed, and then would shift to the next job.

Can this really be justified? You bet. When I first learned about this, I was working with a company that was having difficulty getting new products released. They would go along for most of the year and nothing would be released. Then headquarters would call and ask why no new products had come out the back door.

"We're working on them," would be the response.

"Well, we want to see something get to market by the end of the year," headquarters would tell them.

So there would be a big push to release all of the products that were in various states of completion, and they would turn out 10 or 12 new products near the end of the year.

Do you know what happens when you release that many products in December? Absolutely nothing. Manufacturing can't get set up to make them, and even if they could, the sales people couldn't sell them.

But let's pretend that they could both make them and sell them, and let's assume that they were able to sell all of those new products during the entire month of December. If that happened, you would have a sales graph like the one in Figure 9.10. Fine. But it is unrealistic.

F I G U R E 9.10

Sales for All Products in December

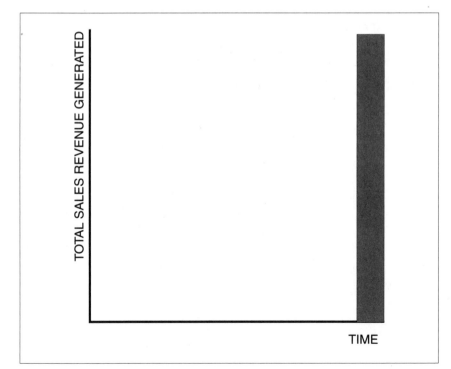

I said to the managers at this company, "You need to prioritize your projects. Work on them one at a time and get them out the back door so that they start selling sooner."

It took nearly 3 years to make it happen, but by that time they were releasing a new product every month or so. That is, they had a steady stream of new products entering the market.

You can do *anything*, but you can't do everything!
— From the cover of *Fast Company Magazine,* May 2000

The result can be shown in another graph, superimposed on the one from Figure 9.10. As you can see, if a new product comes out at the beginning of the year, and we assume flat sales, you get the rectangle labeled *Product 1*. The next month, Product 2 is released, again with flat sales throughout the year. Then Product 3 comes out, and so on. This is shown in Figure 9.11.

As the graph indicates, the sales for the year approximate a triangle. The area under the triangle has the units of money multiplied by time. This is called the time value of money, or interest or cost of capital. So which figure has the greatest area, the rectangle for the month of December or the triangle for the entire year? It's a no-brainer. The triangle has considerably greater value to the company than the rectangle.

What this says is that prioritizing projects is the only economically viable approach that a company can take. To have "all the balls in the air" at once is to confuse activity with progress. When you ask a manager what must be done first, and she tells you "It all has to be done," she is overlooking the time value of money and its impact on the organization.

If you think of this in reverse, when you are late to market with a new product, you have lost the revenue that would have been generated by sales during that period, and also the cost of capital associated with it. That is why it is so important to complete projects on time.

F I G U R E 9.11

Sales of a Constant Stream of New Products

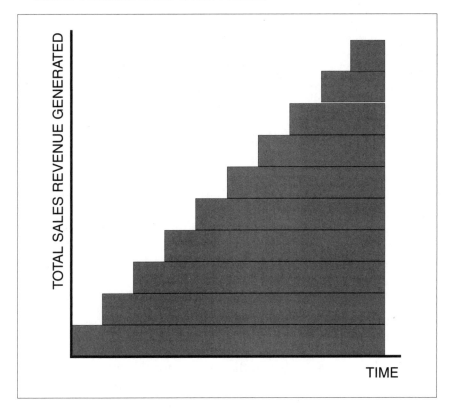

CONCLUSION

In closing, let me say that if you follow the guidelines in this chapter, your schedules should be more workable. The only thing that you have to worry about is whether your estimates of task durations are realistic, and these can usually be improved through consensual estimating.

Whatever approach you follow, the schedule should be used to help you manage the project. It should not make you a slave to the software.

KEY POINTS FOR CHAPTER 9

- **Critical path:** a path that has no float, and is the longest path through the project.
- *Principle:* The real advantage of network diagramming is to help you find all the places where work can be done in parallel, thus creating the shortest possible schedule.
- *Principle:* No system should be loaded beyond 85 percent capacity for very long.

QUESTIONS FOR REVIEW

1. What is the true meaning of critical path?
2. What is the real advantage of using CPM or PERT scheduling technique?
3. Why should you construct a schedule using sticky notes before entering it into scheduling software?
4. What is the difference between time-critical and resource-critical leveling?
5. What is the maximum duration that a task should have in a schedule?
6. What is the usual result of practicing reverse-inferential progress reporting?
7. What is the maximum availability of people to do work as a percentage of the total time they work?
8. What causes resource availability to drop below the 80 percent mark?
9. Why should a system never be loaded beyond 85 percent of its capacity over a long period?

MANAGING THE PROJECT—CONTROL

Keeping the Project on Track—Control

The only reason for doing a project plan (including the schedule) is to achieve control of the project. Remember the definition of control? If you have no plan, you can't possibly have control—by definition! So now we are ready to deal with how control is actually achieved in a project.

> con • trol: Control is exercised by comparing where you are to where you are supposed to be so that corrective action can be taken when there is a deviation from target.

MEASURING PROGRESS

If you are going to have control of a project, you need to know two things—where we are supposed to be and where we are. The

plan tells where we are supposed to be. As for where we actually are, that comes from our project information system, which in many organizations is nonexistent.

> Predicting the future is easy. It's trying to figure out what's going on now that's hard.
> — Fritz R. S. Dressler

This system must provide information on all four project constraints. Remember, the relationship between them is given by the formula:

$$C = f(P, T, S)$$

So if you are going to really know the status of the project, you must know what costs have been incurred to date, whether the work meets functional and technical requirements (which is performance), whether the work is on schedule, and whether the scope of work done is at the right level.

> *Principle:* To measure progress you must know the value of all four constraints.

Again, remember that cost is for labor only in this equation. As I have said before, you care about materials, capital equipment, and other project costs (such as travel or insurance), but

they do not enter into this particular equation—they are tracked separately.

The easiest of the four variables to know about is cost. You may not have a system in place to provide that information, but if you wanted to get it, you would be able to do so by having everyone record the hours spent on the project, multiply those hours by the hourly labor rate that they are paid, and then add them up.

What is hard to know is the stuff on the right side of the equation. To illustrate, let's begin with a simple example. Say you are building a brick wall. It is supposed to be one foot thick, 10 feet high, and 100 feet long by today. When it is finished, it will be one foot thick, 20 feet high, and 200 feet long.

The nice thing about brick walls is that you can measure them. So you take a scale out to the wall and determine that it is indeed one foot thick and 100 feet long. You inspect the mortar between the bricks and it looks nice and clean and uniform. In addition, you check to see if the wall is perfectly vertical and it is. This tells you that the quality of work done (functional and technical performance requirements) is okay. Next you measure the height of the wall, and find that it is only eight feet high. This tells you that the scope is not correct. The workers have accomplished only 80 percent of what they were scheduled to do up to now.

That being the case, we also know that they are behind schedule. How far behind? Well, if you assume work is linear over time (which it isn't, but we will assume that it is for now), and they have been working for 10 days on the job, then they have accomplished what they should have done in only eight days, but it has taken 10 days to do so. Therefore, they are about two days behind schedule.

This isn't totally correct, because work is almost never linear. But it is a fair approximation for a wall of this height. This is tangible work. It is much easier to measure than knowledge work.

For example, if you were checking progress on a software task, and the programmer had estimated that she would have written about 10,000 lines of code by today, and she has only written 8000 lines, is she 80 percent complete?

Who knows? She may find that what she has written won't work and have to start over completely. Or she may actually be finished because she found a way to write the code using fewer lines of code than she originally anticipated.

In addition, knowledge work usually proceeds along a progress curve like the one shown in Figure 10.1. Note that very little progress is made for a long time, then the work accelerates quickly, and then near the end it slows down again.

This is sometimes the source of great anxiety for senior managers who do not understand the nature of this progress curve. They expect work to be more linear, so when a knowledge worker seems to be "going nowhere" for a long time, they get very concerned and start putting pressure on the person to get the job done. The net result of this pressure may very well be to slow the person down. As one of my engineers told me once when our

F I G U R E 10.1

Progress Curve for Knowledge Work

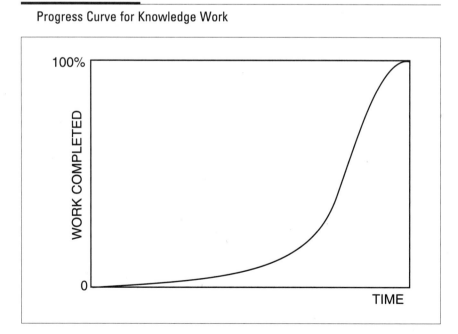

manager was putting pressure on him to speed up, "Putting two jockeys on one horse won't make him run faster."

So how do we measure progress of knowledge work? With difficulty.

If you remember the chunk-down rules that I presented in the scheduling chapter (Chapter 9), they state that knowledge tasks should have durations no greater than one to three weeks. Furthermore, I said that the chunks must have markers that tell you they have been completed. These markers are called exit criteria. For software or engineering design, the exit criteria may be that the design has been reviewed by one's peers, who have reached consensus that it should perform correctly once it is completed. Of course this is a judgment on their part, and they could collectively be wrong, but it is the best we can do with work of this nature.

If the task was to conduct a test, the exit criteria may be raw data that states the part met the technical and functional specifications. Or in an environmental cleanup project, we may have a situation where oil has seeped into the ground and at this stage of the project all the oil in a certain area has been removed. That makes it binary. It has or has not been removed.

In some cases, the exit criteria is a checklist (such as pilots use to ensure that all of their instruments and controls are functioning correctly before they take off). In others, it is a judgment by someone in the organization, as when a marketing vice president approves the aesthetics of a design.

What is really hard is to know if P and S are correct, and if these cannot be determined, then you don't know how you are doing on your schedule. For that reason, I have been told that there is no point in trying to measure progress in knowledge work.

I can't agree with that. If you don't know where you are, you can't have control. My suggestion is that we simply must recognize the limitations in our ability to measure exactly where we are. If we are building a brick wall, we may hold tolerances of ± 5 percent. For knowledge work, the tolerances are more typically ± 20 to 25 percent, and if there is a lot of research involved, we have a situation where the tolerance may be –100 to +20 percent on schedule. In other words, we must accept very large tolerances on poorly defined or intangible work.

THE KISS OF DEATH: REPORTING SCHEDULE ONLY!

Estimates are that over a million individuals have purchased some form of scheduling software. So far as I know, all of the major programs allow you to report progress using your bar chart schedule. The reports typically look like the one in Figure 10.2. Small bars are run through the larger schedule bars to show how far along the work has progressed. For noncritical tasks, the smaller bars are black, and for the critical path, which is usually shown with a solid black bar, the progress bar will be white.

In Figure 10.2, the weekends are shown by vertical shaded areas, which indicate that no work is done during these days. If a project is scheduled to work 7 days a week, the shading would be removed. The "time-now" date is shown as a vertical dotted line between the 19th and 20th. You will note that the 20th is a Monday. Usual convention is to report progress on Monday morning for the previous seven days.

According to this report, task A, which is a critical path task, is behind schedule by 1 day. This immediately tells us that the project is in jeopardy of slipping a day unless something can be done to get this activity back on track, because a delay on the critical path will delay the completion date correspondingly.

Task B cannot be seen because it is scheduled to start at a later date than this report shows. Task C is complete, D is 1 day ahead of schedule, and E is right on target. So says the report.

What is missing from this report is information about cost, performance, and scope. We must take for granted that performance and scope are correct if the schedule is where it is reported to be. But there is nothing we can infer about cost.

To see why this is a problem, assume that task D is a software development task. The work was supposed to take 40 hours (we will assume 100 percent productivity of the programmer). The person doing the work, Sue, says that she is right on schedule. She

288

F I G U R E 10.2

Schedule Showing Progress Page 1

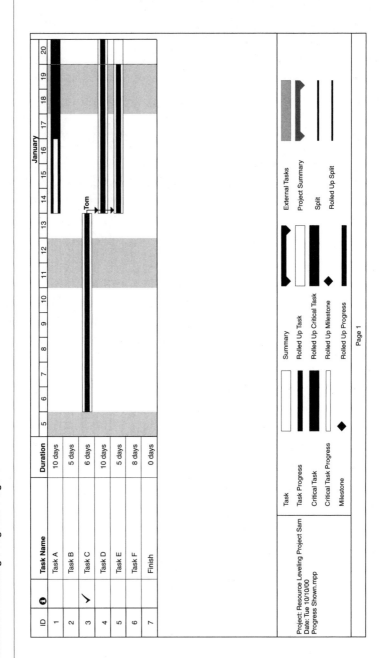

Schedule Showing Progress Page 2

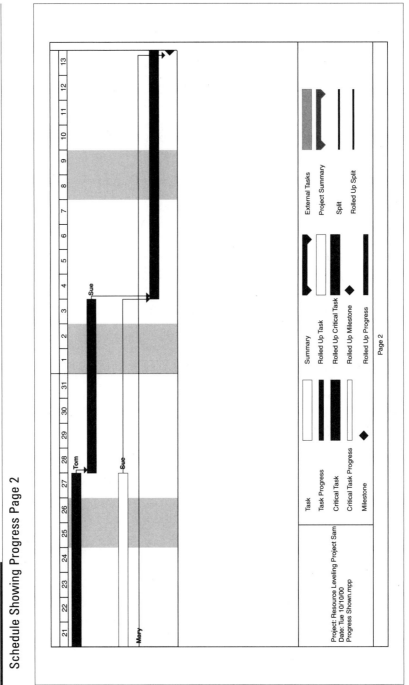

Task		Summary		External Tasks	
Task Progress		Rolled Up Task		Project Summary	
Critical Task		Rolled Up Critical Task		Split	
Critical Task Progress		Rolled Up Milestone	◆	Rolled Up Split	
Milestone	◆	Rolled Up Progress			

Project: Resource Leveling Project Sam
Date: Tue 10/10/00
Progress Shown.mpp

Page 2

gave you this information about 8:30 Monday morning. You are very comfortable with her work. The only one you are concerned about is that critical path activity. Something will have to be done about it.

At 8:45 a.m., Tom comes by and has a brief conversation with you. "I really felt sorry for Sue last week," he confides.

"How so?" you ask.

"Oh, didn't you know? She had a terrible time with the code she was writing. Instead of the 40 hours she expected the work would take, she actually put in nearly 80 hours to get the job done."

"Really?" you say, pondering the situation. "Well, I'm sorry to hear that she had so much trouble, but she is a salaried person, so it doesn't affect my budget, so everything is fine."

Wait a minute! Is that really true? No way!

If Sue missed her estimate by 100 percent last week, perhaps her estimate for subsequent weeks is off in a similar way. If so, how many 80-hour weeks can she work before she burns out and starts making errors and missing deadlines? This is a sure sign of potential trouble, and you had better do something about it right away.

So you go talk to Sue.

"I understand you had problems with your code last week," you say.

Sue seems a bit surprised that you know about this, but she agrees. "Yes. It turned out to be a lot harder than I expected."

"Well, do you think this will continue to be true?" you ask.

There are two possibilities—yes or no. If she says yes, then you must do something right away. There are only a few possibilities. You can get some help for her—if that is possible. You can reduce the scope of the remaining code that must be written. Or you can show that the task is going to take a lot longer to complete than the original estimate, in which case it may use up all of its float and end up on the critical path. You may also decide that Sue is not the right person for this job and replace her.

If she says no, it was a one-time occurrence, and she is confident that the remaining work will go according to plan, then you tell her to keep you posted. If the work does turn out to be as difficult this week as it was last week, you want to do something before Sue gets herself—and your project—into serious trouble.

Notice what happened here. Without knowing how much effort (cost) Sue put into the work you have no indication that there is a problem. This leads to an immutable law of tracking progress: Unless you have an integrated cost-schedule tracking system, you

> *Principle:* Unless you know both cost and schedule, you have absolutely no idea where your project actually is.

don't have a clue where your project is! It is simply not enough to let people report schedule progress alone.

Knowing cost allows you to tell what is going on. If the work is on schedule and less hours were required than estimated, people are working more efficiently than you expected. If work is on schedule and more hours have been expended than planned, this is a sign of trouble. If work is behind schedule and total hours worked are less than planned, then people are not doing what they are supposed to, and you need to find out why. And so on.

We still do not have any measure of scope or quality, however, so we must address that next.

TRACKING PROGRESS USING EARNED VALUE ANALYSIS

There are a number of detractors of the earned-value system for tracking projects. Most of the complaints are that you can't measure the amount of work done when it is knowledge work, and I wholeheartedly agree. You can't, but you must pretend you can, or else you can't possibly achieve control of knowledge projects, and this category probably is the largest in the world at present. As I have said previously, we simply must accept that the precision of our measures will be much worse than is possible for well-defined or tangible work, but at least we have some indication of how we are doing before a disaster occurs.

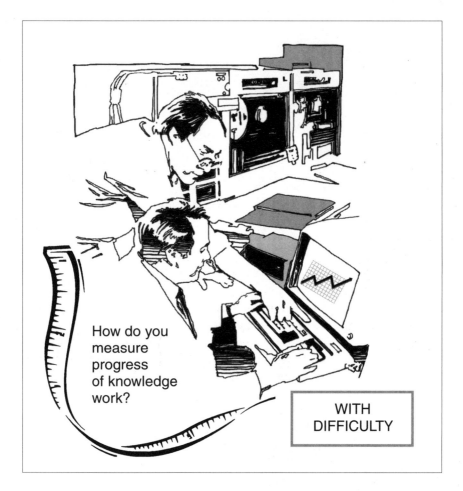

The earned value system provides three measures that allow us to tell where a project is. These are measures of what is supposed to be done, what has actually been done, and the amount of effort or cost that has been expended to do the work. To see how they work, we will start with a very simple example.

Assume for a moment that you have guests coming to stay with you for a few days, and you want to make a good impression by having a spotless house. You don't have time to do all of the cleaning yourself, so you call a cleaning service and ask what they will charge to clean the house from top to bottom. They come out to your house and give you a quote.

"We should be able to thoroughly clean your house with one worker in 40 hours," the agent tells you.

"How much will that cost?" you ask.

"Our billing rate is $20 per hour," says the agent, "so it will cost you approximately $800."

"Is that a fixed price?"

"No, we charge by the hour. If it takes a little less, you will pay less, and conversely."

"Okay, let's do it," you say.

The agent agrees to have someone at your house by 8 o'clock Monday morning. You make a note that the job will cost about $800, and this number is called the budgeted cost of work scheduled (BCWS) to be done.

On Monday morning, around 7 a.m., the phone rings. It is the agent.

"I have a problem," she tells you. "The fellow we were going to send over to clean your house had an accident this weekend and can't make it. However, I have another person available, but we bill him at $22 an hour. Is that okay?"

"You have me at a disadvantage," you say. "I have to get the house cleaned, so go ahead and send him over."

So the alternate worker comes out to your house and starts the job. You have to leave town for a job, so you don't talk with the worker until you return on Friday. He is just wrapping up for the week.

"How did it go?" you ask.

"I'm afraid I didn't quite finish," he says.

"Well how much did you get done?" you ask.

He thinks for a moment. "As near as I can tell, I got about 80 percent of it done," he says.

Notice those words—*as near as I can tell*. In other words, he is *estimating* where he is!

Now as former President George Bush used to like to say, estimating is one of those kind, gentle words that really substitutes for the fact that you are guessing. That's right, an estimate is a guess.

So where are we? We guess we're 80 percent of where we are supposed to be.

How did we know where we were supposed to be in the first place? We guessed at that too.

So let's get this straight. Control is exercised by comparing where you are (which you only know by guessing) to where you are supposed to be (which is another guess) and then taking corrective action to correct for differences between the two. Does this sound like witchcraft and magic to you? It does to me.

Then we may as well not do it if it's just a bunch of guesses. Sorry, as I've said above, that won't fly. It may not be very precise, but it is better than doing absolutely nothing.

Most important, it shows the difficulty of measuring progress even in tangible work. How do you know how much of the house you have cleaned? Can you measure it on a square foot basis? What about cleaning walls or dusting furniture? The truth is, you have no choice but to estimate progress, compare it to the scheduled work (also estimated), and do your best to correct for deviations.

Fine. How do we assign a value to what has been done? Well, if we compare what has been done to the original target, how much should it have cost me to do 80 percent of the total job? The BCWS was $800 worth of work. If the person has done only 80 percent of that, it should cost me $640. This number is called the budgeted cost of work performed (BCWP), and is calculated as follows:

$$BCWP = 0.80 \times BCWS = 0.80 \times \$800 = \$640$$

This number (BCWP) is called *earned value.* The worker has contributed $640 of value to cleaning your house. Of course, he was supposed to have done $800 worth of work, so he is not performing according to plan.

The fact that you got less done than you were supposed to get is bad enough, but then it occurs to you that he has actually worked 40 hours at a higher labor rate ($22 an hour) than you originally budgeted for, so the actual cost of the work performed (ACWP) is $880.

This is not good. Not only did you get less than you were supposed to get, but you have paid more for it as well. So the status of this task is determined using the following equations:

$$CV = BCWP - ACWP$$
$$BV = BCWS - ACWP$$
$$SV = BCWP - BCWS$$

$$\text{Schedule variance} = BCWP - BCWS$$
$$\text{Cost variance} = BCWP - ACWP$$
$$\text{Budget variance} = BCWS - ACWP$$

Using these formulas, we arrive at the following variances:

$$\text{Schedule variance} = \$640 - \$800 = -\$160 \text{ worth of work}$$
$$\text{Cost variance} = \$640 - \$880 = -\$240$$
$$\text{Budget variance} = \$800 - \$880 = -\$80$$

In conventional accounting practice, a negative variance is unfavorable, so this means that the job is behind schedule by $160 worth of work. To convert that to time, you divide by the original $20 per hour labor rate, and you see that the person is 8 hours behind schedule. That makes sense. If he did only 80 percent of the work and it was supposed to take 5 days, he has done what should have been done in 4 days, so he is 1 day (or 8 hours) behind.

But notice the cost variance. Why is it $240? Because you have spent $80 more for the work than originally budgeted and gotten $160 less work done than you were supposed to get. So your cost variance in this case is the sum of the budget and schedule variances, and because the number is negative, you are overspent by $240.

Here is an important point. We have already seen that if you just look at the schedule without knowing the cost, you have no warning that a project may be getting in trouble. In the same manner, if all you were tracking were your budget variance, you would know that you were spending too much, but that alone does not give the true picture. Not only are you spending too much, but you are getting a lot less than you should for what you are spending. This also confirms the need to know both cost and schedule in order to have a true picture of project status.

It is also instructive to notice how this job got into trouble. We failed to check on progress through the week. Rather, we waited until Friday afternoon to find out that the person was not on target. Had we checked progress around midweek and found that the work was already falling behind, we might have been able to get the person to spend some overtime to get it finished by Friday afternoon. Now all we can do is pay for work on Saturday or have the person come back next week to finish the job.

This suggests a guideline that we should follow: The rate at which you monitor progress must be proportionate to the total time the work will take. So a task that is supposed to take a week should probably be monitored daily. That doesn't mean that the project manager should do so, but the individual(s) doing the work should monitor their own progress and they should be told how much leeway they have to take steps to get back on track.

RESPONDING TO DEVIATIONS

In tracking a project, you must always ask three questions, as shown in the box. What is the status? When there is a deviation, what caused it? What should be done about any deviations that exist?

If we apply these to the housecleaning example, the answer to the first question is that we are behind schedule and overspent. When it comes to question two, however, is it clear that we don't know the cause of the deviations? It could be that this person is not as efficient as he should be, or it could be that the estimate was wrong in the first place. How would we figure it out?

Suppose we bring back this same fellow week after week to clean the house, and he can never get it all done in 40 hours. Does this prove it is the person? No. It could be impossible for anyone to do the work in 40 hours.

Then suppose we alternate between two workers. If neither of them can clean the house in 40 hours, we are pretty certain the estimate was optimistic. However, if one can clean the house in 40 hours and the other cannot, then it is clearly the person. Is it?

Well, clearly one person can work faster than the other, but it is important to remember what we said about estimating back in Chapter 7. All estimates are person-specific. It makes no difference what someone else can do. If you want to know when a project will end, you have to estimate for the individuals doing the tasks.

Simply put, there are a few runners who can run a mile in less than 4 minutes. Very few. So it would be totally unreasonable for me to expect an average person to run the mile in 4 minutes just because somewhere there is *someone* who can do it.

Monitoring Progress

When you monitor progress, you ask three questions, as follows:

1. What is the actual status of the work?
2. When there is a deviation, what caused it?
3. What should be done to correct for any deviation that exists?

To answer question 3, note that there are only four responses you can make to a deviation. They are:

1. Ignore the deviation.
2. Take steps to get back on track.
3. Revise the plan to show that the deviation cannot be recovered.
4. Cancel the project.

Given these facts, I can't answer the second question at the moment. All I can do is move on to the third one, which asks what I want to do about the deviation. To answer this question, I actually have to look at my three options at the bottom of the box. I can ignore the deviation, take corrective action to get back on track, or change the plan to accept the deviation.

In the housecleaning situation, it would seem that I have only a limited number of choices—have the person work overtime on Saturday at premium pay or return on Monday to finish the job at regular pay. If I can wait until Monday, that will be the cheaper option. Otherwise, I may have no choice but to pay premium wages. Of course, there is a third option, which is to leave the 20 percent as is, but that isn't a very attractive choice. Neither of the preferred options fits with the second choice. Both are examples of changing the plan. And of course, it is too late to ignore the deviation.

> No matter how far you've gone
> on a wrong road, turn around.
> — Turkish proverb

When would it be okay to ignore a deviation? When it is smaller than the tolerances you can hold and does not show a trend that will eventually take it out of bounds. Consider the deviation chart in Figure 10.3. This chart is showing a project in which tolerances of ± 20 percent are the best that can be maintained. During the first few weeks of the project, the deviations vary randomly within those boundaries. Then there is a definite trend that suggests the project will go outside the 20 percent boundary if nothing is done to get it back on track. Either corrective action must be taken or, if nothing can be done to get back on track, the plan may have to be revised.

In examining deviations, you must always go back to the equation that relates the constraints to each other, namely the following:

$$C = f(P, T, S)$$

If you are trying to get back on schedule, you can increase costs (add labor), reduce scope, or reduce performance requirements. All of these can actually be considered a change to the original plan, except that you may not formally revise the published plan. In the case of reducing scope or performance, you probably have no choice but to revise the plan. In the event that you can increase resources without going over budget, you may be able to leave the plan alone.

F I G U R E 10.3

Deviation Graph for a Project

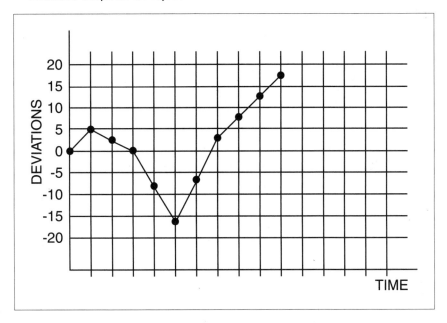

Let me reiterate a point, just so no one misses it. There are *only* four responses you can make when a project is offtrack. You can ignore the deviation. You can take corrective action to get back on target. You can change the plan. And you can cancel the job altogether. This would be done when the project has slipped so much that it is no longer viable in some sense. It will be too late, too expensive, or won't be functional.

When a project is offtrack, you can:

1. Ignore the deviation.
2. Take corrective action to get back on target.
3. Revise the plan to reflect the deviation.
4. Cancel the project altogether.

USING GRAPHS TO TRACK PROGRESS AND FORECAST TRENDS

To get an overall assessment of project status, we can plot earned value data graphically. These graphs will also allow us to forecast where the project will end up in terms of both schedule and spending.

Consider the bar chart in Figure 10.4. There are only three activities. As you can see, task A spends $800 a week for labor, B spends $3000 per week, and C spends $2400 a week. On the first line below the bar chart you see the weekly spending figures, which are obtained by summing the spending on each bar for the week. The final line shows the cumulative spending, and for this project goes to $28,800 at the end of the job. Note that these figures represent the BCWS for the project. If these are plotted, we simply transform the bar graph into a line graph, which shows the cumulative work to be done over time, in dollar value. Because the bar

F I G U R E 10.4

Bar Graph for a Small Project

F I G U R E 10.5

Cumulative Spending for the Three-Activity Project

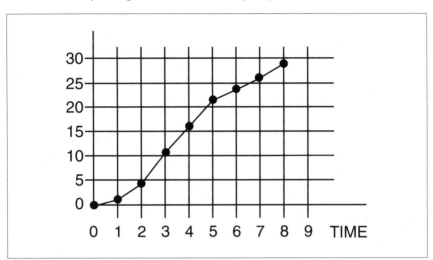

graph is a major component of the project plan, the line graph is also, and is, in fact, called a *baseline plan*. This plot is shown in Figure 10.5.

Once this curve is plotted, we can compare progress to it so that deviations from plan can be spotted. To show this, I am going to use a new curve, one for a larger project than the simple three-activity example.

First Case: Behind Schedule and Overspent

For this project, I have a total cumulative spending of about $90,000. To show progress, I need to find out how much has been accomplished and how much it has cost. To do this, I find out from everyone how much work they have done, expressed as BCWP, and I add up the total value of their work. As you can see from the graph in Figure 10.6, they were supposed to do $50,000 worth of work by the date in question. This was supposed to be 1000 hours of work at a loaded labor rate of $50 per hour. When I total what

F I G U R E 10.6

Plot Showing Project Behind Schedule and Overspent

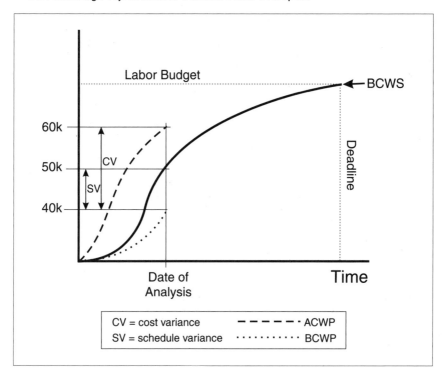

they have actually accomplished, I find that they have done only $40,000 worth of work. In addition, when I collect their time reports, they have put in 1200 hours of labor at a loaded labor rate of 50 dollars per hour, or the ACWP for the project is $60,000.

Returning to our progress questions, we first ask, What is the status of the project? We saw previously that the schedule variance is given by:

$$SV = BCWP - BCWS$$

I suggest that you begin with schedule variance, because cost variance doesn't always make sense until you know what has happened to your schedule.

For this project, the schedule variance is –$10,000 worth of work. This is calculated as follows:

$$SV = 40,000 - 50,000 = -\$10,000$$

If you divide $10,000 by $50 per hour, you find that the project is 200 hours worth of work behind schedule. What this means in calendar time depends on the number of hours per day that are scheduled to be worked. However, you can tell the schedule variance by looking at the horizontal axis. This is shown in Figure 10.7.

Notice that the schedule variance is shown both as a –$10,000 dollar deviation on the vertical axis and also as a time deviation

F I G U R E 10.7

Schedule Variance Shown on Horizontal Axis

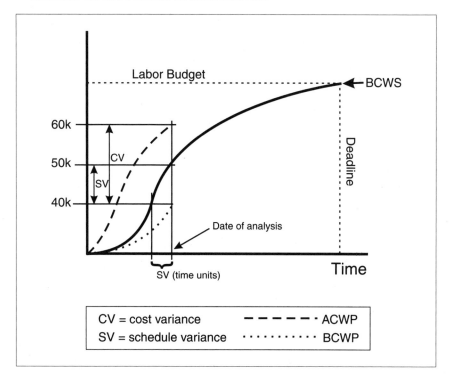

on the horizontal axis. We have done $10,000 less work than was scheduled.

We have also spent $60,000 to do the work, so the cost variance is $20,000. This is calculated as:

$$CV = BCWP - ACWP$$
$$CV = \$40,000 - \$60,000 = -\$20,000$$

Because a negative variance is unfavorable, we are $20,000 overspent. This is most easily understood if you say in words, "We have spent $60,000 to accomplish only $40,000 worth of work." As you can see from the graph, the cost variance is the sum of the budget variance of $10,000 and the schedule variance of $10,000. We have spent $10,000 more for labor than scheduled and gotten $10,000 less work done than scheduled. This is the worst state a project can be in, but unfortunately it happens.

The second question we must answer is, What is the cause of the deviation? As was true for our housecleaning example, we don't know. It could be that people weren't as efficient as they should have been, or it could be that the estimate was optimistic to begin with. And because we don't have the ability to compare this project to another one, we can't answer the question as we could if we compared workers. So all we can do in this case is do a review to determine if there were any factors that caused the work to take longer than expected and try to project from there. And we can also ask, What should be done on the basis of those projections?

This is the third question, which asks, What should we do about the deviation? To answer that question, we need to have some idea what is going to happen to the project. That is, where will it end up? If we had some way to extrapolate the BCWP and ACWP curves in Figure 10.7, we may be able to determine the end state.

To extrapolate these curves, you might do a linear regression, but if you are on the very steep part of the BCWS curve, fitting a linear projection to the BCWP and ACWP curves can be very misleading. It would be better to reestimate where the curves are heading, but I am going to pretend that we can fit a nonlinear projection to each curve, which would give the result shown in Figure 10.8.

Project with BCWP and ACWP Extrapolated

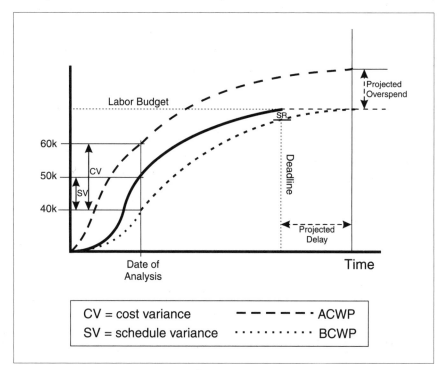

On the basis of these projections, the project is going to be seriously late and overspent, unless something can be done to get it back on target. What to do? The first thing to consider is the worst case, which means that the project can't be "fixed." It is going to be late and overspent. The

> When you're riding a dead horse, dismount.
>
> — Sioux proverb

question in this case is whether it is still viable. If it is product or software development, and we estimate lost sales because it is late and because of increased development costs, we may find that the return on investment (ROI) no longer meets an acceptable level. If that is the case, and unless something can be done to get it back on target, it may be prudent to cancel the job and get on with something that will give an acceptable return. If the ROI is unacceptable, the only reason to continue the project would be because it is mandated by contract or else we are just being masochistic. If the product were a loss leader, or one needed for position in the marketplace, then ROI wouldn't be a factor, and we might continue the job in spite of the projections.

But is there anything that can be done to recover? Perhaps. Notice that if the scope were reduced, the project could be finished by the original completion date, although it will still be overspent. This is shown as SR in Figure 10.8. If that is an acceptable trade-off, we would agree on a scope reduction, which would mean that the plan would be revised, and we would continue.

Suppose, however, that you were told, "It's not acceptable to reduce scope, nor is it permissible to be late. You have to bring this project in on time."

This means that you must somehow make the BCWP curve turn upward so that it intersects the BCWS curve at the deadline. This is shown in Figure 10.9. You will also note that we will most likely incur even greater cost to make this happen, because we will probably have to throw resources at the project to complete it on time.

Of course, you can finish the project on time and on budget if you are dealing with salaried people who don't get paid overtime. That is, you can *appear* to do so. But is that really true? Is nonpaid overtime really free?

You can be sure it is not. You will pay in terms of lost productivity, increased rework, field failures, employee absenteeism, stress-related illness, or turnover. In a job market in which unemployment is only a few percent (which is true of the U.S. economy as of this writing in May 2000) people can fairly easily find new jobs, and may very well leave if the unpaid overtime goes too high. And the cost to replace professionals today is in the range of $100,000 to $200,000. So your unpaid overtime can turn out to be very expensive!

Project Ending on Time But Overspent

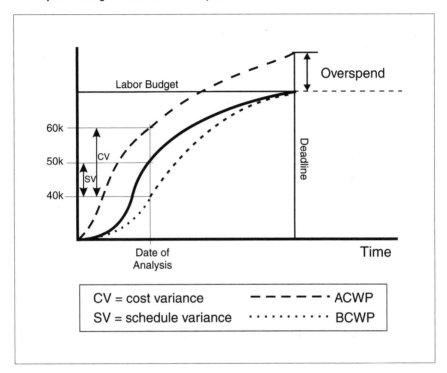

CV = cost variance   – – – – – – · ACWP
SV = schedule variance   · · · · · · · · · · · BCWP

As a final question, you may ask if there isn't something that can be done to get the project completely back on track without going way over budget. I can assure you that it would take a miracle.

There is a rule that says if you are 15 percent into a project on the horizontal time line and you are in trouble, you are going to stay in

> *Principle:* If you are 15 percent into a project on the horizontal time line and you are in trouble, you are going to stay in trouble!

trouble. I call this the 15 percent rule.

This means, then, that if a project is supposed to take 100 weeks to complete, and you are in trouble at the end of week 15, you are going to stay there. Period!

How can I be so confident of this? Aren't there any exceptions? To answer these questions, a study several years ago found that, of 800 defense contract projects that were in trouble at the 15 percent mark, not a single one ever recovered.

I know, I know. You're thinking that's typical of defense contracting. But I can assure you that it applies to your projects as well, even if you aren't in defense contracting.

How can I be sure? Easy. Where did the BCWS curve come from?

The bar chart schedule.

Where did the schedule come from? A bunch of estimates.

Now let's use President Bush's favorite expression. A kinder gentler word than estimate is *forecast*. It's true. Estimating is forecasting. The thing is, we all know that if the weather forecast for tomorrow can't be trusted, there is no need to believe the forecast for six weeks out. In other words, if the near-term forecast (just 15 percent into the project) isn't right, why would it be any better at the end of the job? It won't.

What this means is that we have a good-news, bad-news story. The good news is that you can forecast a losing project very early, so that you can perhaps cancel it and cut your losses early. The bad news is that, if it is doing well at the 15 percent point, it won't necessarily continue to do so.

Second Case: Ahead of Schedule, Spending Correctly

To illustrate another combination, consider the situation shown in Figure 10.10. This time the BCWP curve shows that $60,000 worth of work has been done and that the ACWP is also $60,000. The BCWS target on this date was $50,000. The status is ahead of schedule and the cost variance is zero.

Be careful to distinguish between budget variance and cost variance. The project is above budget by $10,000, but that is because they are ahead of schedule. In words, they have done

F I G U R E   10.10

Project Ahead of Schedule, Spending Correctly

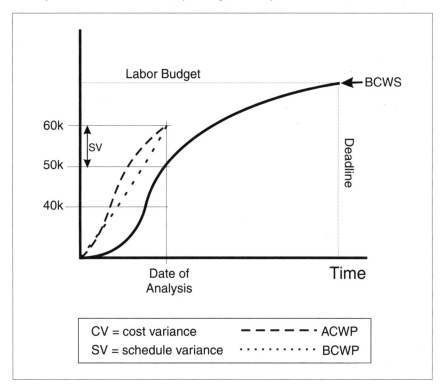

CV = cost variance   – – – – – · ACWP
SV = schedule variance   · · · · · · · · · BCWP

$60,000 worth of work (BCWP) and spent $60,000 to do it. A simple way to keep this in mind is that, when BCWP is larger than BCWS, you have done more than scheduled, so you are ahead of schedule. If you have done less, you are behind.

The second question we must answer is, What is the most likely cause of this variance? Unlike the first one, where the project was behind schedule and overspent, this variance has a generic cause. Remember, this is labor cost. When you are ahead of schedule and spending correctly, it means that you have more resources applied to the project than you had intended, but they are working at expected efficiency.

In shared resource environment, that should raise a red flag. Where did you get extra resources? You don't exactly have them sitting around in the hall waiting for something to do.

There are two possibilities. Either you stole them or somebody got into trouble and couldn't use some people and gave them to you.

In a construction project, there is another possibility. The schedule had some weather delay built into it for safety and the weather has been beautiful, so the work has been progressing ahead of schedule.

Now before I refer you to the third question, I must tell you that I can predict your response, even from here. You are going to think, "Is he crazy?" Let's see if I'm right.

The third question is, What do you want to do about the deviation?

See. I was right. You're thinking, "Wait a minute. I'm ahead of schedule and spending correctly, and he wants to know what I'm going to do about it? Like nothing, man! Hide it maybe. I'm sure not going to slow down."

Before you go too far with that thinking, you have to ask if being ahead of schedule can cause problems later on. And the answer is yes. Suppose you deliver a product to a customer before the customer is ready for it. You may have to pay to warehouse it. You may also have to wait to get paid for it.

Speaking of pay, suppose the project is a construction job. Contractors usually want to get progress payments for their work, so they send you bills totaling $60,000. Your controller may kill you. Your plan stated that you were going to do $50,000 worth of work, but the contractors have done $60,000. Although the difference may be small, the controller may have cash flow problems and tell you to slow down.

Darn. What a thankless job! Just when you thought you were doing something good and everyone starts trashing you.

It's a matter of degree, you understand. If you are a little bit ahead, nobody will get excited. In fact, we all know it is always better to be ahead than behind. But there are definitely situations where being ahead can be a problem. I know of a company that finished some equipment ahead of time and shipped it. When it arrived at the new facility, they hadn't finished building the loading dock, so they had to put it in a warehouse temporarily and pay the rental charges.

Behind Schedule, Spending Correctly

The next scenario is shown in Figure 10.11. In this case, BCWP is at $40,000 and so is ACWP. The target BCWS is still $50,000. What is the status? The project is behind schedule but has no cost vari-

F I G U R E 10.11

Project Is Behind Schedule and Spending Correctly

ance. What is the most likely cause? Lack of resources. Either someone stole your help or, if it is construction, you may be waiting for the weather to clear up. Or you may be waiting for supplies or whatever. In any case, not enough labor is being applied to the project.

What do you want to do about it? Usually you want to catch up. However, you can almost be sure that to catch up you will blow your budget. It is usually better to stay on schedule than to try to recover once you get behind.

Final Scenario

Now examine Figure 10.12. What is the status? Did you get it? The project is ahead of schedule and underspent. How much? The work is $10,000 ahead (BCWP is at $60,000) and spending is $20,000 less than expected. If you say it in words, you have spent only $40,000 to accomplish $60,000 worth of work.

What is the most likely cause of this variance? There are two possibilities. One is that the estimate was very conservative—to the point of sandbagging. The other is that you had a very lucky break. You can bet that sandbagging is far more likely than a lucky break.

Question three is, What do you want to do about it? I know what you're thinking. Leave it alone. Hide it maybe. You sure aren't going to slow down, and if you were to give the money back, they would expect you to do it next time. Nobody in his right mind would do either—or would he?

I submit that you should give some of the money back and reschedule the project. If you don't, the organization will lose the opportunity to make good use of the money until the project ends, and that opportunity cost can be significant.

Remember our first project scenario, in which the job was behind schedule and overspent. We stated that the project may be canceled if it is not viable, but it could be viable and still be canceled simply because there is no money to fund it. However, there would be money to fund that project if we freed it up from this one, which is under budget.

F I G U R E 10.12

Project Ahead of Schedule, Underspent

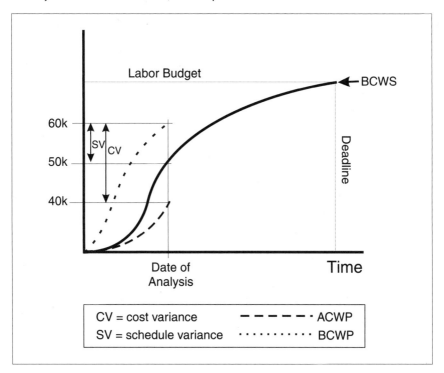

CV = cost variance — — — — — · ACWP
SV = schedule variance · · · · · · · · · · · BCWP

Notice that I said you should give *some* of the money back. This is because all work varies. There is some tolerance that we must accept as normal variation. If it is ± 15 percent, then give all but 15 percent of the money back. Keep some in reserve to cover the variation. This is proper control of variance.

Again, I know what you're thinking. If you give it back, and then hit a rock later on, you won't be able to get it back. This is true in many organizations. What I am advocating is that the organization must change the way it treats project budgets. They must all be examined about once a quarter and adjustments made in either direction. That way, people will be willing to give back extra money, because they know they can get it back later if they need it.

The Sin of Cross-Charging

In many more companies than I care to count, the solution to this problem is to simply tell members of the overspent project to quit charging time to it. They are told to charge to the underspent project instead. That way, both projects will come in on budget.

In defense contracting, if you get caught doing this, you may go to jail. It is illegal, because earned value is used to determine when progress payments should be made to a contractor, and you are charging for work you haven't done in one case. So it is lying, and it is illegal.

Principle: Cross-charging contaminates databases. The proper approach is to rebudget aboveboard.

Most seriously, it destroys our ability to tell when we have a "sick" project so that we can do something to help it. Or, if it is too sick to be saved, we may cancel it. But we can't tell it is really bad off if no one charges time to it.

In addition, cross-charging contaminates both history databases. Next time you do similar projects, you will underestimate one and overestimate the other. And you will be in trouble again.

What should be done is to make an aboveboard adjustment to both project budgets. The funds are transferred from one to the other. This does not contaminate your databases, and is acceptable.

USING A SPREADSHEET TO TRACK PROGRESS

The graphic method of tracking progress is good for showing trends and visually seeing what is going on overall in a project, but it is not a very effective method of actually determining the true state of the job. The reason is that the graph presents composite data for the project, and that data is not good for seeing problems that exist with individual tasks.

Consider the situation shown in Figure 10.13. There are three tasks going on in parallel. One is $100 overspent, the second is

Three Tasks in Parallel

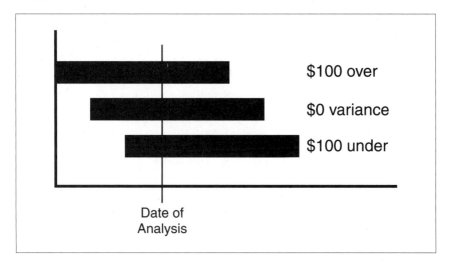

right on target, and the third is $100 underspent. What you see on the bottom line will be a zero variance in spending, because one deviation cancels the other. This would tell you that the project is fine when it is not. To really track progress, you need to look at every task, and the best way to do that is with a spreadsheet kind of report.

Most scheduling programs today allow you to report progress using earned value analysis and present it in spreadsheet format. However, not all of them have one feature that I find very useful, and that is the critical ratio. This is a performance index that is actually the product of two individual indices. One is the schedule performance index (SPI) and the other is the cost performance index (CPI). These are shown as follows:

$$SPI = \frac{BCWP}{BCWS}$$

$$CPI = \frac{BCWP}{ACWP}$$

Before continuing, I think it is helpful to consider the meaning of these equations. First of all, BCWP is called earned value, and is a measure of *what you got.* The amount of work you were supposed to get is BCWS. So the SPI is simply *work efficiency,* or fraction of work done. Finally, ACWP is the actual cost of work performed, so the CPI can be thought of as *spending efficiency.*

If the two ratios are multiplied together, you get a combined index called the critical ratio (CR), as is shown by the following equation:

$$CR = SPI * CPI$$

Like all ratios that indicate performance, these will have values of 1.0 if work is going exactly as planned. If work is going better than planned, the ratios will be greater than 1.0 and if worse than planned, they will have values of less than 1.0. When you multiply the two together, one of them may be slightly above 1.0 and the other slightly below 1.0 and the CPI can still be 1.0. This is shown in the following equation:

$$
\begin{aligned}
CR &= SPI * CPI \\
&= 0.9 * 1.11 \\
&= 1.0
\end{aligned}
$$

A spreadsheet that uses the critical ratio to indicate progress and suggest actions to be taken is shown in Figure 10.14. Note that the critical ratio is calculated in the next-to-last column, and then the last column is headed *Action Required,* which has the following meaning. (This spreadsheet can be downloaded from my website free of charge.)

In manufacturing, a process can be monitored by taking measures on the things produced by the process and plotting those measures on a deviation graph. So long as those measures fall randomly around the centerline, the process is in control. When the deviations cease to be random, there is a probability that the process is either out of control or about to go out of control. The tests for nonrandomness are outside the scope of this book, but a good reference is Walpole (1974).

Spreadsheet for Tracking Progress

Earned Value Report

Date: _____
Page _____ of _____
Signed:

Project No.:
Description:
Prepared by:

FILE:

WBS # or Name	Cumulative-to-date			Variance		At Completion			Critical Ratio	Action Required
	BCWS	BCWP	ACWP	Sched.	Cost	Budgeted (BAC)	Latest Est. (EAC)	Variance		
				0	0			0	NA	NA
				0	0			0	NA	NA
				0	0			0	NA	NA
				0	0			0	NA	NA
				0	0			0	NA	NA
				0	0			0	NA	NA
				0	0			0	NA	NA
				0	0			0	NA	NA
				0	0			0	NA	NA
				0	0			0	NA	NA
				0	0			0	NA	NA
				0	0			0	NA	NA
TOTALS:	0	0	0	0	0	0	0	0	NA	NA

NOTE: Negative variance is unfavorable || If Critical Ratio < 0.6, INFORM MANAGEMENT!   ( ) = NEGATIVE VALUES

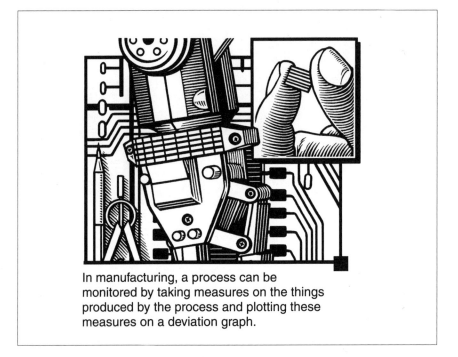

In manufacturing, a process can be
monitored by taking measures on the things
produced by the process and plotting these
measures on a deviation graph.

Critical Ratio Greater than One

A similar idea has been developed for keeping track of the critical
ratio over time. The control limits are shown in Figure 10.15. If the
critical ratio is between 0.9 and 1.2, we consider the deviation to
be acceptable. If it falls between 1.2 and 1.3, we are told to check
the task (or project), and if the ratio goes above 1.3, we are told to
red flag it. The term red flag means that the ratio is seriously out of
line.

However, I said earlier that ratios greater than 1.0 mean that
work is going better than planned. So why would a critical ratio
above 1.3 be cause for concern? First, you have heard the saying
that if something seems to be too good to be true, it probably is.
So the first concern is whether the data is actually valid, or are
people deceiving themselves? If the data is valid, then what is
going on?

F I G U R E 10.15

A Critical Ratio Control Chart

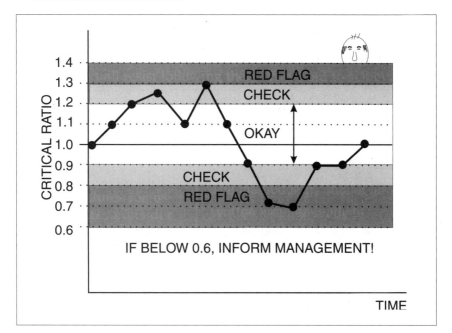

In all likelihood, the project is very much ahead of schedule and underspent when the critical ratio goes this high. Wonderful, you say! Well, maybe.

But this is the last situation we just examined in the section on tracking progress graphically, and we said that the project should be rescheduled and some of the money given back. So the critical ratio is flagging you that something should be done about the project.

Critical Ratio Less than One

When the CR is between 0.8 and 0.9, it is in the check range. If it is below 0.8 it becomes a red flag, and if it drops below 0.6, we are told to inform management. The reason is that this project is really sick, nigh unto death. For a critical ratio to be around 0.6, the project is most likely way behind schedule and seriously overspent. It is a good candidate to be canceled (if that is an option), and cancellation decisions are usually made by senior management, so we are being told to inform them, so that they can decide what to do.

Of course, this only applies to the overall project critical ratio. If a single task has a critical ratio around 0.6, you wouldn't tell senior management about it. It is you, the project manager, who should be alarmed and who should take action. Chances are that, if this task had any float, it probably doesn't have much left, and if it becomes critical and slips any more, it will impact the finish date for the project, so you need to take action immediately.

The spreadsheet shown in Figure 10.14 has an "if" formula in the cell to test the critical ratio against the specified limits, and it prints the words Okay, Check, or Red Flag in the cell so that you can scan the right-hand column and immediately see where your trouble spots are. In addition, you can set up conditional formatting of the cell to make it turn red, yellow, or green, to correspond to the words, and distribute color prints that make it very easy for people to spot problems.

Forecasting Final Cost and Schedule Results

There are a couple of ways to forecast final results for a project. One is to replan on the basis of what has been learned to date. Another is to calculate forecast results using earned value data. Perhaps the best would be to do both.

The most common and most accepted of the statistical forecasting methods is to use the cumulative CPI estimate at completion. The formula for making this projection follows:

$$\$EAC = \frac{BAC - BCWP}{Cumulative\ CPI} + ACWP$$

If we go back to the first project status example we used, in which the project was behind schedule and overspent, and ask what the $EAC (monetary estimate at completion) will be, we would get the following. The original BAC (budget at completion) is about $90,000. The current BCWP is $40,000, the ACWP is $60,000, and the CPI is therefore 0.533. (Numbers below are expressed in thousands.)

$$\$EAC = \frac{90-40}{0.533} + 60$$

This calculates to a $EAC of $153,800. If nothing is done to bring spending in line, the project is going to be overspent a bunch! The only problem with this formula is that it is a more or less linear projection, which depends on the slope of the curve at the present time for its forecast. It is better to reestimate each task and forecast from those estimates, but this is a quick way to find out how much trouble you are in.

ALTERNATIVES TO EARNED VALUE

As far as I am concerned, there is no completely adequate alternative to earned value tracking. I showed at the beginning of the chapter that, unless you know both how much effort has gone into a project and where the schedule is, you can't tell you have problems. However, there are some approaches that can be used in lieu of earned value if you simply can't find a way to measure BCWP, for example.

Using Run Charts

One of these is the run chart. You can plot any four of the project variables (P, C, T, S) using this approach. The chart in Figure 10.16 shows a plot of fraction of work completed each week for a hypothetical project called Echo. To plot fraction of work completed, you divide the amount of work completed to date by the amount of work scheduled to be completed. This could be called percent of scheduled work actually completed, and is equivalent to the ratio BCWP/BCWS. From this chart you can see that starting in week 3 there is a downward trend. People are clearly having trouble. Then they somehow begin to recover and there is an upward trend that peaks in week 15, then falls back a bit. Because work

F I G U R E 10.16

A Run Chart for Project Echo

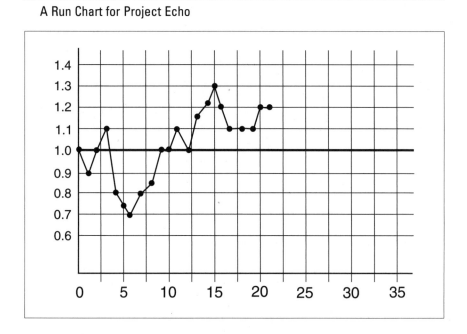

following week 12 is being performed at a greater rate than scheduled, it is likely that the project will finish early, possibly by week
21, rather than as scheduled on week 23. This chart is highly unlikely to occur in reality, because the team is in a lot of trouble
early on, but it illustrates the approach.

There are two guidelines for interpreting run charts in order
to detect meaningful systemic changes:

    a. Since it is expected that there would be approximately
    the same number of points above the *average* line as there
    are below it, a good rule of thumb is that if there is a run
    of seven consecutive points on one side of the average,
    something significant may be happening and it would
    probably be a good idea to call "time out."

    b. A second test is to see whether a run of seven or more in-
    tervals is steadily increasing or decreasing without rever-

sals in direction. As in (a), such a pattern is not likely to occur by chance, thereby indicating [that] something needs to be investigated (Kiemele and Schmidt, 1993, p. 2-25).

To track quality, you might want to record rework hours. It is likely that most projects will incur from 5 to 40 percent rework. If you are improving your project management process, you should see a decline in rework. A run chart that tracks hours spent on rework is shown in Figure 10.17.

To track quality you might want to record rework hours.

A Run Chart for Project Echo Showing Rework

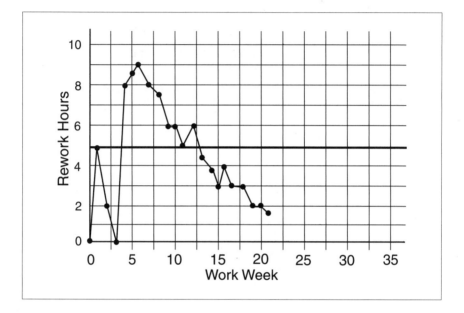

If you compare Figure 10.16 with Figure 10.17, you will notice that the curve showing rework hours is almost a mirror image
of the progress curve. This suggests that one reason the team was
not making good progress prior to week 10 is because they were
making a number of errors that had to be corrected. After week
10, they had reduced the rework significantly, and progress re-
flects this. These figures would be for a very small team.

Other indicators of project quality might be documentation
changes, engineering changes, design revisions, customer complaints, test failures, number of software bugs, and so on.

It is also useful to track the number of scope changes in a
project, but you need to capture the impact of a scope change for
this to be meaningful. You might be able to absorb a dozen small
scope changes with almost no project impact, whereas a single
change in scope might nearly sink the project. Because scope

changes results in additional work, you can track impact by looking at the dollar value of the extra work required (or the number of working hours, if you don't have dollar figures). You can also show impact by any slip in schedule that results.

The other issue that should be addressed is what caused the scope change. If it was environmental changes that no one could foresee, then the changes are probably legitimate. On longer-duration projects, the world is going to move around before you can finish the project. Competitors bring out products that necessitate changes in your design if you are going to be able to compete. This is understandable, although you sometimes should go ahead and freeze a design without the competitive feature, release it, and then start a new project to add that feature. It all depends on how critical that feature is for product sales.

On the other hand, if changes were required because not enough time was spent up front in defining the project, these are wasteful and should be avoided in the future.

GUIDELINES ON TRACKING PROGRESS

Although it seems obvious, there is very little need to go to the trouble of tracking progress unless you keep accurate records. If you don't want the information to be used for control, but rather want to make your project look good, then why bother to collect data? Just write down what you want people to see and save yourself a lot of effort.

There are two major sins committed in tracking progress. One is to let people record their time once a week. I know. I did this 30 years ago when I didn't know any better. We had to record time to the nearest quarter hour, and we turned the reports in on Monday morning.

Even when I was younger, I could never remember what I did the previous Monday. Now I can't remember what I did yesterday. So when it came time to do the report, I guessed at it the best I could, but you can be sure it was highly inaccurate. That means that the database was a bunch of fiction that would subsequently be used to estimate future projects. It's useless!

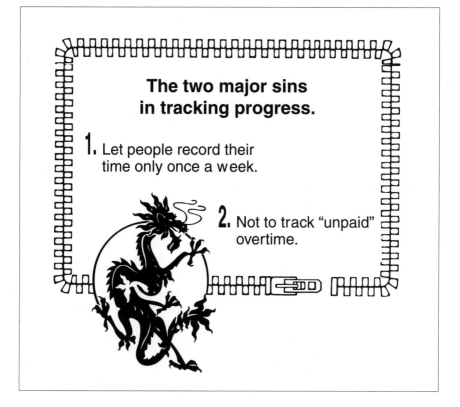

The only reasonable way to record work is to do it daily. No, it doesn't take that long. If it takes longer than five minutes, you are being obsessive. I don't think it makes sense to record time in increments much less than a half hour. If you work an eight-hour day, that is 16 entries into your time log. It should take less than 15 seconds to write each one down, so that is about four minutes. (Okay, you're slow–allow yourself 10 minutes, but that's it!)

The second deadly sin is to not track unpaid overtime. In some organizations, salaried personnel are allowed to report only 40 hours a week, because that's all they are paid for. That is a payroll issue, not a project one. For project purposes, you need to know exactly how many total hours are spent on a task so that your database will reflect actual hours for use in future estimating. In addition, if you strip off the overtime, you can't tell that you have problems, as was shown at the beginning of this chapter.

CONDUCTING PROJECT REVIEWS[1]

There are three kinds of project reviews that can be conducted: status, design, and process. Each has a different purpose. A status review concentrates on whether the P, C, T, and S targets are being met. Are we on schedule, are we on budget, is scope correct, and are performance requirements okay?

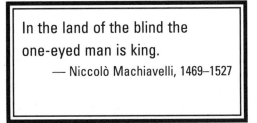

In the land of the blind the one-eyed man is king.
— Niccolò Machiavelli, 1469–1527

A design review only applies to those projects in which something is being designed, such as a product, service, or software. Some of the questions asked during such a review are: Does it meet specifications? Is it user-friendly? Can we manufacture it? Is the market still looking for what we are developing? Are return on investment and other product justifications still in line?

A process review focuses on *how* we are doing our work. Two questions are asked: What are we doing well? What do we want to improve? We will discuss how this review is conducted later in this chapter.

During status and design reviews, a project may also be evaluated. An evaluation is usually focused on software or hardware development projects and tries to determine if the total end result that is supposed to be achieved will be accomplished. Will the return-on-investment target be met? Will the product be manufacturable? Can we sell it? The answer to these questions determines whether the project will be continued or canceled. Table 10.1 shows a summary of the three project reviews.

---

[1] The material on project reviews has been adapted from my book, *The Project Manager's Desk Reference*, 2d.

T A B L E 10.1

The Three Kinds of Project Reviews

Project Reviews and Their Nature	
Status	Looks at the status of cost, performance, schedule, and scope
Design	Examines a product, service, or software design to see if it meets requirements
Process	Reviews project processes and asks if they can be improved

Following are some of the general reasons for conducting periodic project reviews:

- Improve project performance together with the management of the project.
- Ensure that quality of project work does not take a back seat to schedule and cost concerns.
- Reveal developing problems early so that action can be taken to deal with them.
- Identify areas where other projects (current or future) should be managed differently.
- Keep client(s) informed of project status. This can also help ensure that the completed project will meet the needs of the client.
- Reaffirm the organization's commitment to the project for the benefit of project team members.

Process Reviews

The objective or purpose of a process review is to improve performance of the team. In reviewing performance, note that we do not ask, "What have we done wrong?" Asking that question simply raises defenses in team members and they are going to try to hide anything they think is wrong, because they assume that they will be trashed for any mistakes that have been made. The purpose of a process review is to learn from experience so that we can avoid those things that were not done well and continue doing those things that have been done well. It is not a witch hunt. If you go about it in a "blame and punishment" way, people will hide their faults.

> *Principle:* The purpose of a process review is to learn how to improve performance. If you go on a witch hunt, you will create witches where none existed before.

The other reason for not asking what has been done wrong is that the answer may be "Nothing," and everyone may think this means a review is unnecessary. This is not true. The best-performing team must always attempt to get even better, because their competitors are not sitting idly by maintaining the status quo. They too are improving, and if you stand still for very long, they will pass you.

> The ability to learn faster than your competitors may be the only sustainable competitive advantage.
>
> — Arie P. de Geus

It is also a fact that the most dangerous place a team can be is successful. That may sound wrong, and even may be a bit depressing, but it is true. A successful team can easily get complacent. Coaches of sports teams know this. When you have won every game of the season, your very next game is risky because you may get cocky and careless. For that reason, you can never be satisfied with the status quo.

> There is a big difference between an excuse and an explanation. Excuses are unacceptable. Explanations are not.

One of the favorite expressions of some managers is "no excuses." When something goes wrong, they regard any explanation of what happened as an excuse. I find this attitude very dangerous, and totally counter

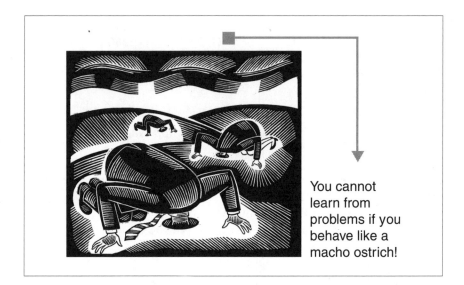

You cannot learn from problems if you behave like a macho ostrich!

to learning. There is a big difference between an excuse and an explanation. Comedian Flip Wilson used to have a wonderful excuse when he did something he shouldn't do. "The devil made me do it," he would quip. That is an excuse.

Saying that El Niño caused so much rain in California one summer that construction of a new plant fell far behind schedule is an explanation, not an excuse. To say that there has been a fire in an auto parts plant, and that parts are not available for production is an explanation, not an excuse.

You cannot learn from problems or failures if you behave like a macho ostrich and stick your head in the sand or hold your hands over your ears, refusing to listen to the facts. And the person who refuses to learn from history is doomed to repeat the mistakes of history, to paraphrase the old saying.

Process Always Affects Task

It is very important to understand that process will always affect task outcomes! That is, the *way* you do something will always affect the results you get. As the old saying goes, "If you always do what you've always done, you'll always get what you always got." And the corollary is, "Insanity is continuing

> **Process will *always* affect task!**
> — Marvin Weisbord

to do what you've always done and hope for a different result." In terms of process, these statements mean, "If you aren't getting the results you want, change your process!"

In any project team, the processes we care about include those shown in the box. One of the most important of these is meetings. Projects cannot succeed without periodic meetings.

However, as we all know, the large majority of meetings are badly run, leaving participants drained, frustrated, and wishing they would never have to attend another one. In his video, "Meetings, Bloody Meetings," John Cleese makes a profound comment about meetings. He says, "The essence of management is in how we run meetings." (This video can be purchased from Video Arts. See the resources list following the Appendix.)

Team Processes

- Leadership
- Decision making
- Problem solving
- Communications
- Meetings
- Planning
- Giving feedback to team members
- Conflict management

Now if that doesn't make you depressed, you haven't thought about the implications. Meetings typically lose focus, have no clear direction to begin with, last ad nauseam, and don't accomplish anything. If you can't manage a meeting, how can you manage an organization?

If you want to improve the management of your meetings, read Chapter 16 and follow the model presented there.

The Process Review Report

When a project is reviewed, the lessons learned should be shared with other teams. By doing so, they can avoid the mistakes made by the team being reviewed and they can take advantage of the things they are doing well. The lessons learned report should contain as a minimum the following:

1. *Current project status.* This is best shown using earned value analysis. However, when earned value analysis is not used, status should still be reported with as great accuracy as possible.

2. *Future status.* This is a forecast of what is expected to happen in the project. Are significant deviations expected in schedule, cost, performance, or scope? If so, the nature of such changes should be specified.

3. *Status of critical tasks.* The status of critical tasks, particularly those on the critical path, should be reported. Tasks which have high levels of technical risk should be given special attention, as should those being performed by outside vendors or subcontractors, over which the project manager may have limited control.

4. *Risk assessment.* Have any risks been identified which highlight potential for monetary loss, project failure, or other liabilities?

5. *Information relevant to other projects.* What has been learned from this review that can/should be applied to other projects, whether presently in progress or about to start?

6. *Limitations of the review.* What factors might limit the validity of the review? Are any assumptions suspect? Is any data missing or suspect of contamination? Was anyone uncooperative in providing information for the review?

As a general comment, the simpler and more straightforward a project review report, the better. The information should be organized so that planned versus actual results can be easily compared. Significant deviations should be highlighted and explained. In Figure 10.18 is a form intended to be used for a milestone pro-

Process Review Form

Project Process Review
Project:
Prepared by: Date:
For the period from   to:
Evaluate the following objectives: Performance was on target ❐, below target ❐, above target ❐ Budget was on target ❐, overspent ❐, underspent ❐ Schedule was on target ❐, behind ❐, ahead ❐
Overall, was the project a success? Yes ❐ No ❐
If not, what factors contributed to a negative evaluation?
What was done really well?
What could have been done better?
What recommendations would you make for future project application?
What would you do differently if you could do it over?
What have you learned that can be applied to future projects?

cess review. For an end-of-project review, the form will be too small to capture all the data generated, so it should be used as a guide for what questions to ask.

PROJECT CHANGE CONTROL

One of the major causes of project time and cost overruns is scope creep. Stakeholders ask for "small" changes. They aren't very significant, so you absorb them. The problem is, five cent changes add up to dollars, and the next thing you know, the project has grown considerably larger than it started out to be. Feature creep is also the cause of scope creep. The interesting thing is that the very people who ask for all of the changes have very convenient amnesia at the end of the project. To protect yourself and everyone else, you have to control changes to the project.

This is done through a formal project change approval process. When someone asks for a change to the project, you should let that person know the impact if the change is made. What will it do to schedule, cost, or performance? Then ask if the individual really wants to accept the impact. If she says yes, then you initiate a formal change procedure.

This procedure requires that changes be approved by more than just the person who asked for it. The change may impact inventory of parts that have already been purchased for the project. It may affect market introduction of a new hardware or software product, which could severely impact sales. It may affect tooling. So a formal change process requires that an approval board review all of these possible effects and sign off on them.

A form is shown in Figure 10.19 that can be used to control changes to a project. Note that tic boxes are placed in front of signatories, so that the person does not have to approve the change unless the box is checked. The rule is that only those individuals who have a need to review the change should sign the form. That way, you cut down on the endless rounds of approvals that can delay the process.

F I G U R E 10.19

A Project Change Approval Form

PROJECT CHANGE APPROVAL

Project Name: _____

Project Number: _____ Date: _____

Project Manager: _____

Requested by: _____

Department: _____

Change in: ❑ Scope ❑ Schedule ❑ Budget ❑ Performance

Deviation Information

Description of change being requested:_____

Reason for change:_____

Effect on schedule: _____

Effect on cost (budget): _____

Effect on performance (quality): _____

Effect on scope: _____

Justification: _____

Class: _____

Capital: Distribution of estimated cost deviation _____

The requested change is: ❑ Absolutely necessary to achieve desired results

❑ Scope reduction that will not impact original targets

Noncapital: Distribution of estimated cost deviation _____

The requested change is: ❑ Discretionary—provides benefits beyond the original targets

❑ Scope reduction that will impact original target

List of Required Approvals—Signed and Dated

❑ Project Leader/Manager _____ Date _____

❑ General Manager_____ Date _____

❑ Concerned Dept. Manager_____ Date _____

❑ Controller _____ Date _____

❑ Concerned Vice President_____ Date _____

❑ President _____ Date _____

❑ Other _____ Date _____

KEY POINTS FOR CHAPTER 10

- *Principle:* To measure progress you must know the value of all four constraints.
- *Principle:* Unless you know both cost and schedule, you have absolutely no idea where your project actually is.
- *Principle:* If you are 15 percent into a project on the horizontal time line and you are in trouble, you are going to stay in trouble!
- *Principle:* Cross-charging contaminates databases. The proper approach is to rebudget aboveboard.
- There are two major sins committed in tracking progress. One is to let people record their time once a week.
- The second deadly sin is to not track unpaid overtime.
- *Principle:* The purpose of a process review is to learn how to improve performance. If you go on a witch hunt, you will create witches where none existed before.

QUESTIONS FOR REVIEW

1. How many of the PCTS variables must you measure in order to know the true status of a project?
2. Give the definition of control.
3. What part does a plan play in controlling a project?
4. What is wrong with reporting schedule progress only?
5. What is meant by BCWP?
6. There are only four things you can do when a project is offtrack. Tell what they are.
7. What is the 15 percent rule?
8. Why is cross-charging bad practice (even if it weren't illegal in defense contracting)?
9. Give the basic expression for the critical ratio.
10. When the critical ratio for a project falls to 0.6, we are told to inform management. What is the reason for this instruction?

11. What is meant by $EAC or simply EAC?
12. List the three kinds of project reviews.
13. In conducting a process review, why do we not ask, "What have we done wrong?"

SECTION FIVE

OTHER ISSUES IN
PROJECT MANAGEMENT

CHAPTER

Managing Multiple Projects

In Chapter 7, we saw that the difference between program management and project management is an order of magnitude. A program is actually a large job that consists of a number of projects. Examples include airplane development projects, the space shuttle development, large weapons systems, and building a housing development.

Program managers do not actually manage the individual projects that make up the program. Rather, they manage the project managers of those jobs. They must see to it that interdependencies between projects are coordinated, that no project manager loses sight of the fact that his or her job is just part of the whole, and that the program cannot succeed unless all parts function together adequately. In fact, a program manager who got too involved with the details of a project would probably cause more problems than would be solved.

HOW MUCH WOOD CAN A WOODCHUCK CHUCK?

I have shown in Chapter 9, on managing resources, that most of the people who attend my seminars are managing two to four projects, with a few having as many as 10. It is never clear that everyone answers the question correctly, when asked how many projects they are managing. The reason I say this is that they sometimes have 10 projects in the works, but only three or four are actually active at the time. So six of them are just waiting to be started, or some preliminary work has been done but they are in a state of limbo at present.

When I am asked how many projects a person should manage, I have to answer, "It all depends." There are a couple of reasons for this answer. One is that we differ in our ability to deal with complexity. The human mind can deal with only five to nine bits of information at once. That means some people can deal with nine, but others can only deal with five.

I also showed in the same chapter that multitasking causes setup time to be increased significantly, which reduces productivity accordingly. So working on multiple projects can certainly be expected to affect the productivity of the project manager adversely.

Another factor in the equation is whether you are actually managing the project or whether you are doing some of the work in the project. I have pointed out in Chapter 3 that a *working project manager* almost always gets into a double bind. If you have a conflict between working and managing, the work always takes precedence, and the managing suffers. Yet, at review time, you get judged badly for not managing better. I believe that, if you are a working project manager, you probably can't manage more than one project, and you may not be able to do that very well.

> *Principle:* In general, two or three small projects are all one person should manage.

The general guideline is that two or three small projects are all any person can handle effectively, because the degree of com-

plexity quickly exceeds his or her ability to keep up with every-thing. Further, there is a certain amount of overhead associated with each project. You have to attend status meetings, deal with bottlenecks, handle political issues, and so on, and these can quickly snowball if you get involved in too many projects. As with any principle, the number of projects a person can handle varies with the individual and is based on mental ability and how many hours a week the person is willing to work to get everything done. It also depends on the maturity of team members. When you have a very capable team, you have to do less managing than if they have low job maturity.

IF YOU GET OVERLOADED

If you find that you have more than you can do effectively, I would advise you to inform your boss. If you work for a person who will see this as a sign of weakness, I would also suggest that you try to find a new boss to work for. Any manager who is overly "macho," and who doesn't understand the basic premise stated in the chapter on managing time, is not the kind of boss you want to work for. Remember, you may be able to do anything, but you can't do everything. The manager who is overly fond of saying there are no problems, only opportunities, is practicing ostrich management and won't see the freight train coming down the tracks until it knocks him on his butt. Many problems are opportunities, but some are simply too much for one person to handle.

> Your boss probably can't keep up with what you have to do. If you don't tell him or her that you're overloaded, he or she has no way of knowing.

I also speak as a former department manager. I could never keep up with how much all of my people had to do. If they didn't tell me they were overloaded, I couldn't do anything to help them. And if they missed a deadline because they couldn't handle everything, then my neck was on the line as well.

> *Principle:* Everything has a capacity!

Everything has a capacity. We know that a machine can perform only so many operations per hour. The same is true of people. It does no good to challenge people to do the absolutely impossible. Stretch objectives should be just that—stretch objectives, not impossible targets.

MANAGING YOUR TIME

When you are managing several projects at once, time management becomes even more important than ever. I would especially recommend that you try to avoid multitasking, because it increases your setup time and decreases your productivity. Try to concentrate on one thing at a time and get it done. I know this is nearly impossible to do in some situations. There are so many people making demands on you that you really can't protect your time from interruptions, but the more you can do so, the better off you will be. It isn't a matter of adhering to any principle absolutely, but to approximate it as much as you can.

KEY POINTS FOR CHAPTER 11

- *Principle:* In general, two or three small projects are all one person should manage.
- Your boss probably can't keep up with what you have to do. If you don't tell him or her that you're overloaded, he or she has no way of knowing.
- *Principle:* Everything has a capacity!

QUESTIONS FOR REVIEW

1. How much information can the mind deal with at once?
2. Why will working on multiple projects affect the productivity of a project manager?
3. What is the general guideline for how many projects a person can manage?

12

CHAPTER

Developing a Project Methodology

I am often told by managers that everyone in their company does projects a different way, using different documentation, and to varying levels of detail. There are some who think that a to-do list with a few dates on it is an adequate project plan. They also run project kickoff meetings differently. Some expect the meeting to clarify what is going to be done. Others come fully prepared to tell everyone the project mission.

If your organization is going to be ISO (International Standards Organization) certified, you must have a consistent, documented way of running projects, and this documentation is called a methodology. It prescribes what kinds of steps must be taken, what kinds of documents must be produced at each step, what kinds of approvals are needed for certain aspects of the project, how changes will be handled, what records must be filed when the project is closed out, and so on.

At the beginning of this book, you saw a flowchart which I call the Lewis Method for running projects. It is not a methodology because it does not spell out many of the items mentioned above. However, it is the basis for a methodology. If a document is developed that tells what is required at each step in the Lewis Method flowchart, then you have a project methodology.

DOES ONE SIZE FIT ALL?

I have argued elsewhere that my flowchart or method is universal. It can be applied to brain surgery, marketing, product development, cooking a meal, construction, information systems, or any other kind of project you may want to do. That is because the flowchart outlines a thought process that should be followed in doing a project, and that thought process is universal.

> *Principle:* The thought process for running a project is universal. A methodology is not. A methodology will be unique for each organization, because it outlines the procedures that must be followed in that environment.

What is not universal are those specific practices unique to your organization. When you sign off a project plan in step eight of my model, for example, just who is required to sign? When should this be done? Has any work already started? Are there monetary levels for projects that require additional signatures?

These are operating issues specific to your organization, and cannot be addressed by my flowchart. They must be documented by someone in your organization so that everyone follows a consistent approach to their project work.

Now let's go back to the original question—Does one size fit all? If that applies to a methodology, I would say no, not even within an organization. The amount of documentation required

Does "one size" fit all?

for a very small project is inadequate for very large projects and that required for a large project would inundate a small job. So the methodology must be flexible in its requirements, and must be clear about breakpoints where requirements change. The number of approvals on a $5000 project are no doubt fewer than for a $1 million job.

PRODUCT DEVELOPMENT VERSUS PROJECT MANAGEMENT

I was once told by some people in a company that they were going to adopt the Software Institute's Maturity Model for their project management methodology. I told them that the Maturity Model is a product development methodology, not a project management methodology. They asked what the difference is. It is a big one.

A product development methodology deals with such things as how you design for manufacturing, how you run tests, what kinds of qualifications must be met before the product can be sold, and so on. It deals mostly with engineering issues (or in the case of software, with programming issues). A project management method may be applied to nonproduct development projects, but a product development methodology can't be applied to all projects.

It is important to note that you certainly need product and software development guides, in addition to a project management guide. Further, keep in mind that good project management practice will help you do better product and software development. So project management is a supporting practice that will help improve the performance of other areas of the organization's operations.

WHAT A METHODOLOGY SHOULD CONTAIN

A project methodology must unambiguously specify what a manager must do to document, execute, and control a project. It must also specify what approvals are needed for various actions, such as procurement, changes to plan, budget variances, risks, and so on. It should tell who is responsible for various aspects of the project, and should spell out the limits of each stakeholder's authority, responsibility, and accountability.

> *Principle:* Leave nothing to guesswork! The methodology must be unambiguous.

If requirements for documentation, actions, approvals, or whatever vary with kind or size of project, this should also be stated in an unambiguous way. Always use the word "shall" rather than "should." If it is required, say so. Otherwise, you give the impression that an action is at the discretion of the person doing the job.

The methodology should spell out how a kickoff meeting is to be held, who should attend, what they are required to have ready for the meeting, and when it is to take place. The same is true for status, design, and process review meetings.

A methodology should be as simple as possible to get the job done. If you make the requirements a burden, rather than a help, then people will resist following them. You want to achieve a consistent, workable approach to managing projects, not hang a noose around the manager's neck.

The methodology should be written independently of software tools. Otherwise, should you decide to change software, you will have to revise your methodology. If you need procedures for using software, consider putting them in an appendix to the methodology or setting them up

> **The methodology should be written independently of software tools.**

as a stand-alone document. Forms to be filled out should be included. These can be a great help to people who are new to project management.

I would suggest that you consider putting your methodology on-line so that project managers can fill out forms and enter information into their computers. If you use a program like Lotus Notes, it will also replicate the project plan across all user platforms, so everyone has access to data in a current form.

KEY POINTS FOR CHAPTER 12

- *Principle:* The thought process for running a project is universal. A methodology is not. A methodology will be unique for each organization, because it outlines the procedures that must be followed in that environment.
- *Principle:* Leave nothing to guesswork! The methodology must be unambiguous.
- The methodology should be written independently of software tools.

QUESTIONS FOR REVIEW

1. What is the difference between a method and a methodology?
2. Why is a product development methodology different than a project management methodology?

MANAGING PEOPLE
AND TEAMS

Exercising Leadership as a Project Manager

The majority of this book deals with the tools of project management—PERT/CPM, work breakdown structures, earned value analysis, and so on. These are all needed to run projects successfully. However, they are a necessary, but not sufficient, condition for success. Very simply, if you can't get people to use the tools appropriately, then they are of little value to you. This means that you have to exercise leadership. You must be able to influence people to do what needs to be done in the project, and the ways of doing this will be covered in this chapter.

MANAGING VERSUS DOING

One of the traps into which project managers sometimes fall is the "doing" trap. If you have been a technical person for a long time (meaning you do some kind of specific work, whether it be engineering, programming, carpentry, plumbing, or whatever), and you are made a project manager, the temptation is to continue doing that technical work. The technical job is comfortable. Managing is not.

Furthermore, you are seen by the people in the team as a technical person, not a manager, and they may trap you by asking for your help with technical problems, and the next thing you know, you are doing and not managing. I don't mean that you shouldn't help people occasionally, but you must be careful not to do so to the detriment of your management responsibilities.

The really big trap is when the organization puts you into the position of being a *working project manager*. They expect you to both manage the project and carry a significant part of the work itself. The problem is that, when there is a conflict between managing and doing work, the work always takes priority and the managing is pushed aside. The double bind is that, come review time, you get trashed for not doing a better job of managing.

Although we all manage our own work, even as members of a project team, when several people are involved in a project, it quickly becomes a full-time job just to manage. My personal opinion is that organizations are much better off if they designate a few people to be full-time project managers, rather than try to have everyone manage projects and do technical jobs simultaneously. An individual can easily manage several small projects or one large one, but trying to manage even one job while doing the work itself is almost always a problem.

LEADING VERSUS MANAGING

The next issue is whether you are a leader or a manager. In Chapter 3, on the role of the project manager, I stated that being a project manager is a proactive job, as opposed to reactive. You must think like a manager if you are going to be effective, and managers must be essentially

> Leadership is the capacity to translate vision into reality.
> — Warren Bennis

Not all managers are leaders.

proactive. They must be forward thinking, always trying to antici-pate where things might go wrong in the project so that steps can be taken to prevent problems or, if they are unavoidable, to re-cover from them as quickly as possible.

The terms "leader" and "manager" are often used almost synonymously, although we know, on reflection, that not all man-agers are really leaders. It is also true that not all leaders are really good managers. The question is, What is the differ-ence?

Vance Packard de-fined leadership as "the art of getting people to want to do something

> Leadership is the art of getting others to want to do something that you are convinced should be done.
>
> — Vance Packard

that you are convinced should be done." This definition is loaded. The key word is *want*. Dictators get people to do things they want done. Guards over prison work crews get them to do what needs to be done. But that doesn't mean that the people want to do what the dictator or guard tell them to do. They are complying because they are being *coerced.*

> You are only a leader if you have followers.
> — James McGregor Burns

James McGregor Burns (Burns, 1978) wrote that it seems obvious, although it is often overlooked, that you aren't a leader unless you have followers. I would modify that slightly to say *willing* followers.

> We don't need any more leadership training; we need some followership training.
> — Maureen Carroll

He also pointed out that we have studied leadership to the exclusion of followership. We know less about the nature of followership than we do about leadership.

There is a basic premise in understanding human behavior that guides my thinking, and it is that all behavior is an attempt to satisfy needs. All animals, including humans, are goal-oriented. If you are familiar with Maslow's (Maslow, 1970) work, you know that human needs can

> All behavior is an attempt to satisfy human needs.

be grouped into five categories: physical or biological, security and safety, social, self-esteem and recognition, and self-actualization or achievement.

In terms of leadership, this means that if a person is going to want to do something, then the person's needs must be met in the process. Therefore, a leader must know what people need, and must show them that they can satisfy their needs by following his lead, if he is going to exercise leadership.

prestige

• personal growth

The most powerful motivators tend to be those intangible needs that people have.

• recognition   • achievement

Good leaders, then, understand what drives people, and are able to enlist their self-interests in the pursuit of the leader's own goals. Later in this book I discuss the building of pyramids, Stonehenge, and the Mayan temples as examples of projects that required superhuman effort over long periods, and you can't attribute that effort to

> You don't lead by hitting people over the head—that's assault, not leadership.
> — Dwight D. Eisenhower

just feeding the workers three meals a day. The leaders of these people somehow convinced them that the effort was worthwhile and got them excited enough about it so that they labored under sometimes harsh conditions to achieve the leader's goal.

F I G U R E 13.1

Vision, Involvement, Persistence

Leaders adopt a three-phase strategy in getting people to follow them.

Vision

Involvement

Persistence

In fact, the most powerful motivators tend to be those intangible needs that people have. One reason is that physical or biological needs are easily satisfied, whereas intangible needs are virtually insatiable. We can't get enough recognition from others. We can't ever achieve enough. In fact, there is another premise that says the more of some rewards we have, the more we want. This is true of power, money, prestige, and recognition. The more of it people get, the more they want. We sometimes refer to people as power crazy, because the more power they get, the more they crave. It becomes an obsession.

The actual way in which people satisfy their needs is to engage in certain patterns of activity. This is covered in detail in Chapter 14, so I encourage you to read that chapter carefully, to learn how to find out what motivates an individual. In any case, you can see that leadership is essentially an influence process. The question is, How is it actually done in practice?

To answer this question, Kouzes and Posner conducted an extensive study of leaders and documented their findings in a book entitled *The Leadership Challenge*.[1] They write that leaders appear to adopt a three-phase strategy in getting people to follow them, which they call VIP—vision-involvement-persistence. Leaders have dreams or *visions* of what could be. They also recognize that they cannot get there alone, so they work to create the *involvement* of others. Finally, they are *persistent* in working toward their goal. This is shown in Figure 13.1.

THE PRACTICE OF LEADERSHIP

Kouzes and Posner say that vision, involvement, and persistence are expressed through five fundamental practices that enabled the leaders they studied to get extraordinary things done. When they were at their personal best, those leaders practiced the steps shown in Figure 13.2 (Kouzes and Posner, 1987, pp. 6–7).

---

[1] See References and Reading List.

Kouzes & Posner's Steps

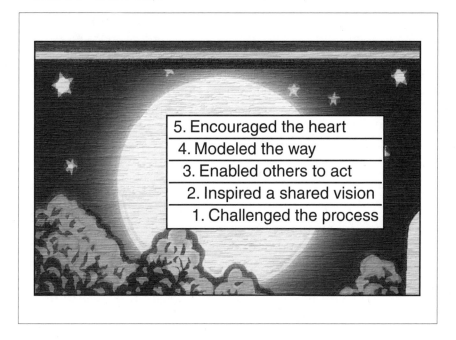

| 5. Encouraged the heart |
| 4. Modeled the way |
| 3. Enabled others to act |
| 2. Inspired a shared vision |
| 1. Challenged the process |

Challenging the Process

Kouzes and Posner[2] state that every case they studied in which a person performed at their personal best involved some kind of challenge. It might have been a business turnaround, some innovative new product, or whatever, but there was always a change in the status quo. Rather than be satisfied to let things continue the way they had always been done, these leaders pushed for a new way.

---

[2] Kouzes and Posner have instruments available to measure how closely a leader conforms to the practices they advocate. These can be ordered from University Associates. See page 531 for phone numbers.

Inspiring a Shared Vision

James McGregor Burns, in his study of political leaders,[3] pointed out that people only follow someone they believe can take them to a destination that they want to reach. Another way of saying this is that they must see something of value in following the other person—they must have some of their needs met.

A sense of purpose, mission, or vision creates in people a great motivation, and leaders are able to create such a shared vision. As Kouzes and Posner state, "A person with no followers is no leader, and people will not become followers until they accept a vision as their own. You cannot command commitment, you can only inspire it.[4]

Enabling Others to Act

A number of years ago David McClelland studied the motivations of corporate executives and found that the need for power is a dominant driving force among those individuals.[5] However, McClelland found that the power motive can be expressed in two ways—the *personal power* motive and the *social power* motive.

He argues that the most effective leaders are those who appeal to what he called the social power motive, which is expressed as the drive to do things together. In today's vernacular, we would say that such leaders *empower* their followers. Rather than tie their hands through domination and restriction, effective leaders make people feel stronger.

Reinforcing McClelland's position, Kouzes and Posner say that there is a one-word test to determine whether someone is on the way to success as a leader. That word is *we*. Leaders can't do it alone.

Some try, however. McClelland found that ineffective leaders are inclined to use the personal power motive, which is character-

---

[3]   See References and Reading List.

[4]   Op.cit., p. 9.

[5]   McClelland, *Power, the Inner Experience,* see References and Reading List.

Leaders empower their followers.

ized by the word I. These leaders tend to be authoritarian, self-centered, and insensitive to the wants and needs of their followers.

By listening to leaders talk, McClelland found that you can tell which power motive they generally adopt. You hear the word *we* with those leaders who have social power as a driving force, whereas the word *I* predominates for the others.

The Chinese sage Lao Tse knew about this aspect of leadership and described it several thousand years ago, as the quotation in Table 13.1 shows.[6]

Modeling the Way

Effective leaders lead by example. They are role models for their followers. They practice what they preach, and they also live their values. Employees are very quick to point out the discrepancies

---

[6]   R. L. Wing, *The Tao of Power*. Doubleday, NY, 1986.

T A B L E 13.1

The Way of Subtle Influence

Superior leaders are those whose existence
   is merely known;
The next best are loved and honored;
The next are respected;
And the next are ridiculed.

Those who lack belief
Will not in turn be believed.
But when the command comes from afar
And the work is done, the goal achieved,
The people say, "We did it naturally."

between a manager's stated values and her behavior. When a manager's behavior is not consistent with her stated beliefs, people ultimately will lose respect for her.

Encouraging the Heart

Difficult objectives can cause people to become frustrated, exhausted, and disenchanted. Leaders must encourage them in order to keep them from giving up. The leader has to show them that they can win. In addition, leaders must give themselves encouragement.

THE SELF-FULFILLING PROPHECY

The self-fulfilling prophecy is one of the most important principles from psychology, at least for leaders. The principle is that you tend to get what you expect from others. Thus, if you expect poor performance from a person, you will tend to get it, and conversely.

Principle: You tend to get what you expect from others.

For leaders, the self-fulfilling prophecy is one of the most important principles from psychology.

Support for the Self-Fulfilling Prophecy

A well-known account of the experiments which indicated that the self-fulfilling prophecy might be valid was published by Rosenthal and Jacobson.[7] Children were given aptitude tests, and were then paired up according to test scores, race, and sex. Thus, two black boys having equal scores would be paired, and so on. Their teacher was not told the actual test scores. Instead, for each pair of children, the teacher was told that one child was average, whereas the other was a "late bloomer." The average child would do all right in school, but the late bloomer could be expected to do really well that year. So the teacher was told.

---

[7]   R. Rosenthal and L. Jacobson, *Pygmalion in the Classroom*, Holt, Rinehart, and Winston, NY, 1968.

Later that school year, the academic performance of the children was checked, and the late bloomers were found to be doing better, on the average, than their counterparts. The only logical explanation for this is that the teacher somehow brought about the expected performance because of the bias presented by the experimenter. But how was this done?

Subsequent studies showed that teachers were more supportive of the late bloomer, more helpful, offered more encouragement, and were more patient when the late bloomer was having difficulty. Thus, the child performed better because the teacher expected it. The average child was not so strongly encouraged, and so did not work as hard as the late bloomer. Thus, the self-fulfilling prophecy comes true.[8]

It Works in Management, Too!

On the basis of this principle, McGregor developed a management model which suggested that the views which managers have of employees might bring about such a self-fulfilling prophecy. He believed that the supervisor's view of employees can be called a "working theory" about employees, and that such views can be placed on a continuum, on one end of which is the Theory-X position, with Theory-Y on the other.

The Theory-X manager thinks employees are poorly motivated, lazy, interested only in pay, and so on. The Theory-Y manager sees employees as motivated, interested in their jobs, and so on. This is shown in Figure 13.3. In other words, it is the opposite of the Theory-X view. According to McGregor, the manager who holds a Theory-X view of employees will tend to get poor performance from them and vice versa.

Although this theory is generally correct, I believe that it needs clarification. It is tempting to view the leader as having uni-

---

[8]   This description of the Rosenthal and Jacobson work has been simplified and stripped of its academic jargon, so the person not familiar with the terminology can follow the essence of the results obtained. Those interested in a fuller exposition will find an excellent treatment in the book by Russel A. Jones, *Self-Fulfilling Prophecies*, Lawrence Erlbaum, Hillsdale, NJ, 1977.

F I G U R E   13.3

Theory X, Theory Y

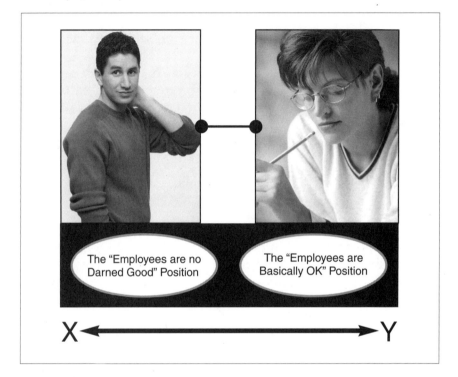

directional influence in the interaction with followers, whereas the influence is really *bidirectional*. That is, the follower influences the leader and is also influenced by the leader. This is shown in Figure 13.4.

No doubt the reason that the self-fulfilling prophecy works in the classroom is that the strength of the teacher's influence is greater than that of the student. In the workplace, however, the supervisor does not always have greater influence on employees than they have on him. For that reason, the supervisor's expectations do not always bring about the predicted result.

In my experience as a manager, I found the X-influence seemed to be a bit stronger than the Y-influence, so the X-employ-

Bidirectional Influence

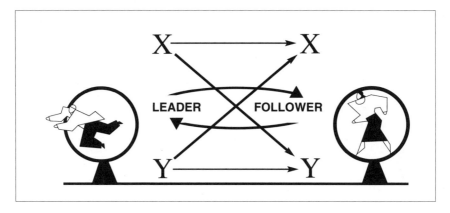

ee eventually caused the supervisor to lose her normal Y-outlook. However, it is a matter of degree. If the supervisor can maintain a Y-outlook in the face of an employee's X-behavior, then she may turn that employee around. Certainly, one is generally likely to get better results with the Y-outlook than its opposite.

Actions Speak Louder than Words

As was previously mentioned, a leader who espouses one thing and then behaves inconsistently with the stated position will not be believed or trusted. For that reason, you cannot *fake* a Theory-Y outlook. You can't tell your followers that you trust and have confidence in them when you

> You can't fake being Theory-Y. People see through your charade.

don't, because your behavior will contradict your words. For example, if you really don't trust someone, you will let them know it by looking over his shoulder fairly often, asking questions that convey your distrust, and in many other ways.

Organizations tend to convey a Theory-X or Y outlook in the policies and procedures that they establish. To illustrate, consider that most adults can make major purchases on their own volition (perhaps in consultation with their spouses, of course). They do not have to obtain permission from their parents to buy a new car or house, which might amount to many thousands of dollars.

That same individual, however, finds that she cannot spend $15 of the organization's money without permission from the "powers that be." (These are our organizational parents!) Heaven forbid! She might spend that $15 unwisely, and after all, you can't expect management to meet profit objectives if every person in the company can just spend money willy-nilly.

Interestingly, managers will tell employees that they must have approval to spend $15, and in the very next breath tell them that they must all behave *responsibly!* Isn't that incredible? If you treat people as though they are irresponsible, how can you expect them to behave responsibly?

It seems to me that the way to deal with this problem would be to give every employee who might have the discretion to spend

Let her be responsible for her own budget and hold her accountable.

money an individual budget. After all, the organization essentially has to create such a budget anyway. Each employee costs the company so much to support, so why not let the person have his own budget and *hold him responsible for it!* So long as he spends the money wisely, he can spend it any way he chooses, in support of his job. If he proves untrustworthy, then his manager should deal with him individually, rather than make a policy to tie the hands of everyone.

> If you treat people as though they are responsible, they tend to behave that way.

In Chapter 14, when motivation is discussed, it will be clear why I am advocating this. For now, suffice it to say that the best way to get people to behave responsibly is to treat them as if they are. The self-fulfilling prophecy works in all arenas of life.

CHOOSING A LEADERSHIP STYLE

Of course there must be controls. There must be accountability. Certainly a manager cannot just turn everything over to the follower. The question is, How is a manager to know just how to supervise an employee? Should the person be supervised closely? Would a participative style be best? Or could delegation be employed?

I think the answer is provided by a model of leadership developed originally by Hersey and Blanchard,[9] which I have modified, using my own terms. Their model was based on the fact that there are two primary components in the *behavior* of leaders toward their followers. One is the emphasis which leaders place on getting the *task* done. The other is how they deal with their followers in terms of interpersonal or *relationship* dimensions. These are defined as follows:

---

[9] Instruments which measure a leader's conformance to the Hersey and Blanchard model can be ordered from Pfeiffer. See the Resources section after the Appendix.

Task behavior is communication on the part of a manager aimed at the task itself. When task behavior is high, the supervisor defines the follower's role, tells the person what, when, how, and where to do the job, and then closely supervises performance.

Relationship behavior is the way in which the supervisor attends to the follower at the personal level. When relationship behavior is high (strong), the supervisor listens, provides support, and involves the follower in decision making.

The two dimensions can be combined, using only high or low levels of each, into four "styles" of leader behavior. These are illustrated in Figure 13.5.

F I G U R E 13.5

My Model of Leadership

	High
Participative	Influence
LT-HR 3 2 HT-HR	
4 1	
Delegative	Hand-Holding
LT-LR	HT-LR

Relationship

Low   Task   High

The word *behavior* is very important to note. This model deals only with how a leader behaves toward a follower, not with her attitude or feelings about the follower. Blake and Mouton have a model called the GRID™, which emphasizes the leader's *attitude* toward task and relationship, and is based on the self-fulfilling prophecy, which says that you will get from people what you expect, so you should have high expectations for task and relationship. There is no quarrel with this. The situational leadership model emphasizes how a leader should actually behave toward a follower, and also advocates that the leader expect both high task and high relationship outcomes. The two models are very different, and should not be confused. See References and Reading List for citation of Blake and Mouton's work.

The *hand-holding* style would sound something like this: "I have a job for you to do. Here are the details (leader outlines task details). It must be done by 3 o'clock today. I want you to do it this way (tells follower specifically how to do the work). I'll check back in a little while, but if you run into a snag, let me know immediately, so I can help you."

The *influence* style sounds exactly like the hand-holding style, up to a point. Here it is: "I have a job for you to do. Here are the details (leader outlines task details). It must be done by 3 o'clock today. I want you to do it this way (tells follower specifically how to do the work). [Here it changes.] The reason I want you to do it this way is (explains rationale for procedure). I'm sure you'll do a good job. I'll check back in a little while, but if you run into a snag, let me know immediately, so I can help you."

The *participative* style sounds like this: "I have a job for you. Here's what it's all about (describes the job). Let's kick around some ideas about how to do it. What do you think?"

Finally, *delegative* sounds like this in the extreme case: "I have a job for you. Here it is. You need anything from me? Any questions? Great! Drive on!"

The style which is best depends on the nature of the situation, which is a combination of the follower's skills and the difficulty of the job to be done.

Note that the proper style depends on how you answer the questions:

Can the person do the job?

Will the person take responsibility for doing it?

The dimensions of *can* and *will* combine to yield what might be called the person's job *maturity*. If the person's job maturity is very low, you need to do a lot of hand-holding. On the other hand, you can delegate to a high-maturity follower.

By combining the *can* and *will* answers, the appropriate style to use can be determined using the following guide:

Hand-holding: Follower is unable and unwilling
                  or insecure.

Influence: Follower is unable but willing to
                  do the job.

Participative: Follower is able but unwilling or
                  lacks confidence.

Delegative: Follower is both able and willing.

Following this model, an interesting point can be made. As an employee's job maturity increases, the supervisor can eventually delegate to him. This frees the supervisor to attend to other matters. For that reason, it is clear that delegative management would be the ideal style, despite the strong advocacy for participative management. However, it is difficult to get all employees into quadrant four, so participative style is probably a good "average."

Nevertheless, part of a leader's responsibility is to develop people over time so that they are moved from quadrant 1 to 2, then to 3, and finally to 4. At that point, the follower can be promoted or given more responsibility. This will cause his/her job maturity to drop, so that a quadrant two or three style will have to be adopted until the person is pulled back into quadrant four, where the process starts again.

Over time, leaders continue to "slide" followers back and forth along the curve (as shown in Figure 13.5), until the follower arrives at the same competence level as the leader. (One hopes that by the time this happens, the leader will have advanced because his or her boss applied the same model to him or her.)

Of course, not all people want to advance beyond a certain level, so for them, this process cannot continue indefinitely. Note also, that if an employee is promoted "too far, too fast," then that person may become a victim of the Peter Principle, which states, "Employees eventually rise to their level of incompetence" (Peter, 1969).

It is up to managers to see that employees are not promoted to a level of incompetence and then just left there. If a person is put into a position that is over his head, then the supervisor should begin pulling that person back up or remove him from that position.

In a project environment, this model can be used by a manager to decide just how much freedom members of a project team can be given. If they work for a functional manager, then that person should be practicing this model. However, if they do not know the model, the project manager can explain it and suggest to the functional manager how the person should be supervised.

If a very inexperienced person is assigned to the project and her supervisor does not provide hand-holding supervision, the project manager would have cause for alarm, and should discuss his concerns with that functional manager. If the manager is the kind of person who prefers to loosely supervise everyone, then the project manager might have to request that a more experienced person be assigned or, if possible, supervise the person himself.

Whatever the case, the model provides a practical way of deciding how to supervise people, and emphasizes that no single style is adequate.

KEY POINTS FOR CHAPTER 13

- One of the traps into which project managers sometimes fall is the "doing" trap.
- The really big trap is when the organization puts you into the position of being a *working project manager*.
- Leadership is the art of getting others to want to do something that you are convinced should be done.

- You are only a leader if you have followers.
- The self-fulfilling prophecy says that you tend to get what you expect from others.
- You can't fake being Theory-Y. People see through your charade.
- The appropriate style of leadership depends on the maturity of the follower. No single style is "best."

QUESTIONS FOR REVIEW

1. What is the difference between leading and managing?
2. On what psychological premise is McGregor's Theory-X, Theory-Y model based?
3. What is the one flaw in the self-fulfilling prophecy when applied to management?
4. You have a "green" college graduate working on your project. She has never worked anywhere before. What leadership style is likely to be best for her initially?

How to Motivate
Almost Anyone

When the Egyptians built their pyramids, the project leaders probably didn't have to worry much about motivating the people who worked on the job. Many of them were slaves. Their motivation was to stay alive.

However, that does not explain the accomplishments of hundreds of other project leaders who built astonishing monuments that inspire awe in us today. Through the centuries, they have been able to coordinate the efforts of thousands of people to build the henges in the British Isles, the beautiful temples of the Mayas, and others too numerous to mention. How did these project leaders motivate the people to do backbreaking work without using threats of punishment or death or the great carrot of today—money?

In my 10 years of teaching seminars throughout the United States, Canada, and San Juan, the most frequently asked question is undoubtedly, "How do you motivate people?" There seems to

How to Get People Started

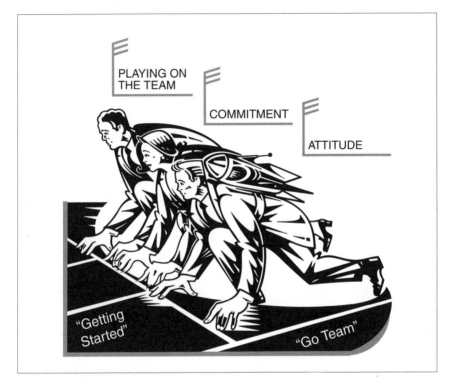

be almost universal concern that people are not motivated to perform those jobs that need to be done in the workplace. The consensus among managers seems to be that the only reason many
people come to work is to get a paycheck. They have a somewhat
Theory-X outlook, to use McGregor's terminology.

I have concluded from conversations with thousands of people that, in many cases, what they really mean by their question is,
"How do we get people to want to do jobs that no one in their
right mind would want to do?" When it comes to motivation, I'm
afraid we have some very unrealistic attitudes. Perhaps it is because we don't really understand what motivation is all about.

In several of my classes, there have been individuals who engage in cliff climbing as a sport. In one class, someone asked the cliff climber, "What do you think about when you're up there on that cliff?"

"Do you really want to know?" he asked.

"Yes."

"I'm thinking, 'If I ever get off this thing, I'll never do this again!'"

"Really!?"

"Yes. Really!"

The questioner looked puzzled. "Then I don't understand. Why do you do it again?"

The cliff climber thought for a moment, then said, "I don't know. Maybe I'm crazy, but someone tells me about another cliff somewhere that is a real challenge, and I can't wait to see if I can do it."

The cliff-climber enjoys the challenge and continues to do so without being paid.

SELF-MOTIVATION

This example strikes me as demonstrating the essence of what we mean by motivation. The cliff climber has a built-in drive to engage in his sport, and all you have to do is tell him about a cliff that is a challenge, and he can't wait to try it. No one has to pay him. He doesn't have to be begged, threatened, or persuaded. He does it because of a drive from within himself. And that is what motivation is all about.

True motivation comes from within the individual. We call such motivation *intrinsic*. Any attempt to get someone to want to do something by offering him external rewards is an effort to use *extrinsic* motivation.

In my own case, I have no intrinsic drive to climb cliffs. I have vertigo, so if I get 10 feet off the ground, I get dizzy. For that reason, no one can arouse in me a desire to climb a sheer rock cliff.

"Suppose someone gave you a million dollars?" a person asked me once. "Would that motivate you to do it?" My response was, "I might climb a cliff to get a million dollars, but I would not be motivated by the task itself, and once I had finished it and collected my million dollars, I certainly would not likely want to do it again."

This leads people to believe that you can motivate someone with money. It is an argument that probably goes back to the invention of money over 2500 years ago, and it is a very heated argument. Those people who are adamant that they themselves are motivated by money miss a subtle point. It is not the money itself that motivates, but all the things they know they can do with the money that "turns them on."

Money is a *symbol* for many things—power, security, prestige, status, comfort, and all the other things that humans desire. So when you offer people a lot of money to do something, they may perform admirably, because they are thinking of what the money represents—or of what they can do with it. The interesting thing is, if they were not paid again to perform that same task, they probably never would.

The cliff climber, on the other hand, continues to climb cliffs, even though no one pays him to do so. What we should learn from this is that *intrinsic* motivation is durable. *Extrinsic* motiva-

tion exists only so long as the external rewards are available. As soon as they are withdrawn, the individual no longer cares to perform the task.

In my opinion, the real conclusion to be drawn from this is that the only *real* motivation is intrinsic. The term extrinsic, although it is used by psychologists and other professional students of motivation, is a misnomer. For that reason, we need to adopt a realistic approach to motivation in organizations and use intrinsic factors as much as possible.

This is contrary to majority practice, and I believe it is the reason organizations have so much difficulty with motivation. They have relied almost exclusively on extrinsic factors to motivate people, and failed to take advantage of intrinsic factors. What this means is that we should try to place people in jobs that they find intrinsically motivating, rather than give them jobs that are boring, unchallenging, or mindless, and then try to get them turned on by using externals.

Another point that seems to be overlooked is that we all must do some things that virtually no one wants to do. Around our homes, for example, the toilet must be cleaned, the house must be painted, the grass must be cut, and for some people, those chores are no fun at all. Yet they do them because they are necessary. (As someone said to me, the alternatives are unacceptable!)

The thing is, we all know that, although we do those tasks—such as cleaning the toilet—we are not turned on to the task, but are looking forward to finishing it, so we can do something that we really enjoy.

The same thing is true of organizations. There are, figuratively speaking, toilet-cleaning jobs at work. What we must realize is that, although someone must do those jobs, we cannot expect people to be turned on to the task, and it is senseless to beat our heads against the wall trying to find a way to motivate a person to clean toilets.

What we should do is to distribute the toilet-cleaning jobs as evenly as possible, so no one person gets stuck having to do them all the time, and we should attempt to eliminate as many of them as possible.

Given that we do this, the question still remains, "How do you know what kind of work will be intrinsically motivating to a person?" and this is *the* legitimate question we should ask. If we can answer this question for most of the people who work for us—and apply it—then most of the problems with motivation in the workplace will be solved, and the remainder will not be of so much concern.

There are two theoretical models that have been taught for over 30 years in an attempt to help managers find out how to motivate people. One is Maslow's need hierarchy and the other is Herzberg's motivation-hygiene factors. Both have merits, but managers who have attempted to apply them have often had limited success.

What is needed is a method of finding out for each individual what motivates him/her, and that is something that the models do not deliver. Such a technique has been devised, and will be presented later in this chapter. First, however, it is useful to know what Maslow and Herzberg said about motivation, because they provide a conceptual base from which to work.

MASLOW'S HIERARCHY

Human beings have a large number of needs. When those needs are active, we are motivated to satisfy them. Abraham Maslow suggested that human needs can be grouped into five general categories that vary in strength, depending on whether they have been recently satisfied. He arranged those needs in a hierarchy, because he believed that the category at the bottom of the hierarchy (the lower-level needs) must be satisfied before the upper-level needs emerge. His hierarchy is shown in Figure 14.2. The terms have the following meanings:

- *Self-actualization:* The need to be everything one is capable of being. Self-mastery.
- *Esteem:* The need to be thought well of by significant others.
- *Social:* The need to affiliate with other people.
- *Safety:* The need to provide for unexpected happenings and to feel secure from harm.
- *Physiological:* The biological needs, including hunger, warmth, sex, shelter, and so on.

Maslow suggested that the lower three levels of his hierarchy are basic maintenance needs. The individual must have these needs met in order to experience well-being. The top two levels are those that are important in bringing about valued organizational performance. The manager's job, according to the theory, is to help individuals satisfy those basic maintenance needs so that the needs for recognition (or esteem) and self-actualization will become active.

F I G U R E 14.2

Maslow's Hierarchy

In my experience, this is easier to say than to do. It is very difficult to know exactly where in the hierarchy an individual falls and how to help him or her satisfy basic maintenance needs.

In his book about personality types and temperaments, Keirsey (1998) wrote that only some people are concerned with self-actualization, specifically the Idealist temperament. The other three temperaments, called Guardian, Artisan, and Rationalist, are not self-actualizers. Keirsey says that Maslow was an Idealist temperament, so he believed that everyone wants to self-actualize. This is because we tend to believe that others are motivated in the same way that we are, and will, in fact, try to motivate others using our own approach. So it may be that Maslow's top need does not apply to everyone.

Furthermore, there is very little research evidence that supports Maslow's theory that needs are arranged in a hierarchy. Of course, Maslow suggested that all levels of the hierarchy can be active at once, rather than progressing in an all-or-nothing manner. That is, physiological needs do not have to be satisfied completely before higher-level needs emerge. However, it seems intuitively correct to say that a starving person will not be too concerned about higher-level needs until his hunger has been satisfied.

Nevertheless, counterexamples of the hierarchy can be found. The "starving artist" may be said to be self-actualizing, despite the fact that her lower-level needs may not be met. She is so totally consumed by the drive to express herself through her art that she suppresses the lower-level needs. I would add that she is expressing a very strong quadrant D preference for thinking, using the Herrmann Brain Dominance model as a guide. In fact, I believe that thinking preferences go hand in hand with our motivation patterns, but I don't know that there is any research evidence to support my belief.

In any case, this is an interesting example that should serve as a guide to how people are actually motivated. Many people disprove the hierarchy by their actions. The athlete who submits to grueling training exercises in pursuit of excellence in his sport is an example. So is the engineer who spends long hours struggling to solve some very difficult technical problem. Likewise, the entrepreneur who works seven days a week for long periods to build a business disproves the idea that lower-level needs must be satisfied first.

Such examples actually imply that, when people give themselves totally to something that for them is a way of fully expressing themselves (self-actualizing), they are not very concerned about the lower needs. Again, this suggests that we must change our approach to motivation in the workplace. If we can somehow help the individual become self-actualizing, then the lower-level needs become less important.

HERZBERG'S MOTIVATION-HYGIENE FACTORS

Another model of motivation that has gained widespread attention is Herzberg's motivation-hygiene theory. Unlike Maslow's

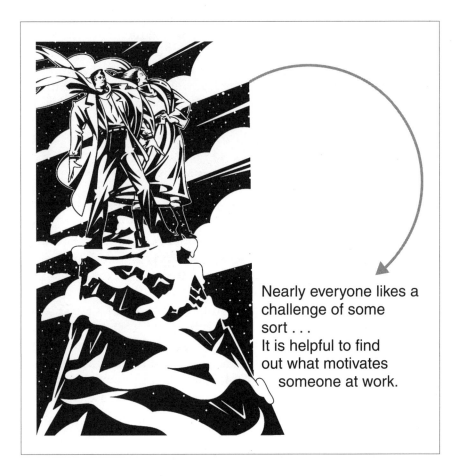

model, which was largely based on theoretical construction, Herzberg's model was derived from empirical research.

Herzberg conducted a number of field studies in which he asked workers to tell what things in their jobs "turned them on" and what things "turned them off." From an extensive analysis of the data, Herzberg concluded that the things that affect motivation could be boiled down to a limited number of general factors. He called those factors that turn people off *hygiene* or *maintenance* factors, and he called the others *motivator* factors. These are shown in Table 14.1.

T A B L E 14.1

Herzberg's Motivation and Hygiene Factors

Motivation factors	Hygiene factors
■ Achievement	■ Company policy and administration
■ Recognition	■ Supervision
■ Work Itself	■ Relationship with supervisor
■ Responsibility	■ Work conditions
■ Advancement	■ Salary
■ Growth	■ Relationships with peers
	■ Personal life
	■ Relationships with subordinates
	■ Status
	■ Security

The hygiene factors, according to Herzberg, will turn people off to their jobs if they are not satisfied, but if they *are* satisfied, they do very little to motivate a person. That is, if they are satisfactory, they are neutral in terms of motivation, but if they are unsatisfactory, they are negative, or demotivators.

The application of Herzberg's model must take into account a characteristic of people that is well understood at the personal level, but seems to be poorly comprehended in work situations. The principle is that, when people are in pain, their pain takes precedence over pleasure. We all know how debilitating a severe headache can be. It is difficult to enjoy activities that would ordinarily be very pleasurable when one has a bad headache.

In other words, a person cannot be turned on and turned off at the same time, and being turned off takes priority. Stated in more formal terms, a person cannot experience two opposite emotions simultaneously.

Given that this is true, Herzberg said that we must take care of the hygiene factors first, before we attempt to apply the motivators. That is, if the hygiene factors in an organization are unsatisfactory, they will cause people to be demotivated, and they must be "cleaned up" before the motivators can be applied.

Of course, it is not an all-or-nothing proposition. The hygiene factors can be a bit unsatisfactory and a person can still be motivated, but if the degree of "discomfort" becomes very high, then motivation will suffer.

However, in some organizations, the hygiene factors are so greatly out of line for so many employees that, if they were taken care of, those organizations would probably find that they actually have very little problem with motivation. Indeed, it is my belief that this is true for most organizations.

For example, the first item listed under hygiene factors is company policy. This is one of the most common offenders, in my experience. As Tom Peters argues in his book, *Thriving on Chaos*, organizations have so many "Mickey Mouse" policies that it is no wonder employees are disgruntled.

Many companies have a policy that establishes a spending limit on employees.[1] The limit goes up as the level of the employee increases, but there is always a limit. There is no quarrel with such a policy in general. The quarrel is with the *level* of the limit.

Tom Peters tells about one newly hired engineering director who discovered that his engineers had a $25 limit. Anything that they wanted to buy for more than $25 had to be approved by someone higher in the organization. He raised the level to $200. The accounting department screamed bloody murder. "Those people will take us to the cleaners," they claimed. "You have no control over spending now." The result? Spending dropped 60 percent.

The reason? The engineers were so insulted at being treated like children (as they saw it) that they were playing "stick-it-

---

[1]   This was discussed in Chapter 13. It is reiterated here with an example which demonstrates that treating employees as though they are responsible does indeed accomplish that result.

to-them." Their response was, let's see how many $24.99 things we can buy—they don't have to be approved.

It might be argued that such action proves the validity of the policy. They were behaving irresponsibly. The evidence does not warrant that conclusion, however. As soon as they were treated as though they were responsible, they began to behave that way.

It is my feeling that most policies represent a "cop-out" on the part of management. Because a few employees behave badly, the organization makes a policy that is intended to limit the behavior of all employees. They do this, rather than deal one-on-one with the offenders, and thereby lose the loyalty and commitment of "good" employees.

Among the hygiene factors, the word "relationship" occurs several times. When employees are in relationships at work that are disagreeable, they are turned off, and one of the most important of those is the relationship with the supervisor. This is why supervisors—in this case, project managers—must work to maintain good relationships with team members.

This does not mean that the manager must run a popularity contest, or that all relationships will be of a highly friendly nature. It does mean that all relationships must be built on mutual respect. Where this is not possible, the employee should be transferred to another supervisor (if possible), both for the benefit of the employee and the supervisor with whom the bad relationship exists.

In support of what was said at the beginning of this chapter about salary, Herzberg found that for 80 to 90 percent of his respondents, pay is a hygiene factor. That is, if pay is satisfactory, it is neutral in terms of motivation, but if it is unsatisfactory, it is negative.

There are two components to whether pay is satisfactory. First, is it in line with what one's peers are making? Women in our society are sometimes victims of this. Why should a man make more than a woman for doing the same job?

Second, is the person's pay adequate to meet her needs? If not, then she will be dissatisfied, and will take steps to correct the problem. That often means leaving the job, because it is sometimes impossible to get a larger salary.

Pay can serve as an extrinsic source of motivation when there is a direct correlation between performance and pay. That is the intention of piece-rate and commission sales jobs and, indeed, people will usually work harder under those conditions to make more money. Unfortunately, numerous stories are told about companies that change the pay or commission scale to keep employees from making more than some maximum level, thereby creating resentment and destroying any incentive to work.

The other factors in the list are fairly straightforward. When people are made to feel like low-status individuals (by treating them as if they are not important, for example), when they feel that their job security is threatened (by automation, among other things), or when working conditions are bad, they will be demotivated.

To sum up Herzberg's "prescription," problems with the hygiene factors should be corrected before an attempt is made to apply the motivators. The problem is, most project managers have limited control over these factors. Still, that does not mean *zero* control, and every manager should do whatever is possible to correct for any hygiene factors that are a problem. If direct control is not possible, one can at least lobby with higher-level managers to have them corrected.

Assuming that the hygiene factors have been taken care of, the motivators can be applied. These are all intangibles, and correspond roughly to the top two levels of Maslow's Hierarchy, as shown in Figure 14.3. The problem, however, is still the same. How do you determine which of these factors will motivate a specific individual?

F I G U R E 14.3

Maslow and Herzberg Compared

Wonder what's happening at the office?

What about unresponsive Al?

WHAT ABOUT UNRESPONSIVE AL?

What indeed? What do you do about Al, who does not respond when you take care of the hygiene factors and try to challenge him? What about Al, who seems to have less drive than a snail? "How do I motivate him?" you ask. Well, before you go too far, you need to answer a basic question, which is, "Is it worth the effort?"

"Gee, isn't that a bit callous?" you may ask. No. We are too easily trapped into trying to "save" employees who cannot and should not be saved. In my opinion, the most respectful and kindest way to deal with another person is to expect of them the best that they can do.

If they choose to not respond to that expectation, which I cannot force on them, I can move them into a job that suits them or remove them from my organization if I have no such match. To keep someone in a slot for which they have no skills, incentive to perform, or whatever, is unfair to the person and to all other employees who are performing adequately, in my opinion.

Two questions must be answered before attempting to motivate Al:

- Does Al have the *potential* to perform adequately in the job?
- Does Al *want* to perform adequately in the job?

Unless you can answer "yes" to both questions, you should consider transferring Al to another job or terminating him.

MOTIVATION PATTERNS: A NEW MODEL OF MOTIVATION

Suppose you decide that Al has potential and wants to do a good job, but for some reason the job doesn't challenge him. How can you determine what *would* challenge him?

You could ask him, but he, like many people, may not be able to tell you. They have never really thought about it. For others, they don't want to tell you—for any number of reasons. You could try giving Al a lot of different assignments, until you find one that turns him on, but that consumes a lot of time, which is something you don't have much of in a project environment. So you need a method of finding out what motivates Al that can be done fairly quickly, and that gives an accurate answer.

Such a method does exist, and I have used it throughout the United States with several thousand people, and have found only a very small number (less than a dozen) for whom the method didn't work. Here are examples of the questions I ask:

- Tell me about some job you've had, during the past six months to a year, that you really enjoyed. You looked forward to working on it, put a lot of yourself into it, perhaps thought about it on the way to work, considering what you were going to do about some particular aspect of the job. I don't need to know a lot of heavy technical detail, but I want to know the part you played in the job, what you feel you contributed to it, and so on.

Note: Don't say, "Tell me about your present job and what you like about it." The person may currently be in a job that is demotivating.

If they can't think of any jobs they have had during that time frame, I ask them to think back over their entire careers and have them tell me about the one job that stands out in their minds.

As they tell me about the job, I pay very close attention—make notes if necessary, and probe for additional information. Next, I ask:

- Now let me ask if you have some hobbies, sports, or other outside interests that you like to spend time with. If they tell me no, I go back and ask for more job examples (or move to the final question that I will present later). When they say they do have some outside interests, I ask them to pick one that they would spend more time doing if they had it. Activities that really motivate people cause them to want to spend more time with them, but most of us have limited time to spend on our hobbies.

The pitfall here is that someone will tell you he likes to jog, which he does because he thinks he should for health reasons, but he wouldn't spend more time doing it if the time were made available. Such activities are not motivators as such, so I avoid them, and ask the person to give me another example.

Finally, I say:

- Now tell me—is there anything you've always wanted to do but never got to do—maybe because you didn't have the time or money, or your family responsibilities prevented it? Call it a fantasy or wish list if you like. Is there anything like that? If so, tell me about it.

These questions can be used as presented, or if the person cannot relate to one of them, you can use the other two. In other words, I could use jobs, hobbies, or wish lists alone or in any combination, so long as I have at least three examples of something that motivates the person.

Now what you do is look for the common thread or pattern that runs through the three motivators, and the important thing here is that it is the *pattern of activity* that is the motivator, not the content of the activity, per se. People achieve self-actualization through engaging in a repetitive pattern of activity. Once you have determined that pattern of activity, you can then try to give the person assignments that contain that pattern.

As an example, some people are motivated by a pattern of activity that can be described as the *troubleshooter* pattern. They love to fix things. Give them a broken *anything* (within reason, of course) and they are driven to repair it.

Another pattern is the *innovator.* The person who is an innovator is always trying to come up with something new. Thomas Edison undoubtedly was motivated by innovation.

There is also the *helper.* Many helpers are found in education, nursing, counseling, and volunteer positions. They are turned on by being able to be helpful to others.

However, I prefer not to create too many labels for patterns. There is a temptation to "pigeonhole" people into categories and miss important characteristics that do not fit a particular mold. For that reason, I encourage people to stay open to whatever information the person offers, and determine the pattern without attempting to label it.

It is also important to note that nearly everyone likes a challenge of some kind. However, what is a challenge for one would not be a challenge for another. The challenge of cliff climbing would be sheer terror for me, for example. So before you conclude glibly that the person likes a challenge, you must be able to say what that means for that particular individual.

Once you know the pattern of activity that motivates a person, you can try to assign work that will contain that pattern. If you have no such job, the information is useful because you now know why she has been unmotivated by the job she has had and you can find another solution.

If this is the case, then transfer or termination are possible. Or—and this is always an option—you may decide that you can live with the person's level of performance. I don't recommend this very often, but there are circumstances that might justify it, such as when the individual has only another year or so until retirement and he has been with the company 25 years and in the past was an acceptable worker. For most people, however, I still prefer to see them work at full capacity (which is a value judgment on my part).

In order to learn this method, I have devised an exercise that I use in my seminars (see Table 14.2). You can also do it yourself, if you follow the instructions. I suggest that you do this with two other people, because if there is just one other person, you have to do everything yourself. It takes some practice to become comfortable with the questioning method, and also to learn to find the pattern that runs through the three examples. By practicing with two other people, you will feel more comfortable when you apply it to an employee.

T A B L E 14.2

Exercise: Eliciting Motivation Patterns

---

1. Get into groups of three people each. One person will be the interviewer, one the subject, and one the observer/timekeeper. In class, you should limit yourselves to about 15 minutes to get information from the subject and process it.
2. The interviewer asks the subject the questions outlined in the text above. The observer should pay close attention, so he or she can help the interviewer process that information when the interview is completed.
3. After all the information has been obtained, the interviewer and observer should put their heads together to see if they can find the pattern. Make sure it seems right to the subject. If the subject objects, look more closely. You probably missed something.
4. Now rotate, twice, so that all three of you "play" all three roles.

CAUTION: Be careful not to "lead" the subject too much, or you will get *your* motivation pattern and not his or hers.

KEY POINTS FOR CHAPTER 14

- Real motivation is internal to the person, and is *called intrinsic*. Extrinsic motivation is an attempt to use rewards such as money or recognition to give the person incentive to do something.
- Motivation is the arousal of built-in drives. If a drive does not exist, there is nothing to arouse.
- Maslow grouped human needs into five categories and arranged them in a hierarchy, and said that the lower-level needs must be satisfied in order for the upper-level needs to emerge.
- Herzberg called hygiene factors those aspects of the work situation that are neutral if they are satisfactory, but that turn people off if they are not okay.
- The hygiene factors should be taken care of first, because a person cannot be turned on and turned off at the same time.
- A person achieves self-actualization by engaging in a repetitive pattern of activity. Once that pattern is known, the person can be given job assignments that contain the pattern.

QUESTIONS FOR REVIEW

1. What is motivation?
2. Why did Maslow say that lower-level needs must be met in order for a person to become self-actualizing?
3. In what way do people self-actualize?
4. If Herzberg's hygiene factors are problems for employees, what might be the result?
5. In what way are motivation and commitment related?
6. Is it possible for a manager to motivate an employee?

Developing the Project Team and Working with People Issues

Because of the tremendous interest in project management just now, the word *team* may well be one of the most misused words in the English language. Everyone has a project team, unless they are doing a one-person project.

I'm sorry, but there are a lot of so-called project teams around that simply don't qualify as real teams. In many cases, they aren't even good herds. At least the cows in a herd will follow the lead cow. Some of our project teams won't follow anyone!

> Why did the chicken cross the road?
> To get away from that team of chickens!

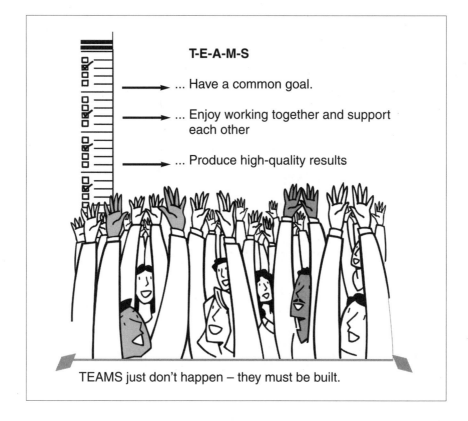

T-E-A-M-S

... Have a common goal.

... Enjoy working together and support each other

... Produce high-quality results

TEAMS just don't happen – they must be built.

At best, some of them are groups. A group can be a collection of people who are aimlessly milling around, each person doing his own "thing," no common goal or objective in sight. But doesn't this also describe some of the project teams you have seen? I think so.

> A team is a group of people who are committed to attaining a common goal, enjoy working together, and produce high-quality results.

A team is a group of people who are committed to a common goal, enjoy working together, and produce high-quality results. Notice the word *committed*.

Here again, some members of the team are like the chicken in a bacon-and-eggs breakfast—they are *involved* in the breakfast, but not committed to it. The pig, on the other hand, was committed. For a group to be a real team, everyone should be committed.

"So, okay, what's the big deal?" you ask. "All I have to do is get them together, make sure they understand the goal for the project, and they'll become a team. Right?"

Wrong. Teams don't just happen. They must be built. If you don't believe it, look at all sports teams, and you'll know that the coach spends a large amount of time working with the players to turn them into a team. It isn't a single weekend affair, like so many team-building efforts that typify efforts by organizations to improve teamwork. It is an ongoing, exhausting struggle sometimes, and one that does not always succeed.

PROJECT TEAMS ARE DIFFERENT

It is tempting to think that whatever you do to build regular teams will work with project teams. Some of it will. But project teams have a couple of significant differences compared to standard teams.

The first difference is that they are temporary, even when the project lasts for a couple of years. There is still the certainty that the team will eventually be disbanded, whereas with regular work groups, the members expect to stay together as long as the work group exists at all. Because of this temporary nature, the members of the team may see very little reason to invest

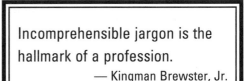

Incomprehensible jargon is the hallmark of a profession.
— Kingman Brewster, Jr.

much in the team itself. This reduces commitment to the team, which will be discussed later in this chapter.

Another difference is that the project manager may not "own" the members of the team. This is true in matrix organizations especially, in which members are drawn from functional groups and actually report on a "solid line" basis to the functional manager and on a "dotted line" basis to the project manager. In that situation, they see their loyalty to the functional department and not to the project. I discuss how to deal with this later on.

Finally, a project team is usually multidisciplinary, whereas standard teams are often single-discipline in nature. In the conventional team, you have a group of mechanics, plumbers, programmers, electrical engineers, painters, or whatever. They speak the same language, think in similar ways, and understand each other. In the multidisciplinary team, the opposite is true, and communication problems are often abundant. Some of the differences between project teams and conventional teams are shown in Table 15.1.

For all of these reasons, managing project teams requires different skills and approaches than those needed for conventional

T A B L E 15.1

Differences Between Project Teams and Conventional Teams

Conventional Team	Project Team
Has permanent membership	Members are assigned temporarily, and often work on a number of teams at the same time.
Team leader may have the authority to reward or discipline team members.	Team leader (project manager) has responsibility for team performance but usually has no authority over team members.
Is often like a basketball team in its interactions.	Is often more like a baseball or football team in its interactions.
May involve only a single discipline.	Often is multidisciplinary.
Usually has deadlines but no rigorous schedules to meet.	Has a critical path schedule to follow in meeting its objectives.
Members may be cross-trained.	Members are usually technical specialists who are not cross-trained.

teams. Most important of all, you need very good "people" skills to manage project teams, because the only way you can get anything done is through influence, persuasion, negotiation, or plain old begging.

> *Principle:* Managing project teams requires different skills than those needed to deal with conventional teams.

As I stated in Chapter 1, if you don't like dealing with "people" issues, you shouldn't be a project manager, because it comes with the turf, and if you hate doing it, project management won't be any fun at all. On the other hand, if you

You need very good people skills to manage project teams.

simply lack people skills but are willing to try to learn, then hang in there. It is possible to learn what you need to be successful in managing a team.

TEAM BUILDING 101

What is one of the primary concerns of every member of a project team? Simple. It's WIIFM. (What's in it for me?)

Every member wants to know what will be expected of her and what she will get out of the experience and for the contribution she makes. Yes, that is true even for a team doing benevolent work. Doing good gives the person a sense of having made a contribution—I call it a "warm fuzzy" feeling, and if you don't get it, you don't do benevolent things. I know some of you may think this sounds cold and callous, but all behavior satisfies some kind of human need (for the person doing the act), and if it does not, then that behavior will eventually fade away.

> *Principle:* If you want people to be committed to your project team, you had better address WIIFM!

So if you want people to be committed to a team, you had better address WIIFM from the very beginning, or you will have a group that may very well go off in search of nirvana someplace else. In fact, I am convinced that the single biggest motivator for human beings is to find meaning in what they are doing. They want to know that the outcome of their efforts is important to someone, that it is valued and appreciated.

To illustrate, I have been to Stonehenge several times, to Avebury, and to Chichén Itzá in Mexico to see the Mayan temples, and I have read countless books on Egypt and the pyramids. Throughout all of these experiences, I have stood in awe of what people did with primitive tools, in searing heat or miserable cold (I nearly froze in the wind looking at Stonehenge one December), and most likely for little more than a subsistence living.

No doubt in some cases they were slaves but, in most cases, the work was done voluntarily. The great pyramid in Egypt is built with stones that weigh more than a modern railway locomotive. There are only a few land-based cranes in the world that can move a load that big, and it takes a week of preparation to do it (Hancock, 1995). As Hancock points out, they didn't need to use stones that big. They could have just as easily built the pyramid with smaller ones. It's as if they were leaving a message for later generations to read: "Look what we did. Let's see you top this one!"

Did they do it just for fun? I think not. So why? It meant something to them. I don't know what. For the Egyptians, there are lots of records that tell us that they were preoccupied with the

Did they do it just for fun?

afterlife. No one knows about Stonehenge or Avebury. The Mayas were concerned about cycles of time and had a calendar more accurate than that of "civilized" Europeans at the time. Hancock claims that they believed these cycles always brought world calamities and that they were trying to predict future events so that they might survive them.

> People didn't build Stonehenge, the Mayan temples, or the Egyptian pyramids just for fun.

Whatever it was, they didn't put all that effort into these projects just for fun. I am certain that they found tremendous meaning in what they were doing. And I submit that if you want people to care about what they are doing at work, they have to find the work meaningful, or they won't be committed to it (Lerner, 1996; Frankl, 1984).

> *Principle:* The primary objective for a manager is to meet the needs of the organization while helping the followers meet their own needs in the process. To do this, you must help individuals find meaning in their work.

So what does that mean for you as a project manager? That you have to help members of your team find meaning in their work. If you can do that, you will achieve the most important objective that a manager has, which is to meet the needs of the organization while simultaneously helping the followers meet their personal needs.

> I want workers to go home at night and say, "I built that car."
> — Pehr G. Gylienhammar
> Chairman, Volvo

In an article written for *Fast Company* magazine, Tom Peters suggests something similar to this when he talks about the WOW! project. According to Peters "WOW projects" are "projects that add value, projects that matter, *projects that make a difference,* projects that leave a legacy—and, yes, projects that make you a star (Peters, 1999, p. 116, emphasis added). Everyone wants to work on those kinds of projects.

But what do you do about the mundane projects? Try to show why they are important. As the old saying goes, "Every cloud has a silver lining," and if we apply this to projects, everyone must embody some importance to the company. However, if you have a project that is not

> Every project is important—or else, why is it being done?

really important why are you doing it? Such projects should be canceled!

I often illustrate this by considering the custodial work done in every organization. Such work is generally regarded as low-status, low-paid, and undesirable work. But how long could your organizations function if the toilets ran out of toilet paper? That may be a bit crude, but I hope it drives home my point. This low-status job is absolutely essential if the organization is going to function. So is it important? You bet!

But do you think anyone ever told one of the custodians that the job was important? I doubt it. Or thanked them for doing it? What do you think?

So let every member of your team know that the contribution they make is important to you and to the project

> Tell every member of your team that his or her contribution is important—every member!

itself, and if you can't do that honestly, perhaps you should ask yourself if the right person has been selected for the job.

MORE ON COMMITMENT

I said above that I want members of my team to be committed to the team, or it isn't really a team. I also said that they must all understand the purpose of the project—why it is important—if they are going to be committed to it, and that their needs must be met through participation. In addition, there are some other conditions that must exist if people are going to be committed to the team.

Frequent Interaction Is Necessary

One condition is that they interact frequently. It is hard to see yourself as a member of a team if you are working out in the boonies somewhere and never see any other members of the team. This can be handled through teleconferencing, videoconferencing, or whatever, but it must be handled through frequent communication. It is most effective face-to-face, but for geographically spread teams, it will have to be done through some kind of media, such as videoconferencing or teleconferencing.

> It is hard to see yourself as a team if you never meet. Bring the team members together once in a while, even if it is by videoconferencing!

Get on the phone and talk with those distant team members almost every day. Send them the same information that your local members get. Keep them informed. Visit them occasionally. Ask for their suggestions about issues that face the team. They may not be colocated with the rest of the team, but if they are really supposed to be part of the team, they have to be treated like real team members and not outcasts.

All Members Must Buy into the Team's Goal

Another condition is that every member of the team must buy into the goals that the group is trying to achieve. If any member is a naysayer, it makes other members feel that they are going to have to do more than their fair share of the work, to "carry" the uncommitted member. Further, the negative attitude of the uncommitted person may be contagious and infect everyone else.

> *Principle:* Every member of the team must buy into the team's goal. If they don't, try to get them off the team.

This is one time when I feel that a project manager has to take decisive action to deal with the uncommitted person. If you can't get her to be committed, then you need—if at all possible—to remove the person from the team, so that the one "bad apple" doesn't "spoil the barrel." I know how hard that is to do. Even when you get to choose your team, it isn't easy to fire someone from a project, and if the person was assigned, it is even harder. But how can I hold a project manager responsible for results if he can't choose his own team members and remove those that don't perform? The answer is simple—I cannot.

Keep Competition *within* the Team to a Minimum

Finally, there is an issue that is greatly misunderstood in general in American society. It is the issue of competition. We love to compete. Most importantly, we love to win. In fact, we have come to see the winner as king and the loser as nobody. Coming in second in a tournament is the same as not even being there.

So strong is this feeling that you see it carried over into organizations. We have to win at all costs. We adopt a "take no prisoners" approach to achieving our organizational goals, and if that means kill the competitor, so much the better.

Interestingly, when we are in school, we are also competitive. You are supposed to do all of your work yourself. Helping other students is cheating, and if you do it on a test, you may be kicked out of school altogether. As a former engineer, I knew engineers

WE LOVE TO COMPETE.

who saw asking for help on a technical problem as shameful. It's a macho thing. If you ask for help, you're a wimp.

But look again at the definition of a team. It is a group of people who *work together* to achieve a common goal. Unless they collaborate and cooperate with each other, they cannot achieve the goal, because it is too big for any one of them to accomplish individually.

Given our social conditioning, however, this cooperation thing somehow seems wrong. We've been taught to compete, to beat the heck out of the other person. So what is this collaboration thing all about anyway?

It seems clear that you can't compete and collaborate with someone at the same time, yet we sometimes promote competition when we really need collaboration. I have seen managers set up competition in their companies and almost destroy them in the process. Yes, there will always be some friendly competition in a team, but how about this—suppose it is expressed in terms of who can make the greatest contribution to overall team performance?

> *Principle:* You can't compete and cooperate at the same time. Keep competition within the team to a minimum.

You see, competition often turns destructive. People are not satisfied to outshine the other person by performing well, they actually try to cause the competitor to fail so that the contrast effect makes them look even better. I know of a manufacturer that set up a shift-to-shift competition for production. The team that had the highest productivity during the week would be treated to a very nice dinner at a local restaurant. This "treat" was something they all looked forward to, so they worked very hard to win.

Soon after the program was kicked off, the people on the second shift got an idea. If they were to adjust the machines so they wouldn't run well, this would slow down the third shift team that followed them, because they would have to readjust all of the machines to get them to run properly.

It did indeed. Of course, it didn't take them long to catch on to what the preceding team was doing, and they did the same thing at the end of their shift. Now the first shift crew had to readjust all of the machines, so they lost ground.

You can guess the next step. The first shift people adjusted the equipment to slow down the second shift. So now it was a vicious circle, with every team trying to depress the performance of the crew that followed them.

The company had to publish a new rule: Each team had to report that the machines all ran properly when they came on duty for the team that preceded them to be eligible for the award.

Study after study has shown that competition turns destructive if it is not controlled. We see evidence of it every day in sports, where fights break out. So if you are going to have competition, try to get your team to beat a team in another competitive company, not your own.

> *Principle:* Competition often turns destructive if it is not controlled.

And try to direct the competition within the team to be expressed in terms of helping the team succeed.

REWARDS

If you want good project team performance, you must have a reward system that balances the rewards for individual performance with the rewards for team performance. As I indicated in the previous section, if you reward rogue behavior, you get it.

We expect to be rewarded if we perform in an outstanding manner compared to other employees. But if we reward *only* individual performance, there is no incentive to cooperate in a team, and competition will be the only thing you get.

> *Principle:* If you want *team* behavior, reward it. If you reward exclusively for individual performance, you won't get people to work as a team.

Most organizations that have successfully solved the reward problem have given a certain percentage of a person's reward for individual achievements and the remainder for team contributions. The exact ratios vary, so you may have to experiment with this to develop the best situation for your organization.

PRACTICING GOOD PROJECT MANAGEMENT BUILDS TEAMS

If you are able to show all members of the team that contributions are valued, then having them participate in developing the project plan is about as good a team-building activity as you can choose. You don't need to do anything special in most cases. Teams develop when people participate in something that they believe in.

> Kick off your project with a purely social event—a dinner, picnic, or softball game.

However, there is one suggestion that will go a long way to getting your team off to a good start. That is to have a social event before the project gets kicked off. Get everyone together for a dinner—or even a lun-

Having a
social event
before project
kickoff is a good start.

cheon—in a purely social manner. Just let them get acquainted with each other. Have them introduce themselves, and have them tell something personal that most other members are not likely to know about them, such as some outside interest that they have. Even if you are sure everyone on the team already knows each other, the party and introductions still serve a useful function.

When your team is spread all over the globe, parties are not always possible, and neither is a face-to-face project kickoff meeting. I much prefer these to be onsite, but if that is not possible, then do the kickoff by conferencing. There are a number of Web-based conferencing facilities available now, that permit you to use voice, video, and presentations to hold the meeting. What you miss are the subtle nonverbal signals that can tell you a lot about a person's reaction to what is happening, but if it is not possible to do onsite meetings, this is a good compromise.

COMMUNICATION: A 13-LETTER WORD

In American culture, the number 13 has long been believed by superstitious people to be unlucky. Ever notice that most buildings do not have a 13th floor? Obviously they do, but it is numbered 14, in deference to people who believe the worst.

> There is nothing that cannot be perverted by being told badly.
> — Terence, c. 190–159 B.C.

The word communication is a pervasive explanation for why teams have problems—communication problems are everywhere. You would think that, after everything that has been written about the need to communicate better, the problems would go away, but they don't.

There is a big difference between communicating and talking. Communication must convey *meaning* if it is to qualify as real communication. Only when there is a *two-way interaction* is there a transfer of meaning between two people. It requires a talker and a listener.

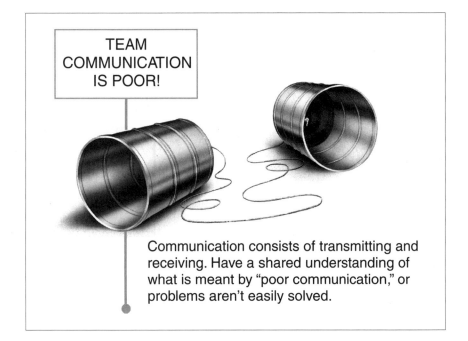

TEAM COMMUNICATION IS POOR!

Communication consists of transmitting and receiving. Have a shared understanding of what is meant by "poor communication," or problems aren't easily solved.

A lot of us are good talkers, and most of us believe we are good listeners, but don't you believe it. If you have ever seen the demonstration of passing a spoken message from one person to another around a circle, you know what I mean. In almost every instance, by the time the message goes around a group of 6 to 10 individuals, it bears no resemblance to the original.

"Then you should say what you mean," the March Hare went on. "I do," Alice hastily replied; "at least—at least I mean what I say—that's the same thing, you know." "Not the same thing a bit!" said the Hatter. "Why, you might just as well say that 'I see what I eat' is the same thing as 'I eat what I see!'"

— Lewis Carroll
Alice's Adventures in Wonderland

> There is a profound difference
> between information and
> meaning.
> — Warren Bennis

It was not always so. Two thousand years ago, when very few people could read or write, people listened to each other and passed along oral traditions. Today rumors fly around like dandelion seeds in the wind, and mutate faster than a virus.

Not only is communication not just talking, but listening is also not just hearing. If you are really listening, you are trying to

> A great many people think that
> polysyllables are a sign of
> intelligence.
> — Barbara Walters

understand, to get the *meaning* of what the other person is telling you. How often have you thought that the person was hearing your words but not your meaning?

I know it is an old saw by now, but real listening is not passive, but active. Yet, in the years that I have tried to teach active listening, I find so many people who don't seem to catch the essential point of the approach

> *Principle:* Active listening is not
> the same as an *inquisition!*

that I wonder if there is a defective gene in them—a listening gene. They go into interviewing, rather than listening. They charge on, asking the person one question after another, without once really understanding what the person has said. This is an inquisition, and it tends to make people defensive if carried on for too long.

If you are really listening actively, you should periodically paraphrase what the person said, to check your comprehension. Say something like this: "If I understand you, you're saying that . . ." Then put into your own words what the person said. Don't parrot. If you repeat exactly what the person said, it appears that you heard her, but that doesn't mean you really understood. If you can say it in your own words, and she agrees that you got it, then you did.

Try to Clarify Assumptions

I was talking with a fellow one day who kept using the acronym ATM. I thought he meant *automatic teller machine,* but somehow, the conversation didn't seem to be going very well, and finally I asked, "What do you mean by ATM?" His response was, "Asynchronous transmission mode." He *assumed* that I understood, because he knew I used to be an electrical engineer, but I had no clue what he was talking about.

Preconceptions

People tend to hear what they expect to hear. During the past week, United Airlines announced that they would buy US Airways. Those people who like United Airlines heard this as a really good thing, and conversely. It is the same deal either way you look at it, but one person sees it positively and the other negatively.

When you are dealing with problems in a project, yours and the other person's preconceived ideas about the situation can greatly influence the exchange of information and prevent a solution that may have been simple, if only information had not been misinterpreted.

THE TEAM-BUILDING CYCLE

I said earlier that team building is not a one-shot affair. It is an ongoing process, and one that is usually overlooked in organizations. We become so focused on the task that must be done that we forget about process. In Chapter 1, I pointed out that process will always affect task. If you want to improve the functioning of a team, you must improve the processes by which they do their work. This is done in a cyclical way, as shown in Figure 15.1.

The Plan-Do-Check-Act Cycle

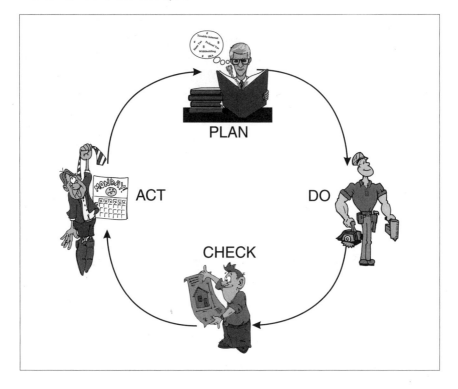

At the Check point in the cycle, you do a lessons learned review, as outlined in Chapter 10. You ask, What have we done well so far? and What do we want to do better in the future? If communication is a problem, you try to improve the process by which you are communicating with each other. If work coordination is a problem, you address this and try to find a better way.

One way to find out where your problem areas are is to do a written survey of all members of the team. A questionnaire that you can use can be downloaded from my website (www.lewisinstitute.com). It is also contained in Figure 15.2 for your convenience.

F I G U R E   15.2

The Team Performance Critique

The Team Performance Critique

Instructions: Indicate how you think the team is functioning by circling the number on each scale that you feel is most descriptive of the team.

1. Goals and objectives
Members do not understand
the goals of the team.

Team members understand
and agree on goals and objectives.

| 1 | 2 | 3 | 4 | 5 | 6 | 7 |

2. Roles and responsibilities
Roles and responsibilities of team
members are not clear.

All team members are
clear about their roles.

| 1 | 2 | 3 | 4 | 5 | 6 | 7 |

3. Procedures
Methods used to do our
work are inappropriate.

We follow sound work
methods and procedures.

| 1 | 2 | 3 | 4 | 5 | 6 | 7 |

4. Relationships
Team members are often
in conflict.

Team members work
together harmoniously.

| 1 | 2 | 3 | 4 | 5 | 6 | 7 |

5. Leadership
Team leadership is
often inadequate.

Team leadership is effective
and shared when appropriate.

| 1 | 2 | 3 | 4 | 5 | 6 | 7 |

6. Planning
We have poor plans
for doing our work.

Plans are well developed.

| 1 | 2 | 3 | 4 | 5 | 6 | 7 |

7. Trust
People don't trust each
other on this team.

Members have a high degree
of trust in each other.

| 1 | 2 | 3 | 4 | 5 | 6 | 7 |

8. Communications
Members don't communicate
with each other very well.

Communications are timely,
open, and appropriate.

| 1 | 2 | 3 | 4 | 5 | 6 | 7 |

9. Creativity/Innovation
We live by the motto "if
it ain't broke, don't fix it."

We are willing to try new
ideas when they come out.

| 1 | 2 | 3 | 4 | 5 | 6 | 7 |

Source: Copyright 1992 by James P. Lewis. This form may be reproduced for use by the purchaser but may not be republished without the written permission of the author.

Principle: Perception is reality. That is, if people believe something is true, they will behave as if it is true, so for all practical purposes it is true for them.

To use this critique, send a copy to each member of your team and ask them to endorse it and send it back. Then tabulate the responses by plotting bar graphs showing the number of individuals who rate an item as a 1 or a 7 or whatever. A resulting graph will look like the ones shown in Figures 15.3 and 15.4.

In Figure 15.3, you can see that most members of the team feel that the process is working well. All of the responses are clus-

F I G U R E 15.3

Frequency Response Graph Showing Good Agreement

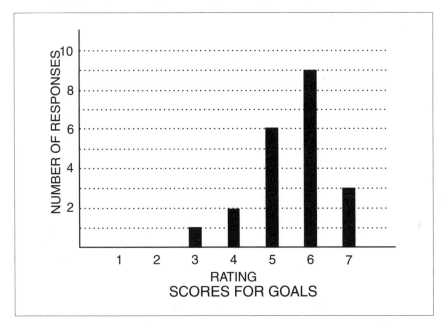

Graph Showing Binomial Split

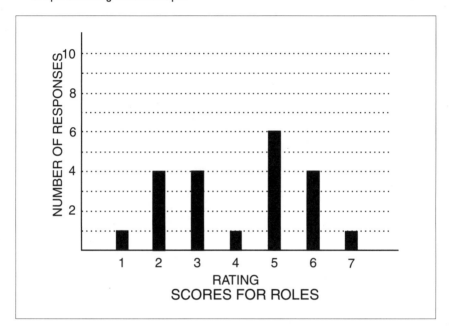

tered toward one end of the scale. In Figure 15.4, however, they are split. Half of them think there is a problem and half do not. When half of your team thinks there is a problem, there is, whether it is objectively true or not. The reason is that perception is reality to people. That is, if they think there is a problem, there is for them. So you need to work to resolve the situation to their satisfaction. You may be able to simply show them that there truly is no actual problem, but whatever you do, you cannot ignore their belief without incurring a cost.

Sequence

There is an important point about the sequence in which you should deal with issues. Note that the first four questions deal with goals, roles, procedures, and relationships. This order is important. All too often, when people are experiencing conflict in a team, or are otherwise not getting along very well, an attempt is made to resolve conflict—that is, to deal with relationships. And all too often, the effort fails.

The reason is that relationship problems are sometimes caused by the fact that goals, roles, or procedures are not being handled properly. For example, as teams develop, they often begin questioning whether they are on the right track.

> It is not necessary to understand things in order to argue about them.
> — Pierre Beaumarchais, 1732–1799

"Are we doing what we are supposed to be doing?" someone asks.

"Of course we are," says someone else.

They argue about this, and each person is convinced that the other is wrong. If the argument gets very intense, hard feelings may result, and we say that they are having a personality conflict. They are, in the sense that they take an affront to their position personally, but it wasn't a personality clash to begin with, it was a disagreement about what they were supposed to be doing.

> It makes me nervous when someone says, "I agree with everything you say." Not even I agree with everything I say.
> — Jeremy Rifkind

So the first thing you must do is help them get clear about the goal they are pursuing (note that I am using the word in its broadest sense—it could be the overall team mission or individual work goals that are in question).

One area that may need to be addressed is when the goal is shifting. In Chapter 5, I discussed the adaptive project. We typi-

Shifting of direction may lead to conflict over goals.

GOAL

cally treat projects as deterministic. We decide what the problem is and how we are going to solve it, and then we march in a straight line until we reach the final destination, and the problem is solved.

This may not be possible in developing software. When we developed my on-line training software, we started with an overall concept of what we wanted to do, but as we neared the end, we began to see features that should be added, so the scope of the job grew considerably. Fortunately, what we wound up with was a far better product than it would have been if we had stuck to the original definition and refused to respond to these new insights.

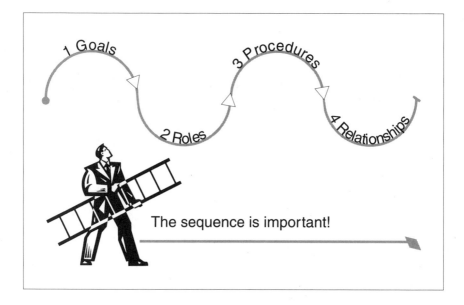

The sequence is important!

The problem is, this shifting of direction may lead to conflict over goals, so if you see that a new direction is necessary, it is time to call a team meeting to explain the reason behind the shift and help everyone maintain a *shared understanding* of where you are going.

Now, for every task that must be done in a project, there must also be someone responsible for getting it done. This is the roles and responsibility question, and if these are not clear, then again, people may fight. So role clarification is the next order of business after goals have been clarified.

> *Principle:* Always deal with the behavior of people, not their attitudes or feelings.

Then we have procedures. How is the work going to be done? "Is that the right way?" someone asks. "I don't think it is."

This, too, is an area that will lead to relationship difficulties if it is not dealt with properly.

Finally, if you still have relationship problems, you can deal with the individuals involved to try and rectify the problem. The general principle to remember is that you may not be able to get people to like each other, but you can insist that their feelings for each other not cause unacceptable behavior that disrupts team functioning. That is, deal with behavior, not feelings.

> *Principle:* Deal with goals, then roles and responsibilities, then procedures, and finally relationships.

Once the first four topics have been worked through, if you have problems with the remaining areas, you can deal with them next. They are not listed in any particular causal sequence.

The Small Team

For teams of perhaps six or more, the procedure outlined above works. When you have only three to six members, however, you can't plot meaningful graphs of responses, so you simply have to ask everyone to respond to the questions and deal with them in the order specified. You may also want to simply have one-on-one interviews to find out what problems you may have. This is hard to do with very large teams, but easy to do with small ones.

What about You?

Don't forgot to include your leadership behaviors as a topic that should be considered. I propose that you ask your team two questions: Is there anything I am not doing that you would like me to do? and Is there anything

> Don't forget yourself as a target for improvement!

that I am doing that you would like me to stop doing?

When you ask these questions, you must be willing to take the heat! If you get defensive about their comments, they will quickly get the message that you were not sincere in wanting answers. And they will clam up and won't tell you anything else.

This is not to say that you have to do everything they suggest. There may be valid reasons why you behave in certain ways that they don't understand, but you can explain that to them, and they should accept it. What I am saying is that you must be careful not to get upset or angry when they suggest a change in your behavior.

The first thing to do is to let them know that you have listened to what they have said. This is easy to do. Simply say, "So you are saying that . . ." and repeat, in your own words, what the person has told you. By responding in this manner, you convey that you are first listening to understand, before trying to be understood (to paraphrase Stephen Covey—see Covey, 1989). If you are not prepared to make the change, you can then explain it in logical terms and hope that they accept your explanation. If you do not first convey that you understand, however, they may see you as just being unwilling to change, and they may lose respect for you.

GIVING TEAM MEMBERS AUTHORITY AND RESPONSIBILITY

In dealing with roles and responsibility, we must understand a fundamental principle that is often violated in organizations. You cannot delegate responsibility without giving people authority commensurate with it! Managers forget this. They want people to be responsible for their behavior when they are in no position to control their work because they have no authority.

> *Principle:* You can't delegate responsibility without giving a person authority commensurate with it.

Authority is much misunderstood. We believe someone must be in charge.

In fact, authority is much misunderstood. Old notions of command and control have been with us for so long that we believe "someone must be in charge," and we won't let members of our teams have any authority to make decisions, spend money, or take unilateral actions. "Check with me before you do anything," we tell them.

There is a very simple cause of this behavior. It is fear. We are afraid that the person will do something wrong—take the wrong step, make the wrong decision, or spend money unwisely. This fear leads to a distrust of people, and the distrust prevents you from giving the person a chance to prove he is trustworthy, so you maintain your distrust. Let me show this with a couple of examples.

Remember when you got your driver's license? You were about 16 years old. You came home with that shiny new license, and what did you want to do? Why, take the car out for a drive, naturally.

With mom or dad?

No way!

You wanted to go solo.

What you didn't realize at the time was what a terrible dilemma this placed on your parents. If they don't let you take the car, they will be hauling you around until you're 40 years old, which is no fun for either of you, and conveys quite clearly that they don't trust you to drive responsibly. If they do let you take the car, they take a big risk, because at this point, the fact that you *can* drive doesn't mean that you will do so responsibly. The point is that, if they don't take the risk, they will never know if you will drive in a responsible way.

There was an experiment conducted to show how this functions in a work environment. A person was chosen to supervise two workers. They were given a paperwork task to perform, and the supervisor was told to make sure they did the task correctly. There were two rounds in the experiment. In round one, the supervisor was allowed to supervise one worker closely, but could hardly supervise the other worker at all. At the end of the round, the experimenter faked the performance information so that the supervisor was told that both workers had performed almost equally well.

In round two, the supervisor was left alone so that she could supervise the two workers any way she wanted. The question is, which worker was supervised the most, the one who was supervised the most in round one or the other one?

When I ask this question in my classes, most people think the least-supervised worker will be closely supervised in round two. That is the intuitive answer, but it is wrong. The supervisor continues to supervise the worker who was most closely supervised in round one!

Why? Because the supervisor is trying to understand the reasons for their performance, and the reasoning goes like this. They both performed about equally well. In the case of the person who was not supervised in round one, this means he is competent. I don't need to supervise him, because it is clear that he can do the job without supervision.

However, I don't know about the other person. That individual performed okay, but was it because I supervised her closely or because she is capable? Because I am being judged on the outcomes of this job, I had better continue to give her guidance so that she does a good job.

> *Principle:* If you don't take a risk, you will never learn if a person is trustworthy or competent!

Of course, the supervisor will never find out if the person is competent so long as she continues to supervise closely. In addition, this micromanaging ultimately means that one of them is redundant. We may as well replace the worker with the supervisor and save a salary.

Situational Leadership

If you have read Chapter 13, you will remember that situational leadership prescribes how much latitude you can give a person on the basis of answers to the two questions, Can the person do the job? and Will she take responsibility for it? The answers to these questions tell you how much authority you can give an individual. When the answers are both "no," you have to deal with the person in a telling or directive way. If the answers are both "yes," then you can be completely delegative. Other answers tell you to be selling or participative.

What this means is that delegating authority and responsibility are a function of where the person is in terms of job maturity. The low job maturity person needs more guidance and supervision than the high job maturity individual. So delegation is not an across-the-board situation. Everyone does not get the same amount of authority, or the same level of responsibility.

Conditions for Assigning Authority and Responsibility

For a person to be able to do an acceptable job in a project team, five conditions must exist. These are listed in Figure 15.5.

Conditions for Acceptable Job Performance

Conditions for Acceptable Job Performance

1. The individual must have a clear goal or objective with the purpose stated.
2. He/she must have a plan for how to achieve the goal.
3. He/she must have the skills and resources needed to do the job.
4. The person must have feedback on performance.
5. He/she must have a clear definition of his or her authority to take corrective action when there is a deviation, and that authority must be greater than zero.

A Clear Goal Must Be Stated. The first condition is that the person must know what is supposed to be done, with the purpose stated. That is, tell the individual not only the "what" but the "why." There are managers who think the "why" is unnecessary. Maybe they got this from their parents. Remember when you asked your mom or dad why they wanted you to do something and they said, "Because I said so." This is a command and control position, but it is dangerous even in the military.

If a person knows why something is being done, and a problem or question comes up, he can think independently about what to do. Otherwise, he will have to come back to you and ask how to respond to the situation. Telling someone only the "what" means that you are employing their hands but not their heads.

The Individual Must Have a Plan. The next requirement is for the individual to have a plan on how she will do her work. The reason is very simple—if she has no plan, by definition, she cannot have control. This rule applies at the individual level as well as at the project level.

The question is, What kind of plan should she have? A simple one. All she really needs is to practice good time management. She should have a to-do list each week that is keyed to the project master plan. She doesn't need a personal PERT/CPM diagram, because the purpose of these is to map out parallel paths in a project, and an individual has no parallel paths unless she is ambidextrous.

Skills and Resources. The third requirement is for the person to have the skills and resources needed to do the job. The resources part is obvious. If you don't have materials, supplies, or equipment, you can hardly do your work. However, one of the most important resources in today's world is information. When people are kept in the dark, when information is withheld from them because it gives the manager power, they cannot perform responsibly.

> An individual without information cannot take responsibility; an individual who is given information cannot help but take responsibility.
>
> —Jan Carlzon

The skills part presents a concern for project managers in matrix environments. You may find that the functional department providing resources to you has no one with certain skills available and the manager is unwilling to pay to have someone trained. In that case, you may have to budget for such training in your project.

Performance Feedback. Because control consists of comparing where you are to where you are supposed to be, so you can correct for deviations, you must know where you are in order to be able to control your own progress. Furthermore, that performance feedback needs to be readily available and in a timely manner.

The other aspect of performance feedback has to do with the level of performance of an individual, which is commonly called performance appraisal. Project managers must have input to the performance appraisals of team members if they are to have any commitment to the team. However, this input is limited to the manager's ability to assess. If the person is in a technical discipline different from the manager's own discipline, then his assessment will be limited to how the team member performed in the team with regard to cooperation, timely completion of assignments, and so on. It would not involve appraisal of technical performance.

Definition of Authority. I stated above that you cannot delegate responsibility without giving the person authority commensurate with it. I also stated that situational leadership enables you to decide the limits of both authority and responsibility. If you practice situational leadership you know that authority and responsibility are not across-the-board for all tasks the person may do in a project. There will be some tasks for which the answers to the "can and will" questions will be a definite "yes" and others for which the answers will be "maybe." So the authority and responsibility that you delegate will vary depending on how you answer those questions.

DECISIONS IN TEAMS

In Chapter 5, I discussed the Abilene Paradox, or false consensus effect, and showed how it can cause major problems for a project team. There are a number of other issues related to how decisions are made in teams that can impact the work done by the team, and a project manager needs to know how to handle these.

Before we continue, it is important to realize that a decision is a choice from among a number of alternatives. This is not the same thing as a problem, which is a gap between

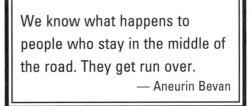

We know what happens to people who stay in the middle of the road. They get run over.
— Aneurin Bevan

where you are and where you want to be, that has obstacles that prevent easy movement to close the gap.

It may be that you are trying to solve a problem and you have identified three approaches that may work. Which one is

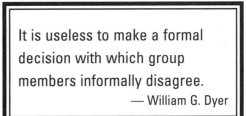

A decision is a choice of an alternative.

best? This is a decision—a choice to be made. The process of making choices is called decision making.

Who Decides?

In this book, we are not going to be concerned with *how* to make decisions. That process requires more space than I have available

for this book. What I want to deal with is the issue of *who* makes decisions. At one time it was considered correct for the team leader to decide almost every issue facing a team. This totally authoritarian ap-

It is useless to make a formal decision with which group members informally disagree.
— William G. Dyer

proach was a command-and-control method that typified the military.

However, even when used in a military setting, this approach can get a leader into serious trouble. So researchers started asking how decisions should be made, and some of the most practical work has been examined by Maier (1955), Vroom and Yetton (1973), and Vroom and Jago (1988). We will take a look at their suggestions in a moment.

First, though, there were some researchers who suggested that decisions be made by consensus. Such an approach was likely to get input from everyone and would lead to greater buy-in once made.

> It's easy to make good decisions when there are no bad options.
> — Robert Half

This is true. The problem is that when a new approach to something is presented, we find people completely abandoning the old way in favor of the new. I call this a knee-jerk response, and it is done without thinking ahead to the consequences.

And those consequences can be serious. In simple terms, if you make all team decisions by consensus, you won't have time to get any work done. You will be spending all your time in decision-making meetings!

As the old saying goes, "There is a time and a place for everything," and this is no exception. There is a time for consensual decisions and there is a time for autonomous ones.

You may remember that in Chapter 1, I discussed the 777 airplane developed by Boeing. During the final testing of the plane, they wanted to do a test that required running the engines at 84,000 pounds of thrust, rather than the 80,000 pounds that had been used in previous tests. Test pilot John Cashman was concerned. This increased thrust also increased the possibility of something going wrong. The test team discussed this issue, and adjourned to consider all the facts. They would come back to Cashman with a recommendation. Cashman's final comment, as the meeting broke up, was, "I still may not do it" (from the video, *21st Century Jet*, fifth series). In this case, because lives were at stake and he had ultimate responsibility for them, he reserved the right to refuse to take a risk that he thought was too severe. (He did finally agree to do the test at the increased thrust, by the way.)

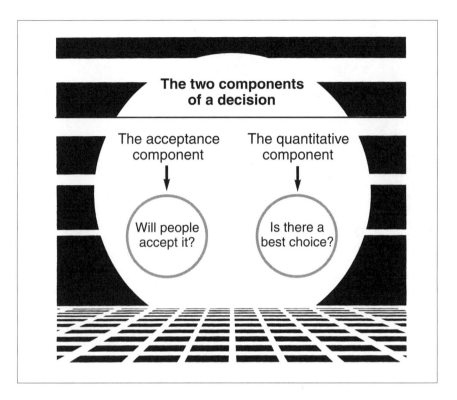

The Two Components of a Decision. Every decision has two components or factors that must be considered. One is how much people affected by the decision will accept it. This is called the *acceptance* component. The other aspect is the quantitative or qualitative component. Is there some way in which one choice can be said to be better than another? The quantitative aspect is obvious—is there a measurable way in which you can say that one choice is better than another? The qualitative aspect is not so obvious. As an example, the color red is considered an action color, whereas blue is more sedate. If you were trying to convey that a company is cutting edge, then red would be a better corporate color than blue. This is a qualitative criterion. For the remainder of this discussion, I am going to use the term quantitative to mean either measurable or qualitative.

It is possible for a decision to be almost 100 percent quantitative or 100 percent acceptance, but in practice, you usually have some of both involved. For that reason, we will think in terms of one being considerably more important than the other, rather than requiring that it be a ratio of 100 percent to zero.

Quantitative More Important than Acceptance. Suppose we begin with a situation in which the best choice can be said to be mostly quantitative in nature. An example might include which manufacturing approach would give the greatest yield per hour. Another would be which mutual fund would give the greatest long-term payback. Or which of three computers will offer the best overall performance for a small business.

Are there any acceptance issues in these situations? Perhaps. For the manufacturing and mutual fund choices, there may be fewer acceptance concerns than would be true if you were trying to select computers. Overall, however, these might be said to be mostly qualitative issues, and the question is, If a team were faced with making a choice of this nature, how should the decision be made?

> *Principle:* Decisions that are primarily quantitative in nature should be made by an expert.

The general guideline is that an expert should make the choice when the issue is mostly quantitative. We may all have opinions about which mutual fund is best, but a securities analyst would be better qualified than most lay persons to pick the fund that would give the best long-term payback.

Acceptance More Important than Quantitative Aspects Now consider a decision that is more of an acceptance issue than quantitative. Suppose our project team has just met a very significant milestone in the project and their performance has been exemplary. As project leader, I have built into my budget some money to pay for an occasional celebration, so the plan is to take the entire team, together with their "significant others," to a restaurant for a really nice evening out. Because there are nearly 15 team members, there will be about 30 people invited to the outing, and I am concerned that no choice will fully satisfy 30 people, so I decide to make the choice myself. I would like to do something unusual, so I decide that we will all go to a Japanese restaurant for a sushi dinner.

Do I have a problem here?

You bet. If you happen to be one of those individuals who turns a bit pale at the mere mention of eating raw fish, you are not going to welcome the outing. In fact, my guess is that, close to the day of the outing, people will start sending me notes saying that they cannot make the outing. That being the case, the dinner will not achieve what it was supposed to do, which was to bring the team together and reward them for their good performance.

This is a perfect example of a choice that should be made by the entire team. But how? The process would be to list a number of possibilities, then have people vote on them. For the majority choice, you then ask the group if everyone can support that choice. If there are members of the team who cannot support the majority choice, then move to the one that had the next-most votes and try again. You will usually reach a suitable choice by doing this.

Note that you ask if everyone can *support* the majority choice. You don't want grudging acceptance, because it won't be a good experience for people who really didn't like the choice at all. As an example, if Mexican food were the majority preference, but there are some people in the group who detest Mexican food, you would not want them to go along just because "most of you wanted to go."

This approach is as close to consensus as you can get. For a large group, consensus is almost never going to mean that everyone totally agrees. All you can ask is that everyone be willing to support the choice, because if you don't get that much, your ultimate outcome is probably doomed.

I once had a superintendent of a school system tell me that this had made her realize why her schools were having trouble. Their normal way of choosing a course of action was majority rule—the "American way." However, when it came time to implement the choice, she would find that some principals were not supporting it. When she called this to their attention, their response was, "Yes, but you will remember that I didn't vote for it, either."

> *Principle:* When acceptance is more important than quantitative concerns, the decision should be made by consensus.

So the rule is that, when acceptance is more important than quantitative issues, you let the group choose, using consensus as much as possible.

Acceptance and Quantitative Concerns about Equal It is actually rare for a decision to be almost purely acceptance or quantitative in nature. More often, both components will be highly important. In this case, a mixture of expert choice and consensus must be used. We call this the *consultative* approach.

> *Principle:* When acceptance and quantitative issues are almost equally important, then a consultative approach should be used.

The expert(s) pick several alternatives that are considered about equally good in a quantitative sense and the team members choose the one that they like the best. The approaches to making team decisions are summarized in Table 15.2.

Avoiding Groupthink

Although it has a similar appearance to the Abilene Paradox, groupthink arises from a different cause. You will remember that the Abilene Paradox happens when a team chooses a course of action suggested by one member, even though no one really liked

T A B L E 15.2

Approaches to Making Team Decisions

Rules for Handling Group Decision Making	
When the issue is:	The decision should be:
Q/A (largely quantitative)	made by an expert
A/Q (largely acceptance)	made by group consensus
A&Q (combination of both)	made by consultation

that choice. The mechanism is the "silence-means-consent" belief. Because no one voiced any concerns, everyone assumed that the members all agreed with the choice.

Groupthink is a similar phenomenon that happens when the group accepts the leader's suggestion, even though they don't all agree with it. How-ever, they reason, she is

> Groupthink is the tendency of a group to accept a leader's suggestion, even though they don't all agree with it.

the leader. Furthermore, they believe that, if you disagree with the leader, you may get into trouble. This is often based on experience, so the fear is not unfounded.

Janis and Mann (1977) researched groupthink and offered a procedure for avoiding it. Their suggestions are summarized in the following steps:

1. The leader should avoid offering a preference in the early stages of the group's discussion. Rather, tell them, I am concerned that we arrive at a course of action that we can all support.

2. Ask that suggested actions be listed in a brainstorming fashion—that is, without allowing any evaluation or criticism until all alternatives have been listed.

3. Encourage all members of the team to be critical evalua-
    tors of each alternative. They should state their concerns
    in objective terms, rather than personal. For example, to
    say, "I think that is a stupid thing to do," only invites the
    person who suggested it to get very defensive, because
    the word *stupid* suggests that he is stupid for offering the
    idea.
4. Have them make a consensual choice, as described previ-
    ously, in which every member can honestly say that he
    or she can support the majority course of action.
5. Ask everyone to come back tomorrow to revisit the
    choice made. If anyone has had second thoughts during
    the intervening time, those concerns should be voiced
    and the choice should be reconsidered.

As you can see, this procedure takes a lot of time, and should
only be applied to issues that are of great importance to the team.
Matters of project strategy, or responses to serious problems may
fit that category.

IN CLOSING

In closing, I should say that the subject of teams can't possibly be
covered in a single chapter. The topic requires a book to do justice,
but I hope I have given you some basics and piqued your interest
in the subject, so that you will continue your reading. There are a
number of helpful books listed in the References and Reading List.

KEY POINTS FOR CHAPTER 15

- A team is a group of people who are committed to attain-
  ing a common goal, enjoy working together, and produce
  high-quality results.
- *Principle:* Managing project teams requires different skills
  than those needed to deal with conventional teams.
- *Principle:* If you want people to be committed to your project team, you had better address WIIFM!

- *Principle:* The primary objective for a manager is to meet the needs of the organization while helping the followers meet their own needs in the process. To do this, you must help individuals find meaning in their work.
- It is hard to see yourself as a team if you never meet. Bring the team members together once in a while, even if it is by videoconferencing!
- *Principle:* Every member of the team must buy into the team's goal. If they don't, try to get them off the team.
- *Principle:* You can't compete and cooperate at the same time. Keep competition within the team to a minimum.
- *Principle:* If you want *team* behavior, reward it. If you reward exclusively for individual performance, you won't get people to work as a team.
- *Principle:* Perception is reality. That is, if people believe something is true, they will behave as if it is true, so for all practical purposes it is true for them.
- *Principle:* Deal with goals, then roles and responsibilities, then procedures, and finally relationships.
- Groupthink is the tendency of a group to accept a leader's suggestion, even though they don't all agree with it.

QUESTIONS FOR REVIEW

1. What is a team?
2. What is one of the primary concerns of a person in a team?
3. What kind of projects do people want to work on?
4. What do you do about mundane projects?
5. Why should you keep competition within a team to a minimum?
6. What is a good way to kick off a project team?
7. It is not enough to convey just information through communication. What is the real intent of any communication?

8. Why do perceptions matter as much as objective facts?
9. Why is it important to deal with goals, roles, procedures, and relationships in that order?
10. Why is it important to provide information to team members?
11. What are the two components that may affect every decision?
12. What is the difference between groupthink and the Abilene Paradox?

CHAPTER

Managing Meetings

You simply cannot manage projects without having meetings. People need information, problems must be solved, and project status must be assessed.

As we all know, the large majority of meetings held in the United States every day are so unproductive that people begin to dread them like the plague. In addition, there are so many meetings being

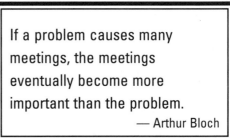

If a problem causes many meetings, the meetings eventually become more important than the problem.
— Arthur Bloch

held that some managers spend nearly all of their time in meetings, and can't get their jobs done as a consequence.

This isn't necessary. A meeting doesn't have to be a fate worse than death. Meetings can actually be productive!

DEVELOP A CODE OF CONDUCT

You may think that this is unnecessary, but one of the first things a team should do is develop a code of conduct for team meetings. It is necessary because, unfortunately, there are those among us who have never been taught how to behave appropriately in team settings.

PLANNING A MEETING

The best meetings have a defined purpose and agenda and are time-limited.

- Circulate the agenda.
- Choose location carefully.
- Take control of the meeting.
- Set a time limit.
- Develop a code of conduct.
- Focus on the issues.
- Discuss the most important items first.
- Minimize distractions.
- Organize breaks.
- Time is costly/appoint a timekeeper.
- Keep the order.
- Arrange for all messages to be taken for participants.
- End on a positive note.
- Record proceedings and decisions.
- Publish minutes promptly.
- Follow up on the "to-do" items after the meeting.

Have the group create the list. Don't do it yourself. If they create it, they will own it. It should contain no more than 10 or 12 items. Usually these will be things like, "Be on time for the meeting." "No side conversations." "Only one person talks at a time."

When the list has been made, ask all members to sign at the bottom of the page indicating that the list is acceptable and that they will abide by it. If anyone refuses to sign, ask why she is reluctant and what must be done to gain her commitment to the list. If you are unable to do this, you may have to deal with her off-line.

Once the signed list is completed, it should be posted in the meeting room. Again, don't use it as a club to beat up people, but in a good-natured manner, point out that they are in violation of a code and ask them to abide by it. Furthermore, you should ask the entire group to help you enforce the code. Ask them to think of themselves as cofacilitators of the group meetings. After all, it is their meeting, and is intended to benefit them, not just you.

REASONS FOR MEETINGS

There are four basic reasons for having a meeting. These are to (1) give information, (2) get information, (3) make a decision, or (4) solve a problem. How about planning? I don't consider a planning session to be a meeting per se, but if you want to think of it as such, then it generally involves a lot of items 3 and 4—making decisions and solving problems.

Purpose of Meetings

1. Give information
2. Get information
3. Make a decision
4. Solve a problem

As a general rule, it is a good idea to never try to deal with more than two of these at once. In other words, a meeting to give and get information is fine. So is one to make decisions and solve problems. It is when you do all four at the same time that everything bogs down.

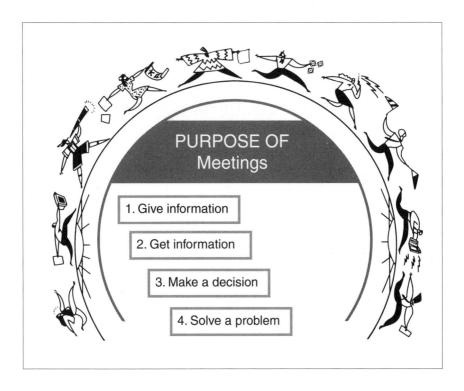

PURPOSE OF Meetings

1. Give information

2. Get information

3. Make a decision

4. Solve a problem

Project status review meetings often involve all four of these, and this is almost always a mistake. A status meeting should limit itself to items 1 and 2. You have called people together to get information from them and to give them information. The trap is that, when they start to give status information on their work, and they are having problems, everything comes to a halt in an attempt to solve the problem that the one individual is having. While this is going on, other members of the team are sitting there spinning their wheels, waiting for their turn to report status.

> When the result of a meeting is to schedule more meetings, it usually signals trouble.
> — Kevin J. Murphy

When there are problems with individual tasks, a separate meeting should be held to deal with those. That way, you don't bog down your status meeting and drive everyone to distraction.

GENERAL GUIDELINES FOR MEETINGS

We all know that a meeting should have an agenda that is published ahead of time. We don't necessarily practice what we know, but we do know it. What we don't all know is that the agenda should have a time allocated for each agenda item, and the overall meeting should be time-limited.

> List each speaker's name beside his or her agenda item.

This is not only courteous to everyone who attends, but makes good business sense. People need to schedule other things in their jobs, and if a meeting goes over the allocated time, it can wreak havoc with the other appointments that people have. One concern that people have is that you may not be able to finish in the allocated time. There are two responses to that concern.

First, if you don't finish, you schedule another meeting to take care of those items. That way, everyone can leave for other business and come back later to deal with unfinished business. This is more efficient in the long run, because when you hold people over to deal with unfinished tasks, they are frustrated and ineffective at their work. When they come back to a later meeting, they do so with a fresh perspective.

Second, Parkinson said that work tends to expand to take the time allowed. There is a flip side to that, however, which is that people will finish in the time allowed if you make it clear that this is necessary. And there is no evidence that the outcomes are any better when you take forever compared to insisting on limited time.

Be generous in your allocation of time to each agenda item. If you finish early, no one will mind, but running over is unacceptable. It is also a good idea to discuss the most important topics early in the meeting, because participants tend to be more alert at that time.

An agenda should usually fit on one sheet of paper. If it won't, the meeting is likely to take far too long. Studies show that people need a break about every 50 minutes, and that 75 minutes is about the upper limit for a meeting. The agenda should tell everyone the date, time, place, and purpose of the meeting.

Appoint a Timekeeper

To keep the group on schedule, it is a good idea to have someone be the timekeeper. This person lets the group know that they are almost out of time, and the group leader holds the group to it. If the group mutually decides to go over on a single item so that it can be finished, later items are simply rolled forward to a later meeting. Allow yourself some flexibility. Use the system as a guideline, not as a club with which to beat people into submission.

Use a Flipchart to Record Proceedings

If you aren't used to using flipcharts to record what happens in the group, let me strongly suggest that you do. Having someone take notes on a desk pad is not nearly as effective as the flipchart. Not everyone can see a desk pad, so they lose track of what has been discussed, but on a chart, everyone can see. Yes, it requires that the chart be transcribed later, but the benefits gained by using the chart greatly offset the cost of transcribing it.

Publish Minutes within 24 Hours

It is a good idea to publish minutes of the meeting within 24 hours, while everything is still fresh in everyone's minds. Be sure to summarize major topics covered, what was decided, action items that were assigned (and to whom), and agenda matters that were rolled forward to a future meeting. If the future meeting was scheduled already, remind everyone of the date and time and who is supposed to attend. It is a good idea to keep the minutes to a page. People have so much to read that, if it is much more than a page, it will serve no useful purpose because most people won't read it.

Tell Every Participant What Is Expected of Them Ahead of Time

There is nothing more frustrating than having participants come to meetings unprepared. They waste everyone's time. But they cannot be blamed if they weren't told what was expected of them before the meeting took place. Furthermore, they must be allowed adequate time to prepare. If you need an extensive report that requires a lot of data, the participants need some time to prepare, and calling a meeting with only 15 minutes notice isn't likely to be enough.

It may also be necessary for a person to go back to his office to get information that you ask for during the meeting, whereas if he knew ahead of time, he could have brought the information along.

FACILITATING THE MEETING

One reason meetings become a fate worse than death is that the facilitator loses control. People get off on tangents. Side discussions take place. Arguments become heated and everything bogs down. Individuals are trying to promote their hidden agendas. Negativity dominates and slows progress.

If you can't deal with these issues, then your meetings will suffer. Let's begin with a common problem, which is tangents.

Dealing with Tangents

The mind works through association. One thing reminds you of another, which reminds you of something else, and that triggers still another thought, and you suddenly realize you have completely lost track of what you started out thinking about. This is normal. It also happens in team discussion.

The chairper-
son keeps
the harmony,
maintains
control, and
implements
acceptable
solutions when
dealing with
disruptive
behavior.

A member suddenly is reminded of something that is associated with what someone said, but is not relevant to the matter under consideration. She injects her thought into the discussion, and
the next thing you know, the group is dealing with her idea rather
than the topic they were supposed to deal with.

It is a good idea to have a flipchart page on the wall labeled
the Parking Lot. When a tangential topic comes up that should be
discussed, tell everyone that it will be put on the parking lot for
later processing. That way, they know that it will be handled, but
you can keep the meeting on target.

Sometimes a person will make a comment that seems to be
tangential, but is actually relevant to the topic at hand. If you

aren't sure it is tangential, say to the person, "I'm having trouble connecting what you are saying to the topic we're dealing with. Can you help me make the connection, or is this something we should put on the parking lot for future discussion?"

This is called a *relevance challenge,* and it allows you to tactfully point out that a person is on a tangent or, if they are actually making a relevant comment, you can get it clarified. This is especially helpful when you have a group member who may not be very good at expressing himself. He can try again, or perhaps someone else may understand him and help him restate the comment in a more understandable way.

Dealing with Emotion

When I worked in industry, there were a lot of managers who would tell people to "Leave your emotions outside," when they came to work. They thought that emotion had no place at work.

I always found this strange, because those same managers wanted their employees to be motivated to do their jobs, and motivation is an emotion. (Note the common root—moti. . . .) What they were really saying was that people should leave their negative feelings outside but bring in their positive feelings.

This is clearly impossible. People bring their entire beings to the table—the good, the bad, the ugly. In fact, without all of that emotion, they would be little better than robots, and a world of robots would be pretty dull and uncreative.

What is important is that we learn to deal with emotion so that it does not impede our work. It is also useful to understand that even anger can sometimes have a positive outcome, if it is channeled properly.

For example, I have occasionally been challenged by someone to prove a point or she may have criticized something I did, and my anger drove me to prove myself or "clean up my act." Ultimately, I produced a better result than would ever have happened if I hadn't gotten angry.

Of course, anger can turn into destructive, vindictive behavior. The angry person invests all of that energy into trying to de-

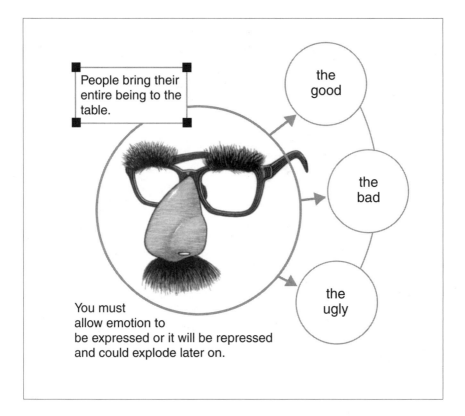

stroy the person who made him angry, and this is certainly not desirable.

So a group facilitator has to deal with anger when it comes up in such a way that it does not block group progress. It is tempting to do this by trying to reason with people. This simply does not work in most cases. You should understand a simple

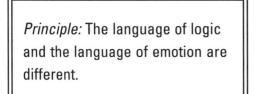

Principle: The language of logic and the language of emotion are different.

rule of human behavior, which is that *the language of logic and the language of emotion are different.* This means that you can't deal with emotion using logical, reasoning approaches. You must allow emotion to be expressed or else it will simply be repressed and explode later on.

The most important lesson is that we allow this expression in a controlled manner. Give people a chance to express how they feel about an issue in a calm way. You can insist on that. No screaming or temper tantrums allowed.

However, you can bet that, if you say to people who are upset, "Calm down," you are just going to make them angrier.

Instead, tell the group to take a few minutes to think about the issue, clarify in their minds what they feel about it, and then call on them individually to express themselves. If another person tries to interrupt someone who is expressing herself, tell the interrupter to cool it. He will have his turn. Furthermore, you can promote listening to understand, rather than listening to rebut, by asking each party to a disagreement to restate what the other has said, in his or her own words. As Stephen Covey stated, one of the habits of highly effective people is to first listen to understand, before trying to be understood.

Once people have had a chance to express how they feel about an issue, you can turn to logically solving the problem. Don't rush it. This is a time when "haste makes waste." Follow this sequence: feelings–facts–solutions.

> Follow the sequence: feelings ⇨ facts ⇨ solutions.

It will save you a lot of time in the long run, even though it seems to take longer.

Let me point out that, if you are a very left-brained, logical thinker, you may not have much patience for this process. Very logical people tend to think that emotion is a waste of time, but I have seen such logical people get more emotional about technical issues than other people get over nontechnical topics. So if you find yourself getting impatient to "get on with it," use your logic to understand that the process is a logical one where humans are concerned.

Dealing With Negativity

I personally have very little patience with nay-sayers. They deplete the energy of a group with their constant sniping at every idea presented. If they are allowed to do this, the group will end up having a totally nonproductive meeting. So again, the facilitator must control this behavior.

In the meeting itself, you can ask the naysayer to suggest a way of dealing with his own concerns. This repeated approach on your part sends a clear signal that you are after solutions, not negativity. If this doesn't work, you call the person aside outside the meeting and have a heart-to-heart talk with him. Here's an approach that may help.

CAUTION obstacles ahead.

You can't solve problems or deal with obstacles unless you can see them.

Have you ever considered that the naysayer actually has a skill? No, I'm sure you haven't. He has been such a pain that this never occurred to you. But it's true. You can't solve problems or deal with obstacles unless you see them, and this person is good at spotting them, so why not use that ability to your advantage?

What you say to him is, "You're very good at spotting obstacles, but when you express them, it sometimes blocks the flow in our discussion, so here's what I would like you to do. I want you to be our official devil's advocate. When you have a concern, write it down. Don't express it right away. Then, later on, I'll call on you to read your concerns to the group, and we will address them."

At the next meeting, you tell the group, "Charlie is going to be our devil's advocate. He will record concerns. If any of you have concerns during our discussion, you can pass them to Charlie, and later on, we will deal with them."

At the appropriate time, you ask Charlie to read the list. You thank him, and then ask the group how those concerns can be addressed. By doing this, you have turned Charlie's negative behavior into a positive. And you may even find that people go to him outside the meeting for advice.

IN SUMMARY

Improving your management of meetings can improve your projects and save you a lot of money. It isn't that hard. All it requires is some discipline. Treat each meeting as a small project. You put together a plan (agenda), publish it, then monitor progress against the plan and control for deviations along the way. That yields control, which is what you are after.

KEY POINTS FOR CHAPTER 16

- A meeting should always use a timed agenda. Start on time and end on time!
- If you don't finish everything in the allocated time, reschedule another meeting to deal with the carryover items.

- Publish minutes within 24 hours.
- Tell every participant what is expected of him or her ahead of time.
- *Principle:* The language of logic and the language of emotion are different.
- Follow the sequence: feelings ⇨ facts ⇨ solutions.

QUESTIONS FOR REVIEW

1. What is the function of a code of conduct?
2. What are the four reasons for having a meeting?
3. What do you do if you can't finish everything in the time allowed for a meeting?
4. How do you deal with a person who gets off on a tangent?
5. When people get upset in a meeting, what should you do?

MANAGING YOURSELF

CHAPTER

Managing Your Time

I said earlier that you can't have control of a project unless every member of your team is in control of his or her own performance. They, in turn, won't be in control of their own performance unless they practice good time management.

Therefore, you can't have good project management unless everyone practices good time management. As it turns out, time management is really project management applied to the individual. You become clear on what you need to do. You plan how to do it. You monitor your progress and try to stay on target. You close out your personal "project," and move on to something else.

> *Principle:* You can't have good project management unless everyone practices good time management.

459

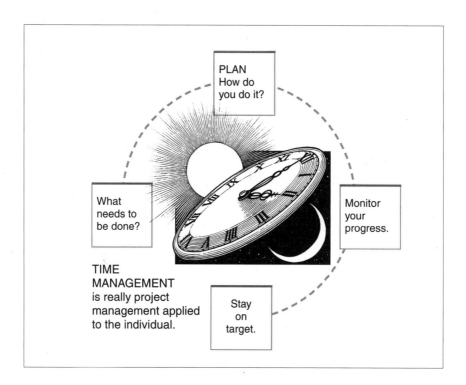

PLAN
How do
you do it?

What
needs to
be done?

Monitor
your
progress.

TIME
MANAGEMENT
is really project
management applied
to the individual.

Stay
on
target.

Because there are a lot of really good books on time management, I don't propose to duplicate them. I don't have the space. What I want to do is present some of the core principles that I think are necessary for project managers to practice.

THE VALUES-BASED APPROACH

Over the years I have looked at various approaches to managing time, and I believe the best is a values-based approach. All systems tell you to list all the things you must do, then prioritize the list, and do the important

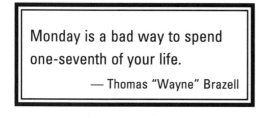

Monday is a bad way to spend
one-seventh of your life.

— Thomas "Wayne" Brazell

things first. They also talk about sorting your to-do list into four categories:

1. Urgent and important
2. Urgent but not important
3. Important but not urgent
4. Neither urgent nor important

Clearly, you should put the urgent and important things at the top of your priority list, but we often get trapped by category two—the urgent but not important ones. This is, in fact, a strange-sounding category. How can something that is not important be urgent.

> There cannot be a crisis next week. My schedule is already full.
>
> — Henry Kissinger

Simple. It's something your boss wants done *immediately,* even though it is not very important to anyone but her. As a maintenance worker said to me, the president has just bought a new picture for her office, and she wants it hung immediately. It isn't very important to the business, but because of her position, she can make it urgent.

The question is, how do you decide into which category things should go? And how do personal things that need to be done fit into the list of work things? That is where values come in.

What Are Values?

First of all, a value is something that is important to you. Some typical things that we value are freedom, financial security, physical security for ourselves and our family, status in our organizations and community, and so on. You would think that we would always behave consistently with our values, but this is not so. We often behave inconsistently, because we simply have not taken time to think through what is really important to us.

A value is something important to you . . . like spending time with your children.

An example of that is how we spend time with our children. I know a number of professionals who spend large amounts of time working, and have very little time to spend with their children. One friend of mine has two boys whom he dearly loves, but he is so wrapped up in his career that he admits he doesn't spend as much time with them as he would like. I hadn't seen the boys for nearly two years because he and I usually meet at work. One evening I visited his home, and his oldest boy had literally grown a foot in that two-year span.

I said to him, "You know, those boys are going to be grown and gone before you know it, and it will be too late to catch up on the time you didn't spend with them."

"I know, I know," he said sadly.

This is an example of not being clear about what is really important in one's life, and it happens when we have not consciously thought about our values.

Identifying Your Values

In his book, *The 10 Natural Laws of Successful Time and Life Management,* Hyrum Smith, CEO of the Franklin Quest company, asks people in his seminars what it would take to get them to walk across a large I beam that is laying on the floor. As you can imagine, it doesn't take much. However, he then asks them to imagine that the beam is suspended between the two towers of the World Trade Center, a height of about 1370 feet above the ground, and asks what it would take to get them to cross it.

Most people immediately say, "No way! You aren't going to get me to cross that thing." But when asked if their child was hanging from the other end, in danger of falling to his or her death, most agree that they would cross the beam. They would put the life of a child ahead of their own safety.

One exercise that I like is to have people imagine being at the end of their lives. In fact, you are just short of being on your death bed, and you are reflecting on how you have lived your life.

Suppose someone were to write a biography about you after your death. Not a small paragraph, but an in-depth article about you. What would you want them to say? What would you like to have accomplished?

> ## Examples of Values
> Children and family
> Education and learning
> Spirituality/religion
> Freedom/independence
> Personal health and fitness
> Spouse
> Financial security
> Quality of life
> Achievement
> Equality
> Forgiveness
> Beauty

I saw a TV biography on Rosalind Carter recently, and she and Jimmy Carter went to Africa to a village where 75 percent of the people suffered from Guinea worm. They ingest the larvae through their drinking water and it can grow to be three feet long. The mature worm then comes out of the body through a joint, and leaves the person paralyzed as if they had arthritis.

By spraying the water, they killed the larvae, and a year later, almost no one had Guinea worm. It has been practically eradicated through the efforts of the Carters. Wouldn't that be a nice thing to put in one's biography?

Try it yourself. Sit down and think about what you would want your biography to say. Then try to list about 10 to 15 values. You can use the list in the box as a guide, but feel free to add others as well. Make sure they are clear. If necessary, write a short sentence to explain what you mean. As an example, Benjamin Franklin listed *justice* as one of 13 values that would govern his life, and wrote that it meant, "Wrong none by doing injuries; or omitting the benefits that are your duty" (Smith, 1994, p. 47).

Ranking Your List

Now summarize each value with a single word or short phrase, and use the priority matrix presented in Chapter 6 to rank the list. You can either make your ranking binary, or you can allocate 10 points between each pair of values. For example, suppose I were ranking only three values. In ranking them, I ask if one is more important than two. If I am doing this in a binary way, and the answer is "yes," then I would put a check beside one. This is shown in Figure 17.1.

You can also allocate points to each item. Suppose, when you compare, you don't want to say that value one is 100 percent more important than value two. Rather, it is perhaps an 80/20 ratio. Then you can allocate points as shown in Figure 17.2.

As you can see, value three has been allocated a total of 14 points, value two has 5 points, and value one has 11. Notice that this makes the ranking three, one, two, as was found in Figure 17.1.

This system works okay for a list of three values, but as I showed in Chapter 6, if you have 10 to 15 values, you need to use

F I G U R E 17.1

Ranking a List of Three Values with Check Marks

|---|---|
1✓	2
1	3✓
2	3✓
The rank order is 3 - 1 - 2.	

F I G U R E 17.2

Points Allocated to the Three Values

VALUE	1	2	3	TOTAL	RANK
1	X	8	3	11	2
2	2	X	3	5	3
3	7	7	X	14	1

the matrix. Go back to that chapter now and create a matrix to use for ranking your values.

NOW WHAT?

Okay. You have your prioritized list of values. Now what do you do with it? I suggest that you ask yourself whether your life is being lived in accordance with your most important values. For example, if success at work was ranked number 6 on your list and your marriage ranked first, yet you are spending most of your time at work and almost none with your spouse, then your life is out of balance.

A basic premise is that your life will be most fulfilling when it is lived in accordance with your values. You need time for work, play, and personal renewal, whether that renewal comes from religion, spending time with your family, taking long walks, or whatever. As Covey likes to say, you must attend to production capability if you are going to have high production (Covey, 1989).

> You must attend to production capability if you are going to have high production.

If you think about the lesson from queuing theory, which is that no system should be loaded beyond about 85 percent of its capacity on a regular basis, then this might well be applied to your own life. There must be some reserve in there so that you can perform "maintenance" on the system called yourself.

THE 80/20 PRINCIPLE

The Pareto Principle says that 80 percent of the outcomes we get will result from 20 percent of our actions. Another way to say this is that about 80 percent of what we do yields negligible results! That means that most of us waste a tremendous amount of time.

> *The Pareto Principle:* Eighty percent of results will result from twenty percent of our actions.

Richard Koch (1998) showed that the Pareto Principle can be applied to almost every activity of our lives. For example, we tend to get the greatest enjoyment from just a small number of our leisure activities. We gain 80 percent of revenues from 20 percent of our customers. There will be an 80 percent return from 20 percent of the ideas we have. And 80 percent of progress in planning a project or developing a product will come from the last 20 percent of the work that goes into it.

For that reason, Koch argued that we must deliberately select those activities that give the "biggest bang for the buck," and concentrate on doing them. It is important to realize that I can do anything, but not everything. By concentrating on those things that give the greatest leverage, and ignoring those that give very small returns, I can greatly improve the outcomes I get in every facet of my life.

However, I think a word of caution is in order. It is tempting to become compulsive and carry any principle too far. As an example of this, the 80/20 principle suggests that when a team is trying to solve problems, they should determine the few that are causing the most grief and tackle them first.

This sounds logical, but overlooks an important human factor. It is likely that the problems causing a team the most grief will also be the most difficult to solve (not always true, of course, but generally so). If a team is not yet very mature, then trying to solve the hardest problems may fail and that early failure can destroy motivation. It is better to always start a team with some successes, and then move on to the more difficult problems. So in this case, the Pareto Principle should be ignored momentarily. After the team has had some "wins," you can move on to the 80/20 rule.

I think this applies to all areas of life. You need to "plan small wins" for yourself, to borrow a phrase from Kouzes and Posner (1987). Furthermore, it may be that a relationship with a certain person may not be very rewarding at the moment, so you may be tempted to sever the relationship, but if you were to develop it more fully, it may turn out to be the most rewarding one in your life. So, as in everything, moderation is in order.

Given this caution, to apply the Pareto Principle, you proceed as follows. In whatever area of your life you are trying to improve the use of your time, make a list of all the activities you engage in. Then identify those that give the greatest return on your investment of time. Concentrate on doing those and drop the others, and you will find yourself getting greater results than you ever dreamed possible.

MANAGING YOUR TIME

Now you need to combine the 80/20 principle with your values to improve your management of time. The usual approach to managing time, as I have said earlier, is to list all the things you must do, prioritize them, then do the high-priority ones first. It is also usual to estimate how many hours it will take to do each activity, add them

> You can do *anything,*
> but not *everything.*
> — From the cover of
> *Fast Company* magazine, May 2000

all up, and consider the implication. If you find, as do many people, that you have 329 hours of work to do and only 40 hours to do it in, then you clearly have a problem that requires more than just prioritization. You need to find someone to share some of the work, or you need to eliminate something from your list.

Your Boss' Priorities

One thing to remember is that you and your boss may not prioritize your list the same way. I would suggest that you try to bring your list into line with how your boss sees things, or you will be out of step with his or her expectations. If you don't agree with the boss' rankings, discuss it and see if you can understand his or her viewpoint. If you can, fine. If you can't you will have to defer to the boss if you want to be evaluated favorably.

In the event that you work for a boss who plays macho manager and says, "It's all got to be done," and refuses to prioritize for you, then you will have to do it yourself and hope you get it right. You may also find that your boss' expectations are unrealistic, and you will have to make some career choices in the long run.

Keep a Time Log

Do you know where your time is going? Do you know how much of every day is productive and how much is wasted? If not, you should keep a time log for a few weeks. About once an hour, make a note of what you have just done. At the end of the tracking period, put things into categories and add them up. If you find that there are a lot of time wasters, try to find ways to eliminate them.

> Whoever admits that he is too busy to improve his methods has acknowledged himself to be at the end of his rope.
> — J. Ogden Armour

How much time are you spending planning? If the answer is none, you have a problem. Most likely, you are going to say, "I don't have time to plan. I'm doing all I can do to keep from drowning."

I'm sorry, that is a false conclusion. One reason you are about to drown is that you have no plans. It is a chicken-and-egg problem. If you have no plan, you tend to have lots of fires to put out, and once you have a lot of fires, you convince yourself that you can't

> There's never enough time to do it right, but there's always time to do it over.
> — Jack Bergman

take time to plan or the fires will get worse. So it goes on and on.

A general rule of project management is that 1 hour spent planning will save 3 hours in execution. The reason is simple: you work more efficiently and effectively when you have a plan, and you reduce rework and false starts. If you think you don't have time to plan, you're wrong, *you don't have time not to plan!*

Learning to Estimate

When you look over your time log, do you find that jobs frequently take far more time than you thought they would? If so, is it because you were interrupted a lot, the scope changed, or you simply guessed wrong? If the answer is that you guessed wrong,

FEEDBACK is important.

When you practice without feedback on results, you could be getting better at doing it wrong.

Principle: No learning takes place without feedback on results.

No learning takes place without feedback on performance!

Suppose you were trying to improve the speed at which you run the mile. Every day you go out and run the mile several times, but you never time yourself. You don't know if you are getting

Principle: When you practice without feedback on results, you could be getting better at doing it wrong.

then you need to keep records for a long period so that you can sharpen your skills. Estimating cannot improve unless you track your actual time spent.

better or worse. You could be getting worse and don't know it. In fact, you may be learning an ineffective way of running! You are getting better at doing it wrong!

Tackling the Big Jobs

There is a tendency to avoid big, especially unpleasant, jobs. This is commonly called procrastination. There are two ways to get out of this dilemma. One is to give the job to someone else to do—if you have that luxury. The other is to approach the job the way you would eat an elephant—one

> How do you eat an elephant?
> One bite at a time.

bite at a time. Trying to eat the whole elephant in one bite is simply overwhelming, and we tend to avoid overwhelming tasks.

Chunk it down, using the same technique as in developing a WBS. After all, that's what it amounts to—breaking down the work into manageable bits. Then tackle a couple of easy pieces to give yourself a sense of accomplishment, and go on from there to the bigger ones.

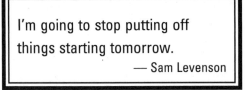

> I'm going to stop putting off things starting tomorrow.
> — Sam Levenson

Achieving Balance

As I suggested in the section on the 80/20 principle, the question we all must ask is, "What am I willing to give up so that I can do those things that really matter to me and that give the greatest return?" Much of life's stress and burnout come from trying to do it all, and not accomplishing anything very well as a consequence.

> No problem is so big or so complicated that you can't run away from it.
> — Charles Schultz
> Speaking as Charlie Brown

Furthermore, even if you manage to reduce your list from 329 hours worth of things to only 40 hours of tasks, you may still have too much on your plate. Remember, you can't work at 100 percent efficiency. And the problem with some time management techniques is that they keep you in a state of perpetual turmoil. A common approach is to rank the to-do list in categories A, B, and C. The A things are urgent and important. The B things are urgent but not important, and so on. But you find that, by the end of the week, you haven't gotten around to the C category at all, and now they are becoming B things and those that were on the B list have moved up to the A list.

For that reason, Covey (1989) suggested that you never fully schedule your week. Leave yourself some slack. You know nothing is ever going to go exactly as planned—or even as hoped for—so if

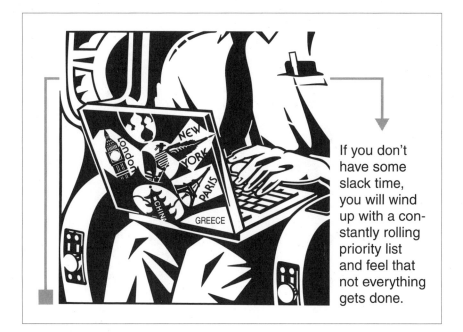

If you don't have some slack time, you will wind up with a constantly rolling priority list and feel that not everything gets done.

you don't have some slack, you will wind up with a constantly rolling priority list, and feel that nothing ever gets done.

Because I travel so much, I see hundreds of people in airports and on airplanes with their laptops and planners, working long days. They sometimes have a harried, fugitive look about them. They have their 20-pound planners out, hurriedly making entries, crossing off things they have done, while simultaneously talking with someone on their cell phones about some situation that has become urgent and important during their absence. The planners are running their lives, rather than being tools that they use to manage their lives themselves.

> The trouble with the rat race is that even if you win, you're still a rat.
>
> — Lily Tomlin

If you don't like being in a rat race, don't feed the rat.

Life lived in an obsessive, compulsive way seems to me to be hardly worth living. But that is my values speaking. I once lived the "go-get em, eat them before they eat you," rat race kind of life, and realized one day that I was living a script laid on me by society. We define success as status and money, and the two often go hand in hand. So I aspired to be CEO of some company.

It was only after considerable soul-searching that I realized what was going on and decided that being a senior manager in a corporation was not for me. I did become a middle manager at ITT Telecom, with 63 people in my department, so I did experience the life of senior managers and confirmed that this was not my career path. I made my choice, and I have been happy with it.

I started my own company, deliberately kept it small, and now I am under almost no stress. I live in the Blue Ridge Mountains, with deer and other wildlife as frequent visitors to my back yard, and I enjoy my work and my life.

You have to make your own choices as well. If you choose to be CEO, then go for it, but it should be a conscious choice, rather than a script laid on you by others—especially your parents, who may be living vicariously through you. Just take time out occasionally to reflect and think ahead. When you reach the end of your life and look back, will it have been everything you wished it to be? Or will you have a long list of regrets?

Only if you take charge of your own life and manage it like a project, are you likely to be able to say, "I did it my way."

KEY POINTS FOR CHAPTER 17

- *Principle:* You can't have good project management unless everyone practices good time management.
- A value is something that is important to you.
- You must attend to production capability if you are going to have high production.
- *The Pareto Principle:* Eighty percent of results will result from twenty percent of our actions.
- *Principle:* No learning takes place without feedback on results.

QUESTIONS FOR REVIEW

1. What are values?
2. How do you apply the 80/20 principle to managing your time?
3. What is the value of keeping a time log?

CHAPTER

Building Personal
Effectiveness

Trying to become a better project manager is a combination of learning more about the tools and techniques of management and increasing your personal effectiveness. We all want to excel at what we do, but learning tools alone won't make it so.

In addition, we sometimes fail to distinguish between *efficiency* and *effectiveness*. Efficiency is doing things well, and effectiveness

> ***Effectiveness:*** doing the right things.
>
> ***Efficiency:*** doing things well.

is doing the right things. Naturally, we want to do both, but it does no good to be 100 percent efficient if you are doing the wrong thing. Or, as someone said, "Digging the world's best hole is not helpful if you don't need a hole in the first place."

If you are working on self-improvement, it is important that you work first on doing the right things, and then on doing them right. In Chapter 17, we discussed managing your time better by focusing on your values. By concentrating on what is important to you, life becomes more rewarding and more successful. We also examined the Pareto Principle, which says that 80 percent of the results you get come from 20 percent of your activities. So your values should first govern what you are concentrating on, and then the activities you engage in, in order to pursue those values, should be chosen on the basis of the 80/20 rule.

STEPHEN COVEY'S SEVEN HABITS

In 1989, Stephen Covey wrote *The 7 Habits of Highly Effective People*. The book was on the bestseller list for several years, and has remained a popular book. Covey clearly struck a chord with readers.

Covey says that most of the success literature of the first 150 years of U.S. history was based on the *character* ethic. That is, if you want to be more successful, you should concentrate on building your character.

Then, around 1940, the literature shifted focus to the *personality* ethic. If you became a nice person, you would win. It was the "me, me, me," narcissistic approach that advocated manipulating others to get what you wanted. If they got hurt by your actions, that was just too bad. The golden rule became, "Do unto others before they get a chance to do you."

Even our schools got into the act. If kids had high self-esteem, it was believed they would perform better. So children were told, "You are special, you are special, you are special." As Charles Sykes (1995) wrote, "There is no evidence that high self-esteem leads to increased performance, but there are plenty of studies that show that good performance leads to high self-esteem" (p. 22).

During the 1980s, we had to introduce ethics courses into business school programs. Why? Because there was an increase in unethical behavior by executives that cost corporate America a lot of money.

Character counts

Boletín Financiero

Be successful.

It seems to me that the ethics problem would not exist if we were emphasizing character development rather than manipulating others. So Covey's seven habits are a move in the right direction.

There is no evidence that high self-esteem leads to increased performance, but there are plenty of studies that show that good performance leads to high self-esteem.

A few years ago a manager at a company I worked with told me that he was reading my book on building project teams during a trip. He was also preparing a Sunday school lesson, so he had his bible with him on the airplane. He laid both books on the seat while he went to the restroom on the plane, and when he returned, the team book had disappeared, but not the bible. Someone had stolen it.

I have often wondered what kind of person would steal a book on team building. I also wonder if he was afraid God would get him if he stole the bible or if, because of his obvious lack of character, he thought he didn't need a bible. In any case, I wouldn't want to be a member of his team. Would you?

PARADIGMS AGAIN

I explained in Chapter 2 that we behave according to what we believe, and these beliefs are called paradigms. Furthermore, I stated that there is a difference between a theory-espoused and a theory-in-action. What we say we believe and what we actually believe are sometimes different, and you can bet that we behave according to what we truly believe, rather than what we say we believe.

> What would you have to believe to behave as you just did?

In fact, if you find that you have behaved in a way that either surprises or disappoints you, ask yourself, "What would I have to believe to behave as I did?" I can promise you that your behavior is in line with your deeply held belief.

The question is, are your beliefs in line with reality? If not, then you will behave in ways that tend to get negative outcomes. This is the problem with the personality ethic. I can tell myself over and over again that I am the world's best athlete, but that won't make it so. Telling yourself lies that you hope to make true won't work, which is why positive thinking can be carried too far. Certainly you are better off thinking positively than negatively, but only if you are realistic about your *capability*.

BEING GOOD AT EVERYTHING

There is a story told by someone (I have forgotten whom) that illustrates a trend in American organizations that I believe leads to serious problems. The animals once decided to start a school. After long discussion, they decided that the curriculum would consist of flying, running, climbing, and swimming. All little animals would have to learn these and would be graded on how well they performed each activity.

Once the school opened, trouble began. There were several little ducklings that excelled in swimming and flying, but running wore out their web feet and climbing was impossible, so they flunked climbing and got mediocre grades in running.

The little squirrels could run, climb, and swim okay, but they could only fly downward (more like gliding, actually), so they got low grades in that subject. The snake children were given credit for slithering, as opposed to running—which was clearly an impossibility—and they too flunked flying, even though they could climb and swim acceptably.

The real trouble started when the chipmunks and groundhogs insisted that the curriculum should include burrowing. The school board refused. They were already having enough trouble with the fact that too many little animals were flunking some subjects, and feared that their graduation rate would be dismal unless they passed them anyway, and they weren't about to add another subject that some of the children would also flunk.

Because they wouldn't include burrowing, the groundhogs and chipmunks dropped out and formed their own school, teaching only those subjects that their children really needed to know.

Does this sound familiar? Have you ever had a performance appraisal? Did the appraiser say, "Well, you've done excellent work in these areas this past year." Then there was a brief pause, followed by, "However, you really need to work on this . . ." And you were told some area of weakness that you should improve if you wanted to advance in the organization.

The net result of this approach is to force everyone to gravitate toward mediocrity! Rather than looking at those areas in which a person excels and developing those talents to their full potential, we insist that everyone be good at everything.

I think this is a serious mistake. Howard Gardner (1993) wrote that there are nine kinds of intelligence, not just the two that we normally think of—math and verbal. These include musical, spatial, bodily kinesthetic, interpersonal, and intrapersonal, to name a few.

> *Principle:* We force everyone to gravitate toward mediocrity by insisting that they be good at everything.

Assuming that this is true, a musical genius like Bach or Mozart might do poorly in a school system that emphasizes math, science, language, and so on, yet excel in a music school. But they would also be evaluated negatively at work. "Yes, I know Bach can write a fugue that moves forward, backward, has inversion, and all, but he is absolutely abysmal at accounting," says his boss. "He really has to work on that if he wants to go anywhere in this company."

> In differentiation, not in uniformity, lies the path of progress.
> — Louis Brandeis

SO WHAT'S MY POINT?

My point is that you should figure out what you are really good at and work to perfect your abilities in those areas. If you try to be good at everything, you will wind up pleasing no one, especially yourself. If you are managing projects and are a really good strategic thinker but are poor at detail work, then try to enlist the help of team members to do the detail work while you concentrate on strategy. In fact, I suggest that you adopt the philosophy and practice of playing to the strengths of all team members and minimize the effects of their weaknesses by helping them in those areas. I believe you will achieve far greater success this way than by trying to force everyone to fit the same mold.

> *Principle:* You will never get ahead of the pack by being just like all other members of the pack.

Please don't misunderstand me. If you can correct some of your weaknesses, by all means do so. I am not suggesting that, just because you may not be good at something

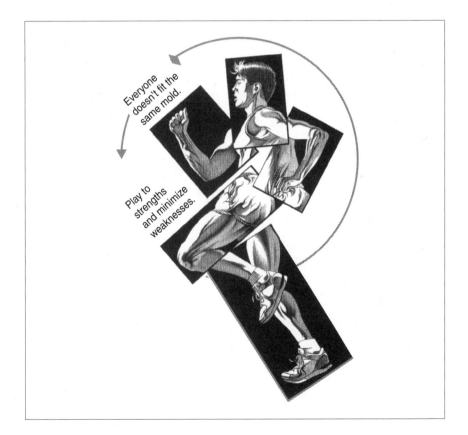

you should ignore it completely. For example, if you are not a very good writer, I definitely suggest that you try to improve this skill, because you cannot get very far in life if you can't write a coherent sentence. But you don't need to aspire to the level of a Pulitzer-prize-winning author.

> *Principle:* Play to strengths and minimize weaknesses.

There is such a thing as *satisficing,* a term coined by James March and Herbert Simon (March and Simon, 1966), to mean that something is *good enough* for the time being at least.

LIFE PLANNING

If you have not done so, I suggest that you go back and read Chapter 17 on managing your time before you go any further. In particular, clarify your primary values. Identify what is *really* important to you.

Next conduct the end-of-life exercise suggested in Chapter 17. If you were to look back on your life, what would you have achieved? Express this as your life goals. Write a mission statement for yourself. Develop a vision of what it would be like to achieve that mission. Be as crisp and clear about it as you can. The more clearly you can visualize the future, the more likely you will be to achieve it. Fuzzy vision leads to fuzzy outcomes.

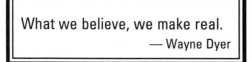

> What we believe, we make real.
> — Wayne Dyer

The mind tends to create what we hold in it over long periods of time. As Wayne Dyer wrote, "What we believe, we make real" (Dyer, 1989). Another way to say this is that, if you can see yourself doing something, you can do it, and conversely, if you say, "I can't see myself doing that," then you won't be able to.

Identify what is really important to you.

This is in line with everything that I have written about para-digms—they become self-fulfilling prophecies. Then you must be careful what you believe, because if you believe negative things about yourself, that is what you will experience.

Once you have your mission and vision developed, you should plan how to accomplish the desired result. What will be your strategy? What will be your implementation steps? Treat your life plan exactly like a project plan, remembering to keep it flexible enough to respond to desirable changes along the way. The world won't stand still while you execute your plan, and situations may dictate that you discard part of the plan and develop some new steps.

Use people you admire as role models. They can be living or dead. If, for example, you think Benjamin Franklin is a worthy role model, read a biography on him and adopt some of his approaches to life.

Engage in lifelong learning. Determine the knowledge and skills that you need to achieve your life's mission, and set about to acquire or develop them. Read Malcolm Knowles' book, *Self-Directed Learning* (Knowles, 1975) and follow his suggestions for developing your own self-education program.

> "You can't believe something that isn't true," said Alice. "Of course you can," said the queen. "Why, sometimes I've believed as many as six impossible things before breakfast."
> — Lewis Carroll
> *Through the Looking-Glass*

As you progress, review your performance and take steps to correct for any deficiencies that you identify. Don't engage in self-flagellation. That is counterproductive. Rather, you should view every "failure" as a positive—you wouldn't have failed if you hadn't tried.

Feedback from yourself to yourself should always be in terms of behavior, not an expression of blame. What was it that you did or didn't do that caused the failure? Once you understand the behavioral deficit, you can set about correcting it.

> *Principle:* You can't fail if you don't try. Failure is evidence that you did at least give it a shot.

You may want to read the following books to help in developing your skills, your life plan, and your career:

Covey, Stephen R. *The 7 Habits of Highly Effective People: Powerful Lessons in Personal Change.* New York: Fireside Books, 1989.

Heller, Robert. *Achieving Excellence.* New York: DK Publishing, 1999.

Keirsey, David. *Please Understand Me II.* Del Mar, CA: Prometheus Nemesis Book Company, 1998.

Smith, Hyrum. *The 10 Natural Laws of Successful Time and Life Management.* New York: Time-Warner, 1994.

KEY POINTS FOR CHAPTER 18

- There is no evidence that high self-esteem leads to increased performance, but there are plenty of studies that show that good performance leads to high self-esteem.
- *Principle:* We force everyone to gravitate toward mediocrity by insisting that they be good at everything.
- *Principle:* You will never get ahead of the pack by being just like all other members of the pack.
- *Principle:* Play to strengths and minimize weaknesses.
- *Principle:* You can't fail if you don't try. Failure is evidence that you did at least give it a shot.

QUESTIONS FOR REVIEW

1. What is the difference between efficiency and effectiveness?
2. What is the difference between the personality ethic and the character ethic?
3. What is the result of insisting that people improve all their deficiencies?

APPENDIX:
SCHEDULE COMPUTATIONS

Once a suitable network has been drawn, with durations assigned to all activities, it is necessary to perform computations to determine the longest path through the project. If start and finish dates have already been "dictated" for the project, these calculations will tell whether the required dates can be met. On the other hand, if a start date is given, the computations will tell the earliest completion date for the project.

The simplest computation that can be made for a network will determine total working time on the longest path through the project and will reveal whether any latitude exists on paths parallel to the longest path. The longest path is called the critical path because a slip on the longest path will cause a corresponding slip in the completion of the project. This computation tells how many weeks (or days or hours, depending on time units being used) it will take to complete the project if no holidays or vacation periods exist.

Naturally, during certain parts of the year, holidays and/or vacations will intervene, so the actual *calendar time* for the project is likely to exceed the *working time.*

It is also important to note that the conventional way to compute project working times is to ignore resources initially. In other words, activities are treated as though they have *fixed durations*, which is based on the assumption that certain levels of resources will be available when the work begins.

Further, these durations are estimated from historical data and are based on a person being available who has a certain skill level to do the work. As was pointed out in previous chapters, if these conditions are not met, the actual working times will deviate from estimated times, sometimes considerably.

NETWORK RULES

In order to compute project working times, there are only two rules that are *universal* in defining how networks function. The software you use may impose additional rules, which will be presented in the user manual. The universal rules follow:

Rule 1: Before a task can begin, all tasks preceding it must be completed.

Rule 2: Arrows denote logical precedence. Neither the length of the arrow nor its angular direction have any significance. (It is not a vector, but a scalar.)

BASIC SCHEDULING COMPUTATIONS

Although no one is likely to do network computations manually in this day of abundant scheduling software, it is important to understand how computations are made by the computer. Otherwise, it is easy to fall into the *garbage-in–garbage-out* problem. Further, the computer output is not easily understandable unless the computation method is understood. What does float really mean, for example?

The following material will explain how the basic computations are performed with no concern for resource limitations. That is, these computations are based on the assumption that the required resources will indeed be available when the time comes to do the work. This is equivalent to saying that the organization has an *unlimited* pool of people, which of course is never the case. For this reason, a schedule that assumes unlimited resources is considered to be the *ideal* or *best-case* situation, and provides a starting point for resource-constrained project scheduling. Chapter 7 deals with the allocation of resources to yield a realistic working schedule.

We will use the network developed in Chapter 5 to prepare a meal to illustrate scheduling computations. That network is repeated here in Figure A.1, using AON notation. A solution will be presented later using AOA notation. The numbers in the duration (DU) cells are working durations in minutes. Each activity contains cells in which we can enter the *earliest start* (ES) and *earliest finish* (EF) as well as the *latest start* (LS) and *latest finish* (LF) for the activity. Other notation schemes are used in other books and with various software packages. This one just seems to me to be very simple to understand.

In order to locate the critical path and compute earliest and latest start and finish times for noncritical project activities, it is necessary to do two sets of computations. These are called *forward pass* and *backward pass* calculations.

Forward Pass Computations

A forward pass is made through the network to calculate the earliest achievement times for each activity in the network. If we remember that each activity has a start and a finish, we can talk about *early start* and *early finish* times, as mentioned above. This really amounts to having start and finish *events* for each activity, but they are not usually shown in activity-on-node diagrams. As was stated above, the durations for the activities in Figure A.1 are *working minutes*. The project is shown as starting at time $t = 0$. For schedules spanning several days or weeks, once activity start and finish times are determined, they can be converted to calendar dates, but that step will be omitted in this chapter. For our simple project, we will compute the total project time in minutes and then convert to hours.

Figure A.2 shows the first steps in the forward pass computation. *Make Menu* starts at time = zero. It takes 30 minutes. That means it has an early finish of 30 minutes after it starts, or $t = 30$. As soon as Make Menu is finished, two activities can start—*Shop* and *Wash Tableware*. This means that the early finish for Make Menu becomes the early start for these two succeeding tasks.

It takes 60 minutes to do the shopping, so the early finish for that task is 90 minutes. You simply add its duration to its early

FIGURE A.1

AON Network for Preparing a Meal

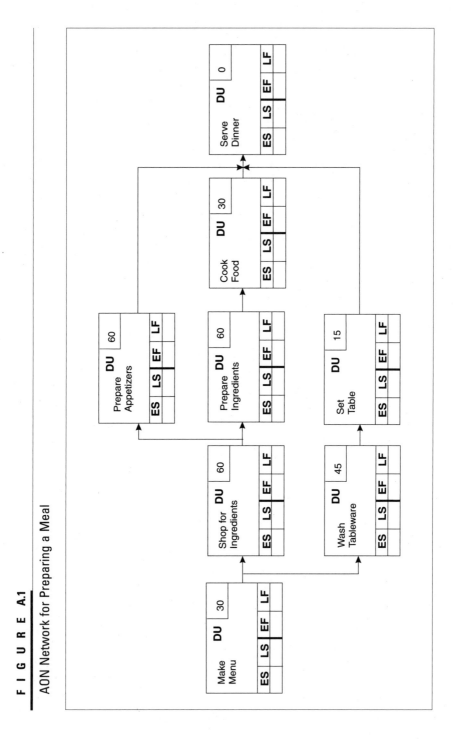

F I G U R E A.2

First Step, Forward Pass Computation

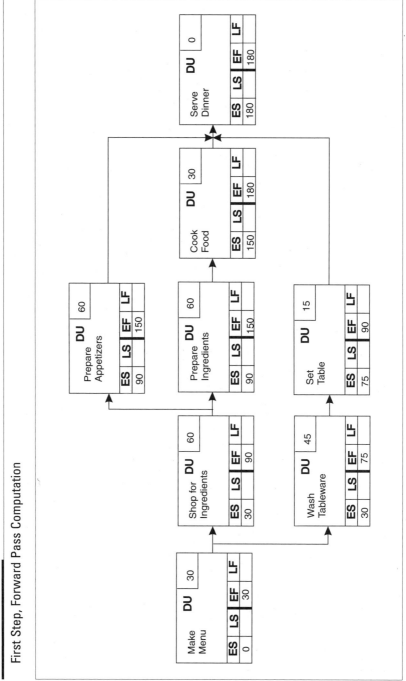

start time to get its early finish. The same is done for Wash Tableware. Again, the early finish for each task becomes the early start for succeeding ones. We continue this process until we get to *Serve Dinner.*

At this point, *Prepare Appetizers* has an early finish of 150 minutes, *Cook Food* has an early finish of 180 minutes, and *Set Table* has 90 minutes for its early finish. Which one becomes the early start for *Serve Dinner?* Remember, rule 1 presented earlier says that you can't start a task until all tasks preceding it have been completed. Because Cook Food ends the latest (has the largest early finish time), its early finish becomes the early start for the serving task.

Given the activity durations shown and the sequences detailed by the network, the project has a completion 180 minutes after it begins. Because we are usually trying to meet an imposed completion time for most projects, this working time can now be compared to the target to see if that target can be met, given an anticipated start date or time. If it cannot, then either the project must start earlier, the end date must slip out, or the network must be changed to compress (shorten) the critical path.

For our example, suppose we had planned to come home from work at 5 p.m. and have dinner prepared to serve at 7 p.m. Because we have found that it will take three hours to prepare the meal, this won't work. Either we will have to shorten the time of some tasks, start the process at 4 p.m., or revise the network in some way. Naturally, we could shave 30 minutes off the project by preparing the menu the day before. For many projects, such a solution would not be an option, so we will pretend for now that this option is not available and see what other approaches are available.

In that case, the question is, How will the network have to change in order to finish in two hours? The answer to this question is never obvious in a complicated network (although it is fairly obvious in this one). As a general rule, in order to see what else in the network might have to change, more information is needed. Specifically, we need to know the latest times by which each activity can be achieved and still meet the 180-minute completion.

You might ask, "Why not use the 120-minute completion, because that is what is required?" The answer is that a *best-case* computation is made first so that we can see which paths have latitude and which one(s) is critical. The best case is considered to be that 180 minutes is acceptable. A shorter time is a worse case because you will have to squeeze time out of something. A longer time is also a worse case, because you are stretching the project out unnecessarily.

For that reason, we assign a 180-minute *late finish* to Serve Dinner, which means that it has the same early finish and late finish times, and zero duration, making it actually an *event*. This is an example of the only kind of event actually shown in activity-on-node networks, and it is called a *milestone*.

Now that the late finish time has been set for Serve Dinner, we do a *backward pass computation* to determine the latest event times on all activities, which will permit achievement of the 180-minute completion.

Backward Pass Computations

Beginning with *Serve Dinner,* and assigning a late finish time of 180 to it, we subtract its duration of zero from that time to get its late start (see Figure A.3). Naturally, that gives a late start of 180. This late start time must be the late finish for all predecessors to Serve Dinner, so that time is entered into the cells for each activity. Now in the case of *Prepare Appetizers,* we subtract its duration of 60 minutes from its late finish of 180, to get 120 minutes. This number becomes its late start time. For *Cook Food,* we do the same and get a late start of 150. In turn, we use 150 as the late finish for *Prepare Ingredients,* subtract its duration, and get 90 minutes for its late start.

Now notice the junction at the beginning of *Prepare Appetizers* and *Prepare Ingredients.* The late start for Prepare Appetizers is 120 minutes and for Prepare Ingredients it is 90 minutes. Which one of these should we use for the late finish of the predecessor, *Shop?* If we allowed shopping to finish as late as 120 minutes, that would mean that Prepare Ingredients could not start until that time, and if you

Backward Pass to Determine Latest Times

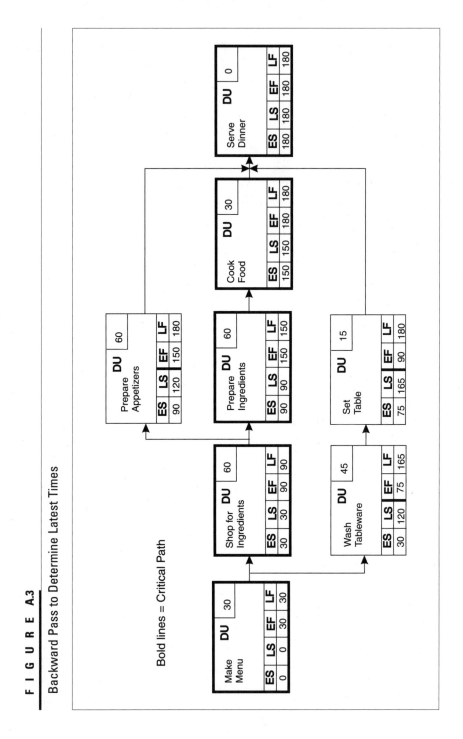

Bold lines = Critical Path

Make Menu	**DU**	30
ES	**LS** **EF**	**LF**
0	0 30	30

Shop for Ingredients	**DU**	60
ES	**LS** **EF**	**LF**
30	30 90	90

Prepare Appetizers	**DU**	60
ES	**LS** **EF**	**LF**
90	120 150	180

Prepare Ingredients	**DU**	60
ES	**LS** **EF**	**LF**
90	90 150	150

Cook Food	**DU**	30
ES	**LS** **EF**	**LF**
150	150 180	180

Serve Dinner	**DU**	0
ES	**LS** **EF**	**LF**
180	180 180	180

Wash Tableware	**DU**	45
ES	**LS** **EF**	**LF**
30	120 75	165

Set Table	**DU**	15
ES	**LS** **EF**	**LF**
75	165 90	180

work forward from there to the end of the project, you will see that this will push the end time out to 210 minutes, instead of 180. We can now offer the following rules for assigning early and late times to activities that have multiple predecessors or successors.

Rule: When two or more activities precede another, the earliest start for the successor will be the *latest* of the late finish times for the predecessors.

Rule: When two or more activities follow a predecessor, the latest finish for the predecessor will be the earliest *late start* for the successors.

Continuing in this way, you arrive at the late activity times shown in Figure A.3.

Activity Maximum Float

Now examine *Prepare Appetizers*. Note that its early start is 90 and its late start is 120. The difference of 30 minutes is called the *activity float*. This float represents latitude for the activity. So long as it starts no later than 120 minutes and takes no longer than its duration of 60 minutes, the project can be finished by 180 minutes.

Note the activities that run through the center of the diagram. They all have the same early and late start and the same early and late finish times. These activities have no float, and are called *critical*.

> An activity is a critical activity any time it has no float.

The path containing those activities is, in turn, called the *critical path*. What we have done is apply *Critical Path Method* to locate that path. By making the final activity late finish the same as its early finish, we have forced one path to have no float. As you can see, it is the longest path.

The term *float* comes from the fact that Prepare Appetizers can start as early as 90 minutes and as late as 120 minutes, or we say it can float around for the difference of 30 minutes. Note that float is always calculated by taking the latest start minus the earliest start, or the latest finish minus the earliest finish. In equation form, you have:

$$\text{Max. float} = LF - EF$$

or

$$\text{Max. float} = LS - ES$$

where LS means late start, LF means late finish, ES means early start, and EF means early finish.

THE VALUE OF FLOAT

It is tempting to think that float is undesirable. The first suggestion people sometimes make is to finish a task that has float as early as possible and move resources onto the critical path to shorten it so that you wind up with no float anywhere. To see why this is not a good idea, we must remember that the durations for all tasks are *estimates*, that they have 50-50 likelihoods if averages have been used, and that we often have made those estimates using poor history, so they are suspect to begin with. Given those facts, it is highly advisable to have float on all but the critical path to compensate for unforeseen problems, estimating errors, and so on.

> The best practice in managing projects is to do whatever is necessary to stay on schedule.

What about the critical path itself? That series of activities must be managed in such a way that all tasks are completed on time or the project will be delayed (unless lost time on one activity can be recovered on a later one). It is very risky to allow a critical path task to slip, under the assumption that you will recover the time later. Murphy's Law invariably prevails when you do this. In fact, the best working rule I know is to *do whatever is necessary to stay on schedule.*

CALCULATIONS FOR AN AOA NETWORK

The calculations for AOA networks are done exactly the same as for AON networks. The only real problem is with notation. Figure A.4 is the same diagram for preparing a meal in AOA format. In the first edition of this book, I learned that people were confused by the notation, because I had split each node in half and placed an early time on the left side and a late time on the right. However, as was pointed out earlier, each node contains at least two events, and if several activities enter or leave, there will be several events contained. I have looked at a number of systems of notation, and no single one is unambiguous. For that reason, I have placed the early and late times on each end of all arrows. On the left end will always be the early start and late start, and on the right end will be the early finish and late finish. Each node is simply numbered for easy reference. See Figure A.4 for this example.

CONSTRAINED END DATE SCHEDULING

As was mentioned above, the usual situation for most projects is that an end time (or date) has been imposed, either by contract with the customer or by management, on the basis of business considerations. This end date may be earlier than the earliest completion date determined by the forward pass computation, in which case the project must be started earlier or the schedule must be shortened somehow.

In many cases, as was mentioned previously, the start date for a project is also dictated by availability of resources or some other factor, so the start date cannot be moved up. When this is true, the critical path must be shortened. When this is done, other paths may become problems as well.

For the network just analyzed, suppose the end time were established as 120 minutes. (Or, as was mentioned previously, you want to serve dinner at 7 p.m., and start the project at 5 p.m.) What would be the overall impact on the project? To answer that question, we will impose a late finish of 120 minutes on the project and do a new backward pass calculation. Note that there is no need to

AOA Diagram for Preparing a Meal

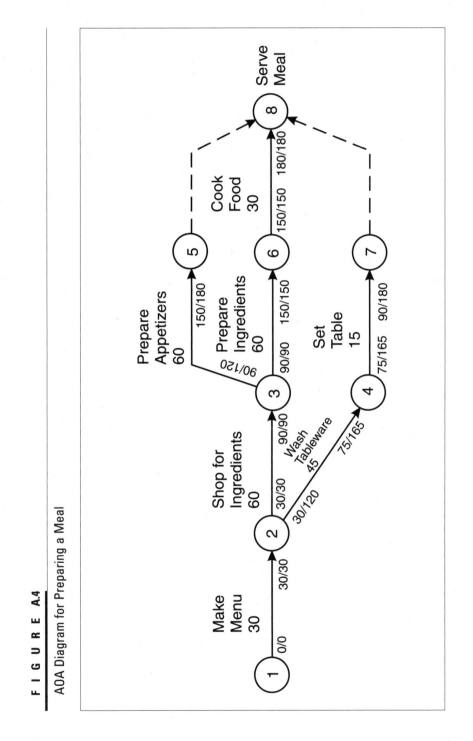

do a new forward pass computation yet, because the forward pass only determines early times, and these will not change until an activity duration is changed or else the network is redrawn.

Figure A.5 shows the network with the latest project completion constrained to 120 minutes. When the backward pass computations have been completed, we find a strange thing. The float on the former critical path is now *negative!* When the float is negative, the activity or path is called *supercritical*. Note also that Prepare Appetizers now has negative 30 minutes of float, whereas before it had positive 30 minutes. Thus we have two supercritical paths. (Wash Tableware and Set Table still have 30 minutes float, because originally this path had 90 minutes of float.)

It is also interesting to examine the late times on Make Menu and Shop. These times are now negative. In the case of Make Menu, this is telling us that the activity needs to start 60 minutes before it is planned to start, which we already knew.

If we cannot start the project early, we will have to shorten the critical path by 60 minutes to meet our deadline. Let's suppose we can do this by taking 30 minutes off the time to Prepare Ingredients and another 15 minutes out of Make Menu and Shop. We might get time out of Prepare Ingredients by buying frozen vegetables rather than fresh, so they don't have to be cut up. If these adjustments are made, we now have the result shown in Figure A.6.

We now have a situation which is not desirable as a general rule. We have two critical paths. Prepare Appetizers is critical, as are Prepare Ingredients and Cook Food. For this particular project, we might not be concerned about having two critical paths, but most of the time this would be very undesirable. The reason is that, when you have no float, you know that if anything goes wrong with the task its duration increases; you will slip your overall project finish time by the amount of the increased duration (unless you can reduce the times taken by subsequent tasks). Having two critical paths increases risk.

For this reason, you should try to get rid of all but *one* critical path. This can only be done by changing the duration of one or more activities, by allowing the end date to be extended, or by redrawing the network to have a new configuration. Assuming that

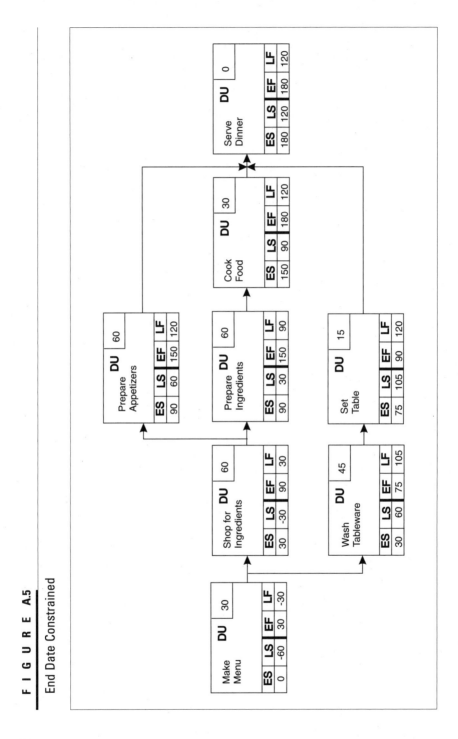

End Date Constrained

FIGURE A.6

Network With Times Reduced

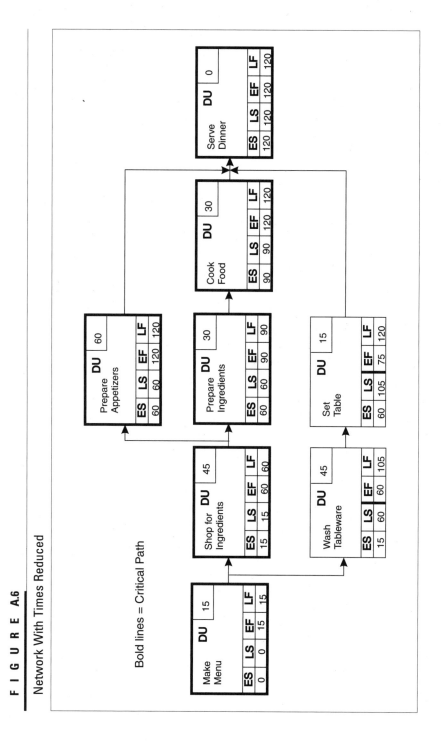

Bold lines = Critical Path

503

T A B L E A.1

Factors to Consider in Eliminating a Dual Critical Path

Number of activities	Path with most activities might be most risky.
Skill level of people	Path with least-skilled people could be most risky.
Technical risk	Path with greatest technical risk should have float.
Weather/uncontrollable	Give float to activities with uncontrollable factors.
Cost	Give float to activities which cost most to do.
Historical data	Least historical data—give float; historically a problem—ditto.
Available backup plan	Give float to activities with no obvious backup.
Business cycle	If business tends to get hectic at certain times, give float to activities affected.
Difficulty	Float given to activities that are most difficult.

one must choose which critical path to eliminate, the issue becomes how to decide which path should be taken off the critical path.

There is no single answer to this problem. Float is only one kind of risk involved in a project. There are also risks from technical problems, poor estimates, weather and other uncontrollable factors, and so on. Table A.1 shows some of the factors that should be considered in making a decision. The comments that follow each factor explain the rationale for deciding what to do.

REDUCING ACTIVITY DURATIONS

When it is necessary to reduce the duration of a critical path, we usually try to reduce activity durations, rather than redrawing the network. That is because we usually believe the logic is more or less sound, so changing sequences might not be an option. When it is, using techniques like lead-lag networks, for example, can be done first.

Whether activity durations can be reduced depends on three factors. Can the work be done faster by increasing *efficiency* (perhaps by using that more productive person mentioned previously)? Can the *scope* of the work be reduced? Can extra effort be applied to the job to get it done faster (by increasing resources). It is not always possible to reduce activity time by adding more resources, because a point of *diminishing returns* is reached, often because people simply get in each other's way.

There are, of course, two ways to increase human resources applied to a project. One is by adding bodies. The other is by working the same number of people more hours per day, which we call working *overtime*. In both cases you tend to get diminishing returns very quickly. I know of one company that measured the impact on productivity of working overtime. They measured productivity for a normal 40-hour week, then again at the end of three weeks in which people worked 50 hours per week. Productivity after working overtime was back down to the normal 40-hour-per-week level, and errors had increased.

When productivity declines without an increase in errors, it is often because people are *pacing* themselves. They think like a marathon runner who knows that if she runs too fast at the beginning and uses up her energy, she will be unable to finish the race. On the other hand, when error rates increase, it is usually because people are truly fatigued.

We also find that people doing *knowledge work* suffer the same kind of problems. One study found that when people put in 12 hours of overtime on knowledge work, you probably get an increase in output from them equivalent to what you would expect in 2 normal working hours!

CONVERTING ARROW DIAGRAMS TO BAR CHARTS

Although an arrow diagram is essential to do a proper analysis of the relationships between the activities in a project, determine activity float, and identify the critical path, the best tool for the people actually doing the project work is the bar chart. People find it much easier to see when they are supposed to start and finish their jobs if you give them a bar chart. The schedule shown as an arrow diagram in Figure A.4 has been portrayed as a bar chart in Figure A.7, making use of what was learned about the schedule from the network analysis.

F I G U R E A.7

Bar Chart for Project to Prepare a Meal

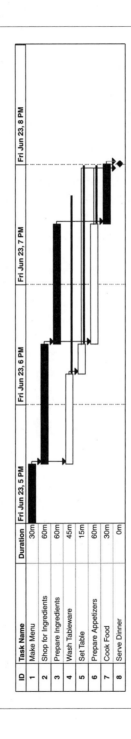

In this figure, the critical path activities are shown as solid bars, whereas those which have float are shown as hollow bars with dots trailing to indicate the amount of float the activity has. Note that each activity is shown starting at its earliest possible time, so that float is reserved to be used only if absolutely necessary. This is the conventional method of displaying bar charts.

Note that Wash Tableware has 90 minutes of float and so does Set Table. Naturally, it is the *same float*, and, initially, before the project begins, there are 90 minutes of float *available* for each activity. However, if all of the float is used up on Wash Tableware, there will be none left for Set Table, and it would therefore be critical.

This illustrates a real pitfall of bar charts. Assume that different individuals are doing two sequential activities that share a common amount of float. Because the chart does not show interrelationships of activities, it is hard for the people performing the work to tell that the float is shared. They look at the chart and think that they each have the designated float. Then, if each tries to make use of the float, the project is in trouble.

In fact, Parkinson's Law can be applied to project float. Parkinson's Law states that work always expands to fit the time allowed. When applied to float, it means

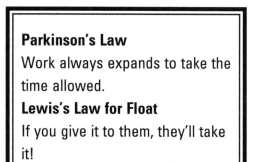

Parkinson's Law
Work always expands to take the time allowed.
Lewis's Law for Float
If you give it to them, they'll take it!

that *when you give them float, they take it!* For this reason, some software can be set up so float is not printed. The implication of such a schedule is simply that the work should be done as shown.

I personally do not like that approach. I prefer to explain to team members that float is shared, and encourage them to keep float in reserve to be used only if necessary. Indeed, it is always a good idea to keep float in reserve to be used if an estimate turns out to be wrong or if an unforeseen problem causes the work to be delayed. As someone told me recently, every project should be planned as if there will be at least some percentage of the total time when the entire city will have a power blackout and nothing will get done.

McGregor formulated a management model some years ago which stated that some managers see workers as undependable, wanting only a paycheck from the job, and so on. He called this a *Theory-X* outlook, and postulated that a manager with such an outlook would tend to get the expected result.

The opposite outlook, which is more positive, he called a *Theory-Y* view. This would naturally be the more desired view, because a manager would tend to get the more positive result. It is easy to see Parkinson's Law and Lewis's Law for Float as Theory-X outlooks. However, I don't see them that way. In today's downsized, right-sized, understaffed organizations, people simply have to do their work in priority order and this leads to putting off things until they absolutely have to be done. Thus, if they have float, they tend to take it, but unfortunately they may take it at the beginning of an assignment, and if they have a problem with the work there is no float left to use in getting the work done on time.

LIMITATIONS OF CRITICAL PATH METHOD

It is important to remember what was pointed out earlier—namely that the conventional critical path analysis which has been illustrated for this network assumes that unlimited resources exist in the organization, so that all activities can be done as planned. As the bar chart shows, however, a number of points exist at which activities are running in parallel. If those activities require the same resources, there may not be enough to get the job done as shown, so the schedule cannot be met. This subject is addressed in Chapter 7.

MULTIPLE CALENDARS

One final subject must be considered in doing basic network computations. Not all project activities can follow the same working schedule. Does everyone work Monday through Friday? Do some people work only weekends?

In some projects there may be activities that require actual working days to complete; others that do not. Pouring of concrete must be done during the workweek. However, that concrete may cure over a weekend. For this reason, it is important that multiple calendars be considered in scheduling.

Consider, for example, the situation in which one group works a conventional Monday through Friday schedule. Another group, however, works only weekends—Saturday and Sunday. This is shown in Figure A.8.

Now suppose the two groups are scheduled to do two sequential tasks, with group 1 working exactly one week (M–F), followed by the people in group 2, who are supposed to finish their work over the weekend. However, group 1 gets behind on their work by one day. How much is the schedule impacted? As Figure A.9 shows, the work will slip an entire week because group 1 gets behind only one day!

F I G U R E A.8

Multiple Calendar Network

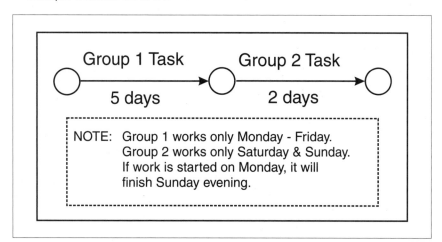

F I G U R E A.9

Slip One Week

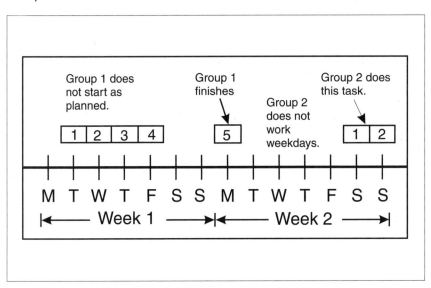

This kind of problem highlights the occasional need for multiple calendars in scheduling. They are called calendars because holiday and overtime dates are different for the two groups. If the software being used does not permit the use of multiple calendars, it may still be possible to "fake it" and force the schedule to reflect correct working dates, but this may be difficult to do. For this reason, selection of software should be made with this potential requirement in mind.

THE BALI BOOK SCHEDULE

In Chapter 4 we developed a WBS for the Bali book project. Figure A.10 is a schedule for that project in AOA format, and Figure A.11 is one in AON notation. This illustrates a much more complex schedule than those presented up to now. Note, however, that times are shown ignoring resource limitations that might exist.

AOA Schedule for the Bali Book Project

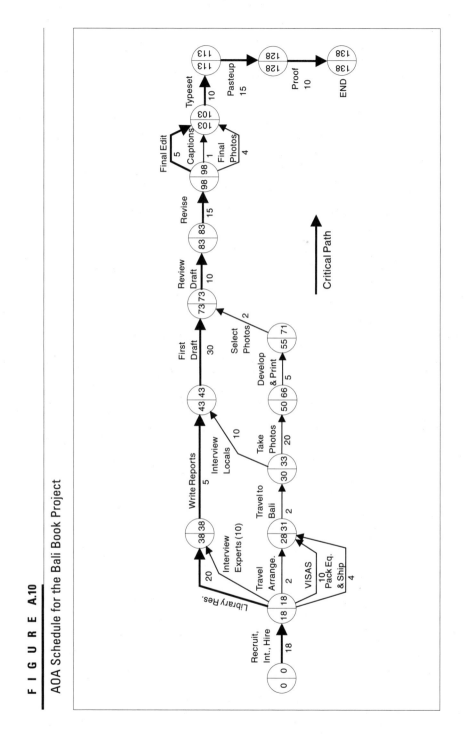

F I G U R E A.11

AON Network for the Bali Book Project

18/18 Recruit, Int., Hire 18

38/38 Library Research 20

28/38 Interview Experts 10

43/43 Write Reports 5

40/43 Interview Locals 10

73/73 First Draft 30

83/83 Review Draft 10

98/98 Revise 15

57/73 Select Photos 2

55/71 Develop & Print 5

50/66 Take Photos 20

30/33 Travel to Bali 2

20/31 Travel Arrange 2

28/31 VISAS 10

22/31 Pack & Ship 4

103/103 Final Edit 5

99/103 Captions 1

102/103 Final Photos 4

113/113 Typeset 10

128/128 Pasteup 15

138/138 Proof 10

138/138 END 0

KEY:

early/late time
xxx/yyy
xx
task duration

non-critical

critical task

KEY POINTS FOR APPENDIX

- Scheduling is done to work out sequencing of work and to show earliest completion for a project, as well as points at which latitude exists in the work.
- Only two rules govern *all* networks. The others are a function of the software being used.
- The *forward pass* computation determines earliest finish times for activities.
- The *backward pass* calculation determines latest finish times.
- Critical path computations assume unlimited resources, and thus may not be achievable.
- Slack strictly applies only to events and float applies only to activities. In practice, the terms are used interchangeably.
- Try to get rid of all but one critical path in a network, because critical activities increase risk.

Questions for Review

QUESTIONS FOR REVIEW

1. What is the difference between a *forward pass* computation and a *backward pass* computation in a network?
2. To find the critical path in a network, what date is used for the final event late time?
3. What is the difference between *float* and *slack?*
4. Of all the ways by which an activity duration can be shortened, what two are undesirable?
5. If an activity duration is to be changed by reducing its scope, what actions should a project manager take before proceeding?
6. In a network, each event or activity has *early finish* and *late finish* times specified. For practical purposes, what is the *real time* by when an activity should be finished?

Network for Scheduling Exercise

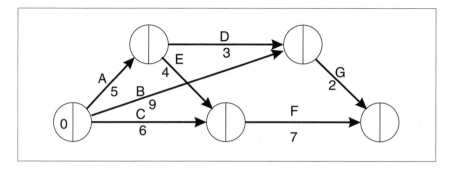

7. In the above network (Figure A.12), calculate all activity
   early and late times and show where the critical path is.

   A. Which activities are on the critical path?
   B. What is the maximum float (in days) for activity D?
   C. What is the minimum float for activity D?

ANSWERS TO QUESTIONS

CHAPTER 1

1. Because every project solves some kind of problem for the customer or the organization that conducts the project.
2. False.
3. Control is exercised by comparing where you are to where you are supposed to be, and taking corrective action when there is a deviation from plan.
4. Scope is the magnitude or size of the project.
5. Because they are interdependent. If values are assigned to three of them, the fourth will be determined by the relationship between them.
6. By improving the process by which the job is done.
7. Prevention, appraisal, and failure.
8. Because you can meet the PCTS targets and not meet all customer expectations.
9. Because people skills form the foundation that holds up the rest of the "structure."

CHAPTER 2

1. A paradigm is a belief about what the world is like. A model of reality.
2. False.

3. False.
4. Theory-espoused is what a person says she believes. Theory-in-use represents what she truly believes.
5. Because the "fat cutting" often goes too far and we start cutting muscle and bone, thus destroying the organization.
6. True.

CHAPTER 3

1. Because they want the status and money a manager's position gives them, but they don't really like the activities that constitute managing.
2. No. If you have no plan, you have no control. Therefore it is necessary to plan. The fact that most managers don't plan doesn't make it right.
3. The tendency to do work instead of managing. It happens most frequently to *working project managers.*

CHAPTER 4

1. False. It measures one's thinking *preferences.*
2. No, except possibly for CEOs. Herrmann suggested that a square profile may be preferred because the individual could relate to people from all four quadrants.
3. You work hard to compensate for those quadrants in which your team has low preferences.
4. You can draw on them to help with issues that are best dealt with using their preferred thinking modes.

CHAPTER 5

1. Failing to properly define the project at the beginning is one of the major causes of project failure.
2. The belief that silence means agreement, and the failure to solicit disagreement.

3. By actively involving core team members in developing a written statement of the team's problem, mission, and vision.

4. You can cut down a tree with a knife, but a saw is better. Some processes are more efficient and effective than others.

5. What the final outcome will look like.

6. What are we going to do? and for whom are we going to do it?

7. A problem is a gap between where you are and where you want to be, which is confronted by obstacles that prevent easy movement to close the gap.

8. False.

9. A closed-ended problem has a single answer and is oriented toward the past. An open-ended one has no single solution and is aimed at bringing about a condition that has not existed before.

10. The scientific approach, which is primarily analytical.

11. Right-brained, synthetic, conceptual thinking.

12. True.

13. Meet with the person to clarify his or her expectations for the project and be sure that they are in line with reality.

CHAPTER 6

1. Strategy is an overall game plan. Tactics are the small steps or actions taken to execute the strategy. Logistics is the transporting of people and materials, feeding people, and so on.

2. A good strategy can save considerable time and money on a job.

3. Technical strategy involves the choice of technology to be employed in the project.

4. Quadrant D, which is holistic, conceptual, synthetic thinking.

5. Both are things that can cause an impact to project success. A threat is something that may be done by an entity (person or organization), whereas a risk is something that can just happen—bad weather, accident, and so on.
6. SWOT stands for strengths, weaknesses, opportunities, and threats.

CHAPTER 7

1. Quadrant B, or detailed thinking.
2. Planning is answering the "who, what, when, how" questions.
3. Three main reasons: First, you may forget something significant, and second, you cannot think of everything yourself. Third, the team will not be fully committed to the plan, because it is yours.
4. Because the more important your deadline is, the more important your plan becomes. If you don't have much time to get a job done, you really need a plan!
5. The duration should be four to six weeks for any task, and one to three weeks for knowledge tasks.
6. The WBS defines project scope; allows time estimates that feed your schedule, and estimates of cost for labor, materials, capital equipment, and other expenses, and assigns resources.
7. The tendency of people to not start early on a task, even when they can.

CHAPTER 8

1. A risk is anything that can happen to create an adverse effect to a project schedule, cost performance, or scope.
2. The three steps are (1) identify risks, (2) quantify them using the RPN, and (3) develop contingency plans to deal with those that cannot be ignored.
3. Probability, severity, and detection.

4. Any severity higher than seven points requires a contingency plan.

CHAPTER 9

1. The critical path is any path that has no float (or slack). It will also be the longest path through the project.
2. The real advantage is to find all of the places in a project where you can do work in parallel so that the job can be done in minimum possible time.
3. So you can see everything clearly. The screen can be too small to see linkages off the screen.
4. Time-critical leveling tries to relieve overloads without slipping the project end date. Resource-critical leveling will relieve overloads by slipping the end date if necessary.
5. The maximum duration for any task is four to six weeks.
6. The job becomes 80 or 90 percent complete and stays there for a long time, because reverse inferences are seldom correct.
7. About 80 percent. It is seldom that high. For knowledge workers, it is usually 50 to 60 percent.
8. Setup time, which comes from having people working on too many things at once.
9. Because you are too far up on the waiting time curve and, if anything happens, you have to wait forever to get access to the system.

CHAPTER 10

1. All four of them.
2. Control is exercised by comparing where you are to where you are supposed to be, then taking action to correct for any deviations that exist.
3. If you have no plan, you cannot have control—by definition!

4. You have no idea of the effort required to stay on schedule. If it is excessive, you have a problem that the schedule alone won't show.

5. BCWP is actually called earned value. It is a measure of the value of the work that has been accomplished in a job.

6. The four responses are (1) ignore the deviation, (2) take corrective action to get back on track, (3) revise the plan, or (4) cancel the project.

7. The 15 percent rule states that, by the time you are 15 percent into a project (on the horizontal time line), if you are in trouble, you will stay in trouble.

8. Cross-charging cuts off your ability to see if a project is doing better or worse than expected and contaminates both project databases so that the data cannot be used for future estimating.

9. The critical ratio is given by the expression:

$$CR = CPI * SPI,$$ or the cost performance index multiplied by the schedule performance index

10. A project with a critical ratio of only 0.6 is in serious trouble and may be a candidate to be canceled, a decision usually made by senior managers.

11. EAC is the estimate at completion, which is the most recent forecast of what the project will cost when it is finally finished.

12. The three reviews are status, design, and process.

13. One reason is that we make people defensive with that question, and second, we may have done nothing wrong, but can always stand to improve, so we ask, "What do we want to do better in the future?"

CHAPTER 11

1. The mind can deal with five to nine bits of information at once.

2. Because they increase the setup time.

3. Two or three small projects are generally all one person can manage.

CHAPTER 12

1. A method can be applied to any project, but a methodology is specific to an organization, and spells out what kinds of documents, approvals, and procedures the project manager must follow.
2. A product development methodology is an engineering procedure that specifies design criteria, test requirements, and so on. A project management methodology indicates how the product development project should be managed.

CHAPTER 13

1. To manage means to handle. It deals with the administrative aspects of one's job. To lead is to get people to go along with you. It involves influence.
2. McGregor's Theory-X, Theory-Y model is based on the self-fulfilling prophecy, which states that we tend to get what we expect from people.
3. The flaw is that the self-fulfilling prophecy treats influence as unidirectional, when it is actually circular.
4. Hand-holding would be best initially, until she "learns the ropes."

CHAPTER 14

1. Motivation is the drive to satisfy one's needs.
2. He believed that a person who is starving (physiological need not met) will be very unlikely to be very concerned about social and esteem needs. Thus, the lower-level needs must be satisfied for the higher-order needs to emerge.

3. People self-actualize by engaging in a pattern of activity.

4. Motivation will be depressed or destroyed.

5. A person is hardly likely to be motivated to do a job if she is not committed to it. Commitment comes from seeing the value of doing something. Motivation comes from having one's needs met through engaging in the activity.

6. All motivation comes from within a person. All a manager can do is try to place an employee in a job that contains his motivation pattern, and the rest is up to the employee.

CHAPTER 15

1. A team is a group of people who are committed to achieving a common goal, enjoy working together, and produce high-quality results.

2. A primary concern is what's in it for me? (Also called WIIFM.)

3. People want to work on projects that make a difference, that are important!

4. Show people why even the mundane project is important. If it is not, cancel it!

5. Because competition and cooperation cannot exist at the same time. Competition within a team is contrary to the definition of a team as a group of people who work together to achieve a common goal. In addition, competition often turns destructive.

6. Kick off a project with a purely social event, so people can get to know each other in a relaxed, casual manner.

7. The real intent is to convey meaning.

8. Because perception is reality to people. They will behave according to their perceptions, regardless of whether the perception is in line with reality.

9. Because there is a causal sequence involved in generating conflict. If goals are not clear, people will fight. Also, if

you don't have a clear goal, procedures can't be defined. Next you need to clarify who is responsible for a task. Then you can work on any relationship problems that may exist.

10. People can't think independently, make decisions, or function well without information. It is one of the most valuable resources we have.

11. Every decision may have a quantitative or acceptance component.

12. Groupthink is the tendency for a group to accept the leader's suggested course of action when they don't all agree with it. The Abilene Paradox arises because we assume silence means consent.

CHAPTER 16

1. A code of conduct establishes guidelines for meeting behavior and, if members violate it, the team can bring them back in line with a gentle reminder that they agreed to abide by it.

2. To give information, get information, make a decision, or solve a problem.

3. Schedule a follow-up meeting.

4. First ask, "How is what you are saying relevant to what we are discussing?" If he can make the connection for you, fine. Otherwise, ask the person to come back to the topic and, if necessary, write his concern on a *parking lot* sheet.

5. Ask people to pause and decide what the issue means to them. You should deal with feelings, then facts, then solutions.

CHAPTER 17

1. Values are things or issues that are important to you.

2. Spend your time doing the 20 percent of things that give you 80 percent of your desired outcomes.

3. A time log tells you where your time is going. If it is being spent on unhelpful activities, you can decide to eliminate them and do something else.

CHAPTER 18

1. Effectiveness is doing the right things. Efficiency is doing them well.
2. The personality ethic advocates influencing people, manipulating people, and perhaps running over them in order to win. It is narcissistic in nature. The character ethic advocates developing one's character to be successful.
3. Rather than capitalizing on what they are good at, we force them to gravitate toward mediocrity.

APPENDIX

1. A forward-pass computation determines early times for activities and a backward-pass finds late times.
2. The final event date is set equal to the earliest finish time determined by the forward-pass calculation.
3. For all practical purposes, they are the same. They mean you have latitude to get work done.
4. Adding overtime in the very beginning and reducing quality of the work.
5. Get approvals in writing from stakeholders. They should be advised of the impact to the project of the change in scope being requested.
6. The final event. The "real time" for an activity *must* be its earliest time. If you allow float or slack to be used up, the activity winds up on the critical path and jeopardizes the project.
   A. Activities A, E, and F are on the critical path.
   B. The maximum float for activity D is six days.
   C. The minimum float for activity D is one day.

GLOSSARY

Activity The work or effort needed to achieve a result. It consumes time and usually consumes resources.

Activity description A statement specifying what must be done to achieve a desired result.

Activity-on-arrow A network diagram showing sequence of activities, in which each activity is represented by an arrow, with a circle representing a node or event at each end.

Activity-on-node A network diagram showing sequence of activities, in which each activity is represented by a box or circle, (that is, a *node*) and these are interconnected with arrows to show precedence of work.

Authority The legitimate power given to a person in an organization to use resources in order to reach an objective and to exercise discipline.

Backward pass calculation Calculations made working backward through a network from the latest event to the beginning event to calculate event late times. A forward pass calculation determines early times.

Calendars The arrangement of normal working days, together with nonworking days, such as holidays and vacations, as well as special work days (overtime periods) used to determine dates on which project work will be completed.

Change order   A document that authorizes a change in some aspect of a project.

Control   Control is exercised by comparing where you are to where you are supposed to be so that corrective action can be taken when there is a deviation from target.

CPM   An acronym for Critical Path Method. A network diagramming method which shows the longest series of activities in a project, thereby determining the earliest completion for the project.

Crashing   An attempt to reduce activity or total project duration, usually by adding resources.

Critical path   A path that has no float or slack and is also the longest path through the project.

Dependency   The next task or group of tasks cannot begin until preceding work has been completed, thus the word *dependent* or dependency.

Deviation   Any variation from planned performance. The deviation can be in terms of schedule, cost, performance, or scope of work. Deviation analysis is the heart of exercising project control.

Dummy activity   A zero-duration element in a network showing a logic linkage. A dummy does not consume time or resources, but simply indicates precedence.

Duration   The time it takes to complete an activity.

Earliest finish   The earliest time that an activity can be completed.

Earliest start   The earliest time that an activity can be started.

Estimate   A forecast or guess about how long an activity will take, how many resources might be required, or how much it will cost.

Event   A point in time. An event is binary. It is either achieved or not, whereas an activity can be partially complete. An event can be the start or finish of an activity.

Feedback   Information derived from observation of project activities, which is used to analyze the status of the job and take corrective action if necessary.

Float   Any path shorter than the critical path will have latitude that is called either float or slack. It provides a measure of how much an activity can be delayed before it begins to impact the project finish date.

Forward pass method   The method used to calculate the earliest start time for each activity in a network diagram.

Free float   The amount of time that an activity can be delayed without affecting succeeding activities.

Gantt chart   A bar chart that indicates the time required to complete each activity in a project. It is named for Henry L. Gantt, who first developed a complete notational system for displaying progress with bar charts.

Hammock activity   A single activity that actually represents a group of activities. It "hangs" between two events and is used to report progress on the composite which it represents.

Histogram   A vertical bar chart showing (usually) resource allocation levels over time in a project.

***i-j* notation**   A system of numbering nodes in an activity-on-arrow network. The *i*-node is always the beginning of an activity, whereas the *j*-node is always the finish.

Inexcusable delays   Project delays that are attributable to negligence on the part of the contractor, which lead in many cases to penalty payments.

Latest finish   The latest time that an activity can be finished without extending the end date for a project.

Latest start   The latest time that an activity can start without extending the end date for a project.

Learning curve   The time it takes humans to learn an activity well enough to achieve optimum performance can be displayed by curves, which must be factored into estimates of activity durations in order to achieve planned completion dates.

Leveling   An attempt to smooth the use of resources, whether people, materials, or equipment, to avoid large peaks and valleys in their usage.

Life cycle   The phases a project goes through from concept through completion. The nature of the project changes during each phase.

Matrix organization   A method of drawing people from functional departments within an organization for assignment to a project team, but without removing them from their physical location. The project manager in such a structure is said to have *dotted line* authority over team members.

Milestone   An event of special importance, usually representing the completion of a major phase of project work. Reviews are often scheduled at milestones.

Mission   The goal or objective that the team must achieve.

Most likely time   The most realistic time estimate for completing an activity under normal conditions.

Negative float or slack   A condition in a network in which the *earliest time* for an event is actually later than its *latest time.* This happens when the project has a constrained end date which is earlier than can be achieved, or when an activity uses up its float and is still delayed.

Node   A point in a network connected to other points by one or more arrows. In activity-on-arrow notation, the node contains at least one event. In activity-on-node notation, the node represents an activity, and the arrows show the sequence in which they must be performed.

Paradigm   A belief about what the world is like; a model of reality.

PERT   An acronym which stands for Program Evaluation and Review Technique. PERT makes use of network diagrams as does

CPM, but in addition applies statistics to activities in order to estimate the probabilities of completion of project work.

Pessimistic time Roughly speaking, this is the *worst-case* time to complete an activity. The term has a more precise meaning, which is defined in the PERT literature.

Phase A major component or segment of a project.

Precedence diagram An activity-on-node diagram.

Queue Waiting time.

Resource allocation The assignment of people, equipment, facilities, or materials to a project. Unless adequate resources are provided, project work cannot be completed on schedule, and resource allocation is a significant component of project scheduling.

Resource pool A group of people who can generally do the same work, so they can be chosen randomly for assignment to a project.

Risk The possibility that something can go wrong and interfere with the completion of project work.

Scope The magnitude of work that must be done to complete a project.

Slack Essentially the same as float (see above).

Subproject A small project within a larger one.

Statement of work A description of work to be performed.

Threat Something that can be done by an outside entity that may cause problems in a project.

Time now The current calendar date from which a network analysis, report, or update is being made.

Time standard The time allowed for the completion of a task.

Variance Any deviation of project work from what was planned. Variance can be around costs, time, performance, or project scope.

Vision   What the final result of the project will look like.

Work breakdown structure   A method of subdividing work into smaller and smaller increments to permit accurate estimates of durations, resource requirements, and costs.

RESOURCES FOR
PROJECT MANAGERS

Following is a list of sources of information, books, and professional associations that may be helpful in managing projects. Not all are specifically aimed at project management, but you may find them helpful anyway.

CRM Films: A good source of films for training, including *Mining Group Gold, The Abilene Paradox*, and many others. 2215 Faraday Avenue • Carlsbad, CA 92008 • tel. (800) 421-0833

Jossey-Bass/Pfeiffer: A source of training programs, training materials, instruments, and books on management. 350 Sansome Street, 5th Floor • San Francisco, CA 94104 • tel. (800) 274-4434 • fax (800) 569-0443 • www.pfeiffer.com.

The Lewis Institute, Inc.: Founded by the author, the Institute provides training in project management, team building, and related courses. The core program is Project Management: Tools, Principles, Practices, and has been attended by over 20,000 managers worldwide. 302 Chestnut Mountain Drive. • Vinton, VA 24179 • tel. (540) 345-7850 • fax (540) 345-7844 •e-mail: jlewis@lewisinstitute.com • www.lewisinstitute.com.

McGraw-Hill Books: Source for other titles on project management. www.mcgraw-hill.com.

MindWare: The store for the other 90 percent of your brain. A source of tools, books, and other materials to help enhance learning and creativity in organizations. They have a nice catalog listing their materials. 6142 Olson Memorial Highway • Golden Valley, MN 55422 • tel. (800) 999-0398 • fax (612) 595-8852

Morasco, Vincent: A newspaper-clipping service that operates on a pay-per-use basis. You pay only for the clippings you actually make use of. A good source of up-to-the-minute information. Vincent Morasco • 3 Cedar Street • Batavia, NY 14020 • tel. (716) 343-2544

PBS Home Video: Source of the video *21st Century Jet.* (800) 645-4727. www.shopPBS.com.

Pegasus Communications: Publishers of *The Systems Thinker,* a monthly newsletter. They also have videos by Russell Ackoff and Peter Senge, among others. P.O. Box 943 • Oxford, OH 45056-0943 • tel. (800) 636-3796 • fax (905) 764-7983

Pimsleur International: The most effective way to learn a language on your own is with the cassettes using a method developed by Dr. Paul Pimsleur. Learning is virtually painless. 30 Monument Square, Suite 135 • Concord, MA 01742 • tel. (800) 222-5860 • fax (508) 371-2935

Project Management Institute: The professional association for project managers. Over 25,000 members nationwide as of July 1997. They have local chapters in most major U.S. cities and a number of countries. 130 S. State Road • Upper Darby, PA 19082 • tel. (610) 734-3330 • fax (610) 734-3266 • www.pmi.org.

Video Arts: A source for management training videos. Originally founded by John Cleese, many of them take a humorous approach to the subjects they cover. 8614 W. Catalpa Ave. • Chicago, IL 60656 • tel. (800) 553-0091.

REFERENCES AND READING LIST

Ackoff, Russell. *Ackoff's Fables: Irreverent Refelections on Business and Bureaucracy.* New York: Wiley, 1991.

Ackoff, Russell. *The Art of Problem Solving.* New York: Wiley, 1978.

Adams, James L. *Conceptual Blockbusting: A Guide to Better Ideas,* 2d ed. New York: Norton, 1979.

Adams, John D., editor. *Transforming Leadership: From Vision to Results.* Alexandria, VA: Miles River Press, 1986.

Ailes, Roger. *You Are the Message: Secrets of the Master Communicators.* Homewood, IL: Dow Jones-Irwin, 1988.

Archibald, R. D., and Villoria, R. L. *Network-Based Management Systems (PERT/CPM).* New York: Wiley, 1967.

Argyris, Chris. *Overcoming Organizational Defenses: Facilitating Organizational Learning.* Boston: Allyn Bacon, 1990.

Axelrod, Robert. *The Evolution of Cooperation.* New York: Basic Books, 1984.

Barker, Joel A. *Future Edge.* New York: William Morrow, 1992.

Bedi, Hari. *Understanding the Asian Manager.* Singapore: Heinemann Asia, 1992.

Beer, Stafford. *Brain of the Firm,* 2d ed. New York: Wiley, 1981.

Bennis, Warren G., and Nanus, Burt. *Leaders: The Strategies for Taking Charge.* New York: Harper & Row, 1985.

Benveniste, Guy. *Mastering the Politics of Planning.* San Francisco: Jossey-Bass, 1989.

Blake, Robert, and Mouton, Jane. *The Managerial Grid*. Houston: Gulf Publishing, 1964.

Blanchard, Benjamin S. *Engineering Organization and Management*. Englewood Cliffs, NJ: Prentice Hall, 1976.

Brooks, F. P. *The Mythical Man-Month: Essays on Software Engineering*. Reading, MA: Addison-Wesley, 1975.

Burns, James McGregor. *Leadership*. New York: Harper & Row, 1978.

Buzan, Tony. *The Mind Map Book*. New York: NAL/Dutton, 1996.

Carlzon, Jan. *Moments of Truth*. New York: Perennial, 1987.

Cialdini, Robert B. *Influence: The Power of Persuasion*, rev ed.. New York: Quill, 1993.

Cleland, David I., and King, William R., editors. *Project Management Handbook*. New York: Van Nostrand Reinhold, 1983.

Covey, Stephen. *The 7 Habits of Highly Effective People*. New York: Fireside Books, 1989.

de Bono, Edward. *Serious Creativity*. New York: Harper, 1992.

de Bono, Edward. *Six Thinking Hats*. Boston: Little, Brown, 1985.

de Bono, Edward. *New Think*. New York: Avon Books, 1971.

Dimancescu, Dan. *The Seamless Enterprise. Making Cross Functional Management Work*. New York: Harper, 1992.

Downs, Alan. *Corporate Executions: The Ugly Truth About Layoffs—How Corporate Greed Is Shattering Lives, Companies, and Communities*. New York: AMACOM, 1996.

Drucker, Peter F. *Management: Tasks, Responsibilities, Practices*. New York: Harper & Row, 1973, 1974.

Dyer, Wayne. *You'll See It When You Believe It*. New York: Avon Books, 1989.

Fleming, Quentin W. *Cost/Schedule Control Systems Criteria*. Chicago: Probus, 1988.

Fleming, Quentin W., and Koppelman, Joel M. *Earned Value Project Management*. Upper Darbey, PA: Project Management Institute, 1996.

Frame, J. Davidson. *Managing Projects in Organizations*. San Francisco: Jossey-Bass, 1995.

Frankl, Viktor. *Man's Search for Meaning*, 3d ed. New York: Touchstone, 1984.

Gardner, Howard. *Frames of Mind: The Theory of Multiple Intelligences.* New York: Basic Books, 1993.

Goldratt, Eliyahu M. *Critical Chain.* Great Barrington, MA: North River Press, 1997.

Graham, Robert J., and Englund, Randall L. *Creating an Environment for Successful Projects.* San Francisco: Jossey-Bass, 1997.

Hammer, Michael, and Champy, James. *Reengineering the Corporation.* New York: Harper Business, 1993.

Hancock, Graham. *Fingerprints of the Gods.* New York: Crown, 1995.

Harry, Mikel, and Schroeder, Richard. *Six Sigma: The Breakthrough Management Strategy Revolutionizing the World's Top Corporations.* New York: Currency, 2000.

Harvey, Jerry B. *The Abilene Paradox: And Other Meditations on Management.* San Diego: University Associates, 1988.

Heller, Robert. *Achieving Excellence.* New York: DK Publishing, 1999.

Heller, Robert, and Hindle, Tim. *Essential Manager's Manual.* New York: DK Publishing, 1998.

Herrmann, Ned. *The Whole Brain Business Book.* New York: McGraw-Hill, 1996.

Herrmann, Ned. *The Creative Brain.* Lake Lure, NC: Brain Books, 1995.

Hersey, Paul, and Blanchard, Kenneth. *Management of Organizational Behavior: Utilizing Human Resources,* 4th ed. Englewood Cliffs, NJ: Prentice Hall, 1981.

Highsmith III, James A. *Adaptive Software Development.* New York: Dorset House, 2000.

Janis, Irving, and Mann, Leon. *Decision Making.* New York: Free Press, 1977.

Jones, Russel A. *Self-Fulfilling Prophecies.* Hillsdale, NJ: Lawrence Erlbaum, 1977.

Kayser, Tom. *Mining Group Gold.* New York: McGraw-Hill, 1995.

Keane. *Productivity Management: Keane's Project Management Approach for Systems Development,* 2d ed. Boston: Keane Associates (800-239-0296).

Keirsey, David. *Please Understand Me II.* Del Mar, CA: Prometheus Nemesis Book Company, 1998.

Kepner, Charles H., and Tregoe, Benjamin B. *The Rational Manager.* Princeton, NJ: Kepner-Tregoe, 1965.

Kerzner, Harold. *In Search of Excellence in Project Management.* New York: Van Nostrand, 1998.

Kerzner, Harold. *Project Management: A Systems Approach to Planning, Scheduling, and Controlling.* 5th ed. New York: Van Nostrand, 1995.

Kiemele, Mark J., and Schmidt, Stephen R. *Basic Statistics. Tools for Continuous Improvement,* 3d ed. Colorado Springs, CO: Air Academy Press, 1993.

Knowles, Malcolm. *Self-Directed Learning.* New York: Association Press, 1975.

Koch, Richard. *The 80/20 Principle.* New York: Doubleday, 1998.

Kouzes, James M., and Posner, Barry Z. *The Leadership Challenge: How to Get Extraordinary Things Done in Organizations.* San Francisco: Jossey-Bass, 1987.

Kuhn, Thomas. *The Structure of Scientific Revolutions.* Chicago: University of Chicago Press, 1970.

Lerner, Michael. *The Politics of Meaning.* Reading, MA: Addison-Wesley, 1996.

Lewis, James. *Mastering Project Management.* New York: McGraw-Hill, 1998.

Lewis, James. *Team-Based Project Management.* New York: AMACOM, 1997.

Lewis, James. *Fundamentals of Project Management.* New York: AMACOM, 1993.

Lewis, James. *The Project Manager's Desk Reference,* 2d ed. New York: McGraw-Hill, 2000.

Maier, Norman R. F. *Psychology in Industry.* Boston: Houghton Mifflin, 1955.

Maloney, Lawrence D. "For the Love of Flying." *Design News,* Vol. 51, No. 5, March 4, 1996.

March, James, and Simon, Herbert. *Organizations.* New York: Wiley, 1966.

Maslow, Abraham. *Motivation and Personality,* 2d ed. New York: Harper & Row, 1970.

McClelland, David. *Power: The Inner Experience.* New York: Halsted Press, 1975.

Michalko, Michael. *Thinkertoys*. Berkeley, CA: Ten Speed Press, 1995.

Miller, William C. *The Creative Edge: Fostering Innovation Where You Work*. Reading, MA: Addison-Wesley, 1986.

Mintzberg, Henry. *Mintzberg on Management*. New York: Free Press, 1989.

Moder, Joseph J., Phillips, Cecil R., and Davis, Edward W. *Project Management with CPM, PERT, and Precedence Diagramming*, 3d ed. New York: Van Nostrand, 1983.

Nadler, Gerald, and Hibino, Shozo. *Breakthrough Thinking*. Rocklin, CA: Prima Publishing, 1990.

von Oech, Roger. *A Kick in the Seat of the Pants*. New York: Warner, 1986.

von Oech, Roger. *A Whack on the Side of the Head*. New York: Warner, 1983.

Patterson, Marvin. *Accelerating Innovation: Improving the Processes of Product Development*. New York: Van Nostrand Reinhold, 1993.

Peter, Lawrence J. *The Peter Principle*. New York: William Morrow, 1969.

Peters, Tom. "The WOW Project." *Fast Company* magazine, May 1999.

Peters, Tom. *Thriving on Chaos*. New York: Knopf, 1987.

Peters, Tom. *Liberation Management*. New York: Knopf, 1992.

Pinto, Jeffrey K. *Power and Politics in Project Management*. Upper Darby, PA: Project Management Institute, 1996.

Pinto, Jeffrey K., editor. *The Project Management Institute Project Management Handbook*. San Francisco: Jossey-Bass, 1998.

Ray, M., and Myers, R. *Creativity in Business*. Garden City, NY: Doubleday, 1986.

Rickards, Tudor. *Problem Solving through Creative Analysis*. Epping, Essex, England: Gower Press, 1975.

Rosenthal, R., and Jacobson, L. *Pygmalion in the Classroom*. New York: Holt, Rinehart, and Winston, 1968.

Saaty, Thomas L. *Decision Making for Leaders*. Pittsburgh: RWS Publications, 1995.

Sabbagh, Karl. *Twenty-First Century Jet*. New York: Scribner, 1996.

Senge, Peter. *The Fifth Discipline*. New York: Doubleday, 1990.

Senge, Peter. Interview in *Fast Company* magazine, May 1999.

Smith, Hyrum W. The 10 Natural Laws of Successful Time and Life Management. New York: Time Warner, 1994.

Smith, Preston G., and Reinertsen, Donald G. *Developing Products in Half the Time.* New York: Van Nostrand, 1995.

Stacey, Ralph D. *Complexity and Creativity in Organizations.* San Francisco: Berrett-Koehler, 1996.

Steiner, Claude. *Scripts People Live By,* 2d ed. New York: Grove Weidenfeld, 1990.

Sykes, Charles. *Dumbing Down Our Kids.* New York: St. Martin's Press, 1995.

Vroom, Victor, and Jago, Arthur. *The New Leadership.* Englewood Cliffs, NJ: Prentice Hall, 1988.

Vroom, Victor, and Yetton, Phillip. *Leadership and Decision Making.* Pittsburgh: University of Pittsburgh Press, 1973.

Walpole, Ronald E. *Introduction to Statistics,* 2d ed. New York: Macmillan, 1974.

Watzlawick, Paul, Weakland, John, and Fisch, Richard. *Change: Principles of Problem Formulation and Problem Resolution.* New York: Norton, 1974.

Weisbord, Marvin. *Productive Workplaces.* San Francisco: Jossey-Bass, 1987.

Wheatley, Margaret. *Leadership and New Science.* San Francisco: Berrett-Koehler, 1992.

Wing, R. L. *The Tao of Power.* New York: Doubleday, 1986.

Wysocki, Robert K. *Effective Project Management,* 2d ed. New York: Wiley, 2000.

Wysocki, Robert K, and Lewis, James P. *World-Class Project Manager.* Boston: Perseus Books, 2000.

INDEX

ABOUT THE AUTHOR

James P. Lewis, Ph.D. is the founder of The Lewis Institute, Inc., an association of professionals providing project management and behavioral consulting and training throughout the United States, Canada, Mexico, England, and the Far East. This includes team building, project management, engineering management, and problem solving to several Fortune 100 and 500 companies in the United States.

An outstanding workshop leader, he has trained more than 20,000 managers and supervisors since 1981, drawing on his many years of firsthand experience as a manager with ITT Telecommunications and Aerotron, Inc., where he held positions including Product Engineering Manager, Chief Engineer, and Project Manager. He also served as Quality Manager for ITT Telecom during the last two years of his industrial career. During his 15 years as an electrical engineer, Jim designed and developed a variety of communications equipment for application in land, sea, and mobile environments. He holds a joint patent on a programmable memory for a transceiver.

He has published numerous articles on managing as well as four books on project management: *How to Build & Manage An Effective Project Team*, *Fundamentals of Project Management*, and *Team-Based Project Management*, all published by the American Management Association; *Project Planning, Scheduling and Control, Revised Edition*, *The Project Manager's Desk Reference, Second Edition*, *and Mastering Project Management,* published by McGraw Hill. He is joint author, with Robert K. Wysocki, of *World-Class Project Manager,* published by Perseus. He holds a B.S. in Electrical Engineering and both M.S. and Ph.D. degrees in Psychology, all from North Carolina State University.

Jim is married to the former Lea Ann McDowell, and they live in Vinton, Virginia, in the Blue Ridge Mountains. Although they have no children of their own, they have three exchange-student "daughters," Yukiko Bono of Japan, Katarina Sigerud of Sweden, and Susi Mraz of Austria.

You can contact Jim at the Lewis Institute, Inc. See the Resources for Project Managers section for phone numbers and e-mail address.